TALL ISLAM AND SHORT MUSLIMS

ABOUT THE AUTHOR

Prof. Dr. Mumtaz Ali Khan obtained M.A. and Ph.D. degrees in Sociology, degree in Law and a degree in Hindi Ratna. He was a Professor of Rural Sociology at Bangalore Agriculture University.

He is deeply involved in promoting Inter-faith activities at the state and international levels. He is a well-known social scientist and social worker. He runs a free Primary and High School at his cost for the poor girls from different social groups.

He is an author of 36 books. He is the publisher of a monthly newsletter "CRUSH". He has visited 29 countries to attend seminars, conferences and discussions.

He is a member of the State Legislative Council and was a Cabinet Minister.

He is regarded as the most honest Minister. He has obtained a number of awards such as Kempegowda Award, Karnataka Kalam Award, etc.

TALL ISLAM AND SHORT MUSLIMS

Prof. (Dr.) Mumtaz Ali Khan

CONCEPT PUBLISHING COMPANY PVT. LTD.
NEW DELHI-110059

ISBN-13 : 978-81-8069-992-4

First Published 2013

Published and Printed by

Concept
Since 1974

Concept Publishing Company Pvt. Ltd.
A/15-16, Commercial Block, Mohan Garden
New Delhi-110059 (India)
T: 25351460, 25351794, *F*: 091-11-25357109
E: publishing@conceptpub.com, W: www.conceptpub.com
Editorial Office: H-13, Bali Nagar, New Delhi-110 015, India.

Cataloging in Publication Data--*Courtesy:* D.K. Agencies (P) Ltd. <docinfo@dkagencies.com>

Khan, Mumtaz Ali.
Tall Islam and short Muslims / Mumtaz Ali Khan.
p. cm.
Includes bibliographical references (p.) and index.
ISBN 9788180699924

1. Islam—Doctrines. 2. Muslims—Religious life and customs. 3. Muslim women Social conditions. 4. Muslims—Violence against. I. Title.

DDC 297.2 23

Dedication

This book, "Tall Islam and Short Muslims" is dedicated to all those who strived to present a true, liberal and secular interpretation of the basics of Islam and as seen through the Holy Quran and the Holy Hadith.

Preface

The present book, *Tall Islam and Short Muslims* is the result of both primary and secondary source of information. The title of the book looks very sensitive and sharp. But when one reads the book one understands that the book has three main issues. The first issue relates to the glorious principles of Islam. *Quran* and *Hadith* contain the message of Almighty God for the benefit of mankind revealed to Prophet Muhammad. It touches various aspects of man's social life. From the birth to death how a man has to conduct himself is enshrined in the holy book. Some of the important aspects are the manner in which men and women should conduct their daily life. There are various prohibitions mentioned in the *Quran* which every man and woman should avoid. Luxury, interest, smoking and drinking, accumulation of wealth, spending of wealth, women's rights and status, marriage and divorce, rights of children, recovery of loan, gambling, violence, patience, tolerance, greed, brotherhood, hardwork and so on.

Besides what is revealed through the Holy *Quran*, the book also deals with the sayings and actions of the Holy Prophet for guidance to men and women. *Quran* and *Hadith* put together form the blueprint for a peaceful and godfearing way of life. When one reads the contents of *Quran* and *Hadith*, one is tempted to embrace Islam. It is very fascinating.

The book then deals with the behaviour of Muslims. It is possible that some people have read and understood the contents of *Quran* and *Hadith*. But the question is do they follow these principles and values in their day-to-day life. Those who have not read *Quran* and *Hadith* might have acquired some knowledge of this. If so, do they follow what they know in their day-to-day life? The book brings out the fact that a majority of Muslims do not follow the message of the *Quran* or the *Hadith*. They are violators. Thirdly, what should be done to correct these deviants? It is necessary to educate them to fall in line with the mandate of Islam. This is the responsibility of the religious leaders, the educated, social workers, educators and others. We should ensure that non-Muslims do not continue to hold a wrong image of Islam. The popular saying that "Islam is good, and Muslims are bad" should be corrected. If Islam is good there should not be Muslims who are bad. The main aim of the book is to bring out the highlights of Islamic principles, scout the deviants and finally educate the deviants to follow the Islamic principles in letter and spirit.

Any writing on religious aspects is very sensitive. This is particularly so on Islam. A large number of Muslims are ignorant of Islam in letter and spirit. The original text of *Quran* and *Hadith* is in Arabic. This is a language of the book, but not that the readers. Arabic has special status, value and sanctity because it is in this language that the Holy *Quran* was revealed through divine voice. But lack of the knowledge of Arabic language had kept a large number of Muslims ignorant of the contents of *Quran*. This necessitated translation of *Quran* and *Hadith* from Arabic to several other languages. The most commonly accepted language is English which has acquired the status of international language.

Though it is generally accepted that there is some difference between *Quran* in Arabic and *Quran* in other languages, some translated books in English, though not all, have been accepted to be almost equal to Arabic version. There is no other alternate channel. At least the basics of *Quran* and *Hadith* can be learnt.

The present book, *Tall Islam and Short Muslims* is in English. The author has extensively made use of primary source of information by observing the behaviour of Muslims, personal and group discussions. The secondary source of information comes from published literature and newspapers. The primary intention of the author is to highlight the glorious principles of Islam through *Quran* and *Hadith*. When people read and understand this 'sociology of *Islam*', they get fascinated and some get converted to Islam. Islamic principles are universal and apply to the entire mankind. It has all positive messages. It does not promote any prejudice or hatred towards other religious or religious scriptures. This is one of the reasons as to why a large number of Europeans in particular embrace Islam which has become the fastest growing religion.

The second aspect of the book is to highlight the actual behaviour of Muslims, the followers of Prophet Muhammad. This is a very, very ticklish and sensitive question. When attempted to say 'spade is spade' this is terrible opposition. Man's tendency is to resist if any one points out his weaknesses. Muslims love and respect Prophet Muhammad. They are ready to die for him. Not a single word against him is tolerated. The entire Muslim world will be in fire. Their attachment to the Holy Prophet does not find any similarity in other religions. Sri Rama, Sri Krishna can be criticized and no Hindu is punished. Even Lord Jesus can be attacked. *Bible* can be questioned. Christianity got divided into Catholics and Protestants. Their rituals can be changed. Jesus's birth and death can be differently presented. Though *Bible* is a revealed sacred book, it can be modified and differently interpreted. But it is entirely a different story in Muslim society. Prophet Muhammad and *Quran* can never be questioned by any Muslim. If ever a non-Muslim does so, Muslims will not be tolerated.

But the one million dollar question is, "are Muslims by and large following the spirit and letter of the *Quran*? Are Muslims, by and large, respecting the words of the Holy Prophet Muhammad? Is it not true that the deviants outnumber the puritans? We see that in day-to-day life, many Muslims are deviants. If someone tries to correct this, he is not spared. He is condemned and called *Kafir*. They do not understand the meaning of the word *Kafir*. They lack patience, tolerance and understanding.

These deviants should be corrected and enabled to understand the elements of *Quran* and *Hadith* in a simple language which they understand. Sermon can be delivered in their own, simple language. It is not necessary for the *moulanas* to address the gathering in high standard non-Arabic language. Who has to encourage this? It is not necessary for the *moulanas* to address the gathering in high standard non-Arabic language.

Who has to encourage this? It is not necessary that only qualified Imam should address. Even well educated people can do this job. I have come across some educated people giving sermon in Urdu or any other non-Arabic language touching the present social concerns to educate and correct the ordinary, not much educated Muslims.

My main attempt in writing this book is to revive Muslim society through pointing out what Islam stands for and whether Muslims are following this. If not following, how to correct them and save the image of Islam. The popular saying, "Islam is good and Muslims are bad" should be replaced with the words, "Islam is good because Muslims are good". I appeal to Almighty Allah to give a good sense to our Muslim brothers and sisters to read my book with an objective approach. Reading in between lines with a negative approach is to be avoided.

Acknowledgements

"Tall Islam and Short Muslims" is the product of cumulative efforts of many people who evinced keen interest in bringing out this book. Though I worked very hard, the credit for this book has to be shared by a few important key players.

I owe my debt to a number of authors of many books throwing light on the precepts and practices of Islam as seen through the Holy Quran and Hadith. I remain grateful to many individuals who spared their precious time with me when I had interview with them.

My office assistant, Mrs. Rukmini Bai deserves my thanks for her efforts in typing this lengthy book with a smile on her face. Ultimately, I remain every grateful to Mr. Sinha, the Chief of Concept Publishing Co. Pvt. Ltd. New Delhi-110059. At a time when my regular publisher for three decades was hesitant to publish this book because of its very title, Concept came forward to publish this book. The editor deserves a particular mention because of meticulous proof correction.

Contents

I
Introduction

The title of the book, *Tall Islam and Short Muslims* is used after a considerable deliberation. Muslim society is very sensitive to religious matter. Any slightest negative reference to *Quran* and the Holy Prophet becomes a matter of intolerable emotions, passions and provocation. It is immaterial whether the author or speaker makes such references wittingly or unwittingly. There is no patience to pause over and find out the intention of the person whose innocence is taken as wickedness. Muslims who have not read and understood the Holy *Quran* or *Hadith* and also the words of the Holy Prophet Muhammad are those who create unrest in the society. When once passions and emotions run high, hooliganism and vandalism reign supreme. Therefore, one has to be extremely careful in using words.

To gauge the possible understanding of the reactions of the Muslim world, I have been telling that I will write a book, *Tall Islam and Short Muslims*. The result is that it is well received. There is absolutely no adverse reaction. People enjoy and appreciate the appropriateness of the title. I asked a few educated Muslims whether the title affects the image of Islam. The answer was "no". They said, 'on the other hand it provides an opportunity to realize what Islam stands for and how Muslims behave in actual day-to-day affairs". Even some religious leaders appreciated. They said, "your intention is positive, you want to present a true picture of Islam. You are rendering yeoman service as a writer. Please go ahead".

Encouraged by this, I picked up courage and set my mind on selection of issues. It would be rather cumbersome to venture to include all issues in life. I had, therefore, to pick up certain major and controversial issues which are in direct conflict with Islamic preaching and practical life. The following issues seem to be the core issues caught in between Islam in theory and Muslims in practice. I would like to clarify here that Islam is not theoretical, but practical.

1. Status of women,
2. Rights of women,
3. Marriage and divorce,
4. Rights of children,
5. Language,
6. Loan and interest,
7. Unity,
8. Wealth,
9. Gambling, drinks,
10. *Fatwas*,
11. Violence, and
12. Religious harmony.

There are two courses of action on which every true Muslim has to set his mind to understand the title of my book and the seriousness of my business. The first is to understand in clear terms the mission of Holy Prophet Muhammad. What message he brought from Allah or to be very precise what was revealed to him through divine voice and why was it revealed. To comprehend this, one should be quite objective and open minded. Secondly, one should be broadminded and prepared to underline the differences between what the message of the Holy *Quran* or the Holy Prophet is for mankind. A little over 1400 years ago Allah, the merciful and most beneficent, sent his message through an illiterate person to correct the erring society suffering from multiple social concern and ills. Allah cannot afford to be a mute witness to the happenings on the earth. He cannot allow his devotees to continue to tread the wrong path forever. Somewhere, some time some medicine has to be applied to prevent further deterioration in the thoughts and actions of the people. With this intention, He sent one lakh twenty four thousand prophets, Muhammad being the last.

The followers of Islam are mandated to adhere to the code

of conduct enshrined in the Holy *Quran* and the *Hadith*. Any deviation from the prescribed path is undesirable, unhealthy and ultimately un-Islamic. Followers of Islam become more emotional when the name of Holy Prophet is mentioned. They show reverence and even fear. They may take Allah, the creator lightly and use singular language. But when the name of the Prophet is mentioned, there will be a total transformation in the mental frame of people. Fear, respect, emotion, tears, shivering, etc., are demonstrated.

But they rather do not take care to know whether they are following the principles of Islam and sayings and actions of the Holy Prophet. Whether there is compatibility between the prescription and practice, between theory and action in practical life? It is here that an ocean of difference is seen. If the differences are marginal, there can be an excuse as we are all just human beings. We are not perfect. But the question is "can the perfection be marginal and imperfection dominant"? If imperfection is dominant, then it sends a clear message that principles of Islam are observed more in breach rather than in observation. This gap cannot be justified and tolerated. When this situation is presented before our very naked eyes, what else we should call the situation other than "Tall Islam and Short Muslims".

I would like to make it clear to the readers that it is not my intention to condemn Muslims. It is not a statement of generalization. Right from the day of creation of this universe, there have been men of varieties. There are good as well as bad people. Where there are angels, there are also devils. We have to live with both. Who are in more number and who are more dominant? It is positively true that humans are more in number and more dominant too. But the presence of evils will definitely affect the virtuous people. It creates an unnecessary situation where the virtuous people have to struggle to overcome the evil minded people. It is also true that ultimately truth will triumph. The good will overcome the bad, however late it is.

Another question connected with the title is how can there be bad Muslims when a Muslim is one who has faith in basic principles of Islam. One has not only to firmly believe that there is one God and there is no parallel God to him. One has also to believe that Muhammad is the messenger of God and he is the last messenger. Muhammad is the last Prophet. Any theory about another Prophet shakes the very foundation of the pillars as well as the structure of Islam. After reposing unquestionable faith in this, the next question is about adherence to the principles and teachings of Islam. These are contained in the Holy *Quran* and the words and actions of the Holy Prophet Muhammad. One should also remember and have firm belief that this is not just a theory but also scientific in its structure. Every principle of Islam is scientific. For instance pork is prohibited in Islam. It should not mean that just because it is prohibited and, therefore, every Muslim should avoid. The reality is that pork contains tapeworms which cannot be easily cooked and, therefore, consumption of pork is harmful to the consumer. But the awareness of this scientific reason is generally not known to people. One more example is that lipstick and nail polish are prohibited. Why? The answer is Islam prohibits nothing more. The truth is that nail polish and lipstick contain poisonous elements and constantly chewing this results in poison which gets into the human system.

Therefore, one should have faith in the principles of Islam. Then another question stems. Is it enough if one has firm faith, one should practice what one believes right in life? It is here one is put to acid test. It is only when believers practice what they believe that they deserve to be called real Muslims. If there is significant gap between belief and practice, such people are exposed. They are not Muslims at all. Or at least they suffer from deficiencies and are dwarfs. Their growth is curtained. It does not mean that they are physically 3 feet or 4 feet. But they are short Muslims because their application of the basic principles of Islam in daily life is nowhere when measured with the noble and glorious principles of Islam. It is in this sense that the title *Tall Islam and Short Muslims* is fully justified. It is also true that the title at least instantly. Does it offend the Muslims? I believe it need not. But if it pricks, it cannot be helped because spade is a spade. One has to suffer some humiliation if one is not true to salt. No one can claim immunity from some degree of humiliation if the basic principles of Islam are not followed in life. One cannot have cake and eat it too. I do not hesitate to say that no Muslim who deviates at least beyond limits, from the principles of Islam and invites disgrace can be saved. No one should claim rewards if he does not deserve it. Should he not deserve some amount of mental agony if he disrespects the *Quran* and *Hadith*. If his code of conduct is repugnant to that of Islam, should he not be exposed? We should protect the image of Islam and in this process some amount of sacrifice is unavoidable. A person who insults the Holy *Quran* and the Holy Prophet deserves punishment. His conscience should prick only when he neglects the principles, but not when exposed for not following the principles.

One thousand four hundred years history of Islam stands before us with voluminous literature since the Holy *Quran* was revealed. How the then Muslims followed the principles of Islam and how the present generation is following these principles will hold a mirror to enable us to know the changes. Changes are not sudden, but gradual. From time to time, changes were witnessed. It is well known that no society has been static. Changes are part and parcel of social life. There are both external and internal factors which force or induce changes. A change for better is most welcome. But when changes start taking place in the society, there is no guarantee that changes are always positive. Changes may produce negative effects too. Islam is a dynamic religion. It has no message that the society remains static. The Holy *Quran* and the Holy Prophet permit certain behavioural changes. Both admit changes surfacing due to the advancement of science and technology. But what is not permitted is a change that negates the basic principles of Islam. Such changes do follow certain definite procedures when getting ready for taking meals. Buffer system is not in Islam. Forks and spoons are alien to Islamic culture. But nowadays these cultural restrictions are not observed. Does it mean that these changes are anti-Islam? If insisted to be so, then life becomes miserable and impractical. For a Muslim in a western society where technological advancement has upset all human calculations and devastating changes in social life are brought about orthodoxical life becomes too difficult.

What is expected of a devotee is adherence to the basic

principles of Islam which envisage a progressive, peaceful and harmonious life guaranteeing a paradise on earth and abode in the kingdom of Almighty Allah. What strikes many outside the domain of Islam is the importance given for social equality and tolerance. The status of woman and universal brotherhood also attract outsiders.

All these values fitted into Islamic social system have enchanting spell of appreciation and attraction to outsiders. Many great scholars who have read the translated version of *Quran* and *Hadith* have expressed their views without any reservation. Bernard Shaw, one of the most celebrated writers and philosophers of modern world says, "I have always held the religion of Muhammad in high estimation because of its wonderful vitality. Islam is the only religion which appears to me to possess that assimilating capacity to the changing phase of existence which can make itself appeal to age. I have studied him—the wonderful man and in my opinion, far from being an anti-Christ, he must be called the Saviour of Humanity. I believe that if a man like him were to assume the dictatorship of the modern world, he would succeed in solving its problems in a way that would bring it the much needed peace and happiness. I have prophesied about the faith of Muhammad that it would be acceptable to the European of tomorrow as it is beginning to be acceptable to the European of today".

Bernard Shaw was not in any sense a sooth-sayer or prophesy maker. He was just an ordinary English man but a great thinker and writer. He was just like the celebrated H.G. Wells who shot into fame when once he published *Things to Come*. Many of his prophesies have come true. Yet he was just an ordinary mortal possessing great proactive mind.

Bernard Shaw was more influenced by the theory and actions of the Holy Prophet. He thought that the followers of Muhammad would strictly adhere to the Prophet's sayings and actions. But he was soon disappointed because he observed fundamental differences between principles of Islam and practices of Muslims. This type of deviation is found in all the religions of the world. Followers of Christianity, Hinduism, Buddhism, and Judaism have enough material to demonstrate that they have not respected the fundamentals of the teachings of their religion. One may say that even Islam is no exception. The followers of Islam of yesterday and the followers of Islam today are significantly different in following the tenets of Islam. In fact, the behaviour of some Muslims is a shameful act. Doubts arise whether they are real followers of Islam. There is definitely some basis for such doubts. One great Englishman made a remark based on his experience "Islam is good, Muslims are bad".

Muslim leaders, particularly religious leaders, have not taken this remark seriously and adopted correctional methods. Some years ago, I met a few young European female youths in a conference in Brazil. It was a Friday. We were getting ready for prayers. Then four girls asked me, "Can we also join you to go to the mosque?" I was surprised, I had five to six men with me. I said, "You are most welcome". On the way we had some time for discussion and knowing the background of these girls I asked, "How is it you are coming for *namaz*"? The answer was, "We are Muslims and we observe prayers, particularly Friday prayers". "Are you converted to Islam?" "Yes, we got converted recently." "Did your parents permit you?"

"We are majors. We take our own decisions. We respect parents. But we need not take their permission. They also do not interfere."

"What made you to opt for Islam when you had other religions also before you?"

"We read the *Quran* in our own language. We also studied the life and achievements of Muhammad. We were fascinated and attracted. In fact, till then, we were not practicing any religion, including Christianity to which our parents belong."

"What was your major attraction in Islam?"

"Equality and status of woman guaranteed in Islam."

"Are you happy now? What is your general observation?"

"We are disappointed. We made a mistake in choosing Islam."

"Why do you say so?"

"There are fundamental differences between what Islam stands for and what Muslims are today."

"How do you say so?"

"Muslims have become conservative with closed mind.

Women are denied their rights. Muslims have no tolerance. In fact, they are deviants."

"What is your stand now?"

"We repent. Had we seen these Muslims first, we would not have embraced Islam. We do respect Islam. But we feel sorry for disgracing *Quran* and the Prophet."

This type of expression of disappointment is not just confirmed to these European handful of girls. There are many such instances. It is not just external expression, but inward feeling too. How much are these girls hurt and disappointed? Their enthusiasm is curbed and erased. On hearing their feelings, what do those who are sitting on the off wall with an intention to jump to Islam wagon feel and react? Will this not affect the prospective converts go back from their stand? This apart, are not these Muslims disgracing the *Quran* and *Hadith*? Are they not disrespecting the Holy Prophet Muhammad? These Muslims who adopt a deviant path are sinners. God will curse them. They have got themselves to Islam without understanding the basic tenets of Islam. They are not torch bearers of Islam, but path breakers of Islam. We cannot raise our heads and walk straight. If we are questioned, we become speechless. They have pumped filthy and nonsense stuff into the mind of the people at large. But the message of Islam is so charming and penetrating that wise people discard the dubious methodology of the deviants and apply their own mind objectively. We have to remember that despite all these deviations, Islam is the fastest growing religion in Europe today. Greatmen of sports, arts, intellectuals, scientists have embraced Islam and the trend continues to grow.

I would like to present the readers some cases of deviations. The main emphasis is on deviations from Islamic basic tenets and values, contradictions and conflicts. One significant caution I would like to stress right now is to make it clear to the readers that it is not the intention of the author to hurt their feelings. I am not generalizing the deviations. I am not offering wrong materials. Let there be no wrong interpretations. I am sincere and God fearing in my presentation. The book is written with the intention of earning the goodwill of people. Let me also make it abundantly clear that I am a member of Bharatiya Janata Party and because of this backward, I am a cabinet minister. Let no one mistake me that this book is written to please my political bosses. No BJP leader has ever tried to influence my mind in religious matter. I have to please Almighty Allah. I want to be a true follower of Islamic tenets and values. There is no question of deviations and wrong presentation just to earn favours. I look to eternal benefits from being a staunch follower of Islam. Being a legislator or a minister is a temporary advantage. I may get some prestige, honour and comforts. But I am realistic. All these are purely transitory benefits. But what is everlasting is that what we get as a reward in the kingdom of Allah for the good works and behaviour as human beings.

My intention is also to reform the present day Muslim society. But the question is who has to reform? There is no question of another Prophet because Prophet Muhammad is the last prophet. This stand is the basic understanding of Islam. "*Laihaha illallahu, muhammed ur rasoolallah*". Then we have to depend upon the mortals to plan their role. Responsibility falls on the shoulder of our *ulema-e-ikram*. They command respect in the society for the scholarly knowledge they possess about Islam. Then the *madrasas*, a place where young children receive Islamic education. It is here that the personality of the children is shaped and moulded. Then the primary school where the teachers have to educate and train the students. Mothers have profound influence on the mind of young kids. A healthy socio-cultural environment has also a place. NGOs can also play a vital role. It is always safer to keep politicians at bay. They spoil the children and youths.

Methodology

The study on the differences between the principles of Islam and the practices of Muslims is of great significance and far reaching consequences. The author has great responsibilities in understanding and presentation of his views. There will be some individuals and groups of individuals who are very keen on pin-pointing the lapses or weaknesses in the presentation.

The main attack will be sources of collection of data. Therefore methodology is very important. The sources of data have to be reliable and free from biases. Keeping all this in mind, I adopted some methods to collect data.

There are two major sources of information. These are the primary source and the secondary source. The primary source is limited. I have to depend upon group techniques. Groups of educated Muslims, both men and women. Further, old people as well as youths were also approached. Observation source is very vital. Born as a Muslim, I had ample opportunities to observe the behaviour of Muslims of different categories. In fact, whatever I could observe in day to day life situation cannot be different from what others observe. The only point to be noted is that objectivity has to be maintained. Since my observation has all along been systematic and unbiased, greater reliance can be relayed upon.

Secondary, sources include mostly books authored by eminent scholars in Islamic theology and sociology of Muslims in practice. In fact, secondary sources are the significant sources to throw light on Islam and Muslims.

The first objective of the study is to create awareness among both Muslims and non-Muslims about the real image of Islam which is formed out of the Holy *Quran* and *Hadith*. This is particularly so in the case of "words of the Prophet Muhammad". For men who have limited time and still desire to know what Islam stands for, words of the Holy Prophet is perhaps more than enough. If one can digest this as contained in a small booklet produced by moulana Wahiduddin Khan, one can really understand the message of Islam for better behaviour in the society. This booklet contains selection from the *Hadith*.

The second objective is to analyze the present behavioural situation and see how far Muslims are deviants from Islamic mandates. What are the main reasons for this? The third objective is to present certain correctional remedies for enabling Muslims to adopt Islamic way of life to suit the requirements of the modern technological society. It is well known that social changes are taking place very fast. When the whole world is changing, Muslims alone cannot remain totally isolated. They cannot escape from the winds of change.

At the same time, they cannot totally surrender to these changes if they are in conflict with the basic values of Islam. Islam is a progressive religion not dogmatic religion. It is dynamic, not static. It provides ample scope for adjustment to modern society. It is quite elastic.

The fourth objective is to ensure that the readers of this book are not misled. The author has absolutely no evil mind to attack or disgrace any group of individuals. While the purity of Islam has to be maintained, wrong perception of Islam has to be removed. While the religious leaders have their own role in society, it should be admitted that they too have to change their mindset in a changing society. Muslim society is a part of the larger society and, therefore, Muslim society cannot remain unchanged at all. Change is a sign of a progressive society. As Karl Marx has said, "Force is the midwife of every society pregnant with old ideas". Islam is quite progressive. It provides for changes. But changes should be healthy. It should maintain moral principles and at the same time adopt progressive and healthy ways of life.

II
Words of Prophet Muhammad

Muslims derive inspiration and guidance for leading a flawless life from the Holy *Quran* and from the words of the Holy Prophet. Those who possess knowledge of these two sources are duty bound to spread the message among those Muslims and non-Muslims who lack knowledge about the basic principles of Islam. Transmission of this knowledge could be through writings and public lectures. If Islamic way of life is not observed because of lack of knowledge, there could be some excuse. But excuses cannot be foı a long time. Efforts should be made at the earliest.

But it is altogether different if people have gained knowledge and still do not bother to put their knowledge into practice. God will not excuse those people who knowingly disregard and disgrace *Quran* and the Prophet.

The material pertaining to this is divided into two aspects, namely social aspect and economic aspect.

Social Aspect

Social aspects of Prophet's words include divine guidance, manners, false evidence, suspicion and envy, visiting the sick, patience and repentance, suspicion and envy, and so on. There are all illustrative, not exhaustive.

Divine Guidance

Prophet admits certain divine guidance offered by God for the welfare of mankind. Prophet reposes unquestionable faith in this. He gives the lead in following God's guidance which is as follows :

> "O God, I seek divine guidance so that I may remain steadfast in what is just;
> I seek divine guidance in order to be firm in righteousness;
> I seek divine guidance in the manner that I express my gratitude for your favours and worship with devotion;
> I seek from you a tongue that speaks the truth and a heart which is pure and clean.

This should be on the tongue of everyone who desires to lead a blessed life. This is the message of the Holiest among the Holy Prophets. Constant utterance of this message will chase away the devils, the evil spirits. The personality development should be based on this. In that case a sound body and a sound mind will result and human society will be peaceful and the individual will be blissful. But the question is do we follow this? Subsequent narration will answer this question.

> "God has imposed certain moral obligations, do not abrogate them;
> He has forbidden certain things; do not indulge in them;
> He has laid down certain limits, do not transgress them;
> He is silent on certain matters; do not knowingly argue over them."

These words of the Prophet are very simple in operation. If followed, nothing but peace and tranquillity would prevail. Worldly pleasure and comforts are at the door of the followers. These permissible and prohibitive words of the Prophet are in the best interest of mankind. Prohibitions are not something impossible and uncomfortable. By observing these prohibitions also man can have access to worldly comforts.

Manners

> "The most perfect of believers in point of faith, is he who is the best in manners."

Human behaviour should be different from animal behaviour. Men are also animals as tigers, lions, deers are. But the difference should not be linked to external appearance. Man is socialized. Right from childhood man is brought up in a different socio-cultural milieu. It is this culture that makes a man distinctly different from the four legged animals.

The term 'manner' refers to human behaviour, not animal behaviour. However, not all human beings are alike in manners. This is so because men are brought up in different situations even in human society. Every human being is a man. But every man need not be a human being. A man becomes a human being when he has acquired certain culture. How he talks, whether politely or impolitely; how he behaves, whether softly or roughly? While eating, drinking, one should acquire refined way. When guests visit, how he treats them. When a man becomes an officer, a minister, a legislator, a rich businessman, how does he conduct himself? When elders, religious leaders are seen or met with, how one treats them? Is it with respect or indifference? How does one behave with an aged man or a poor man, or insane person or handicapped person?

All this would reflect on the cultural training one has received from the parents or to some extent in the schools. Education moulds our behavioural pattern. Simplicity, honesty, politeness, softness, openness, facial appearance is some of the qualities of good manners. The Holy Prophet was himself a model to mankind. And he sends the message of "good manners" to man. But how do we behave? Are we following his message in our daily life? The simple answer is "by and large NO". When once we get some position of importance, we change our colour. We become arrogant, indifferent, change mode of life, style, put on air of superiority. Is this how we should respect the words of the Holy Prophet?

"No one should ask another to vacate his seat for him. Room should be made for him without his asking."

"It is not proper for a man to sit between two men and thus separate them, without seeking their permission."

These two instances form a part of manners which the Prophet is bent upon. Many people do this mostly because of lack of knowledge and understanding. This message carries a lot of significance and value system. To my knowledge such a message is not found in other religious faiths. If Muslims learn this and practice, good message goes to other social groups.

Brutal Behaviour

Abdullah ibn Masud said, "It is as if I see the Prophet Muhammad describing the life of one of the Prophets who is assaulted by his people until the blood runs. He wipes the blood from his face and says, "O God, forgive my people for they know not what they do".

This message of Prophet Muhammad points at the barbaric behaviour of the most uncivilized people who believed in murderous culture. This passage refers to the Prophet Noah who preached peace, but faced hatred and violence. Prophet Noah did not get annoyed and revengeful. On the other hand, he showed mercy. He had nothing but pity. This should be a part of our daily behaviour when we meet hostile group of people who become emotional and senseless at their height of intolerance. Do we learn a lesson from the sufferings of Prophet Noah and correct ourselves? Wait and see.

Bigotry

A man once asked the Prophet if bigotry was to love one's tribe. "No", replied the Prophet. "Bigotry is help your tribe to tyrannise others."

"He who preaches bigotry is not one of us. And not being one of us, he may go ahead and fight in the cause of bigotry. He who dies for such a cause is not one of us either."

We observe that many people who hold high positions

tend to favour their own men in many ways just because of kinship, friendship, religion and caste. This is called nepotism. Here merit is not counted. This is only a blind support which cannot be appreciated. There is no rationality and justification. Prophet discards such an attitude. By discarding, Prophet ensures social justice.

This is what prevails today in our society. The moment a person becomes a legislator or a minister, he tries to overlook the deserving persons and blindly helps his people even if they are not deserving.

Slander and Backbiting

The Prophet explained that slander meant speaking of one's brother in a manner that was hurtful to him. He was then asked what if one's brother was actually at fault. The Prophet replied that, if he was at fault, then what was said against him was just backbiting and, if he was not, it was calumny

Prophet forbade not only indulgence in slander and backbiting, but even listening to such talk. The man who indulges in backbiting will not enter paradise.

Complaints

The prophet said that none of his companions should complain to him of another. "I would like to come to you with a clear heart."

Muslim society has a large number of people who are in the habit of complaining against one another. People create stories to damage the image of those who they do not like. Sometimes they know that they will not gain anything out of this false propaganda. I give my own experience. Till 30th July, 2011 I was the Minister for Minority Welfare besides Wakf and Haj. When the cabinet had to be reconstituted one Muslim, a party worker, wanted to become Minister in my place. He used all possible methods to block my entry. He wrote twenty pages containing filthy language and imaginary instances to ensure my character assassination. Wherever he went he spoke ill of me. I learn he paid heavy amount to some TV channels to show that I will not be included in the new ministry. He went to the extent of canvassing that he should be included, not me. Otherwise, the portfolio can be given to some non-Muslim minister. Where is the fear of God and Rasool? False propaganda sometimes assumes the strength of truth. Such persons should be made to know what the Prophet has said.

The Prophet said, "O my son, if you can act in such a way that you spend your mornings and your evenings without wishing anyone ill, then that is how one should act". Then he added, "O my son, this is my way. And anyone who loves my ways, loves me. And anyone who loves me will live with me in paradise".

Wishing ill will of those who are not on terms with us is very common. We curse them. We even pray Almighty God to throw them in trouble, not to give them peace, to see that their business suffers, and so on. Our prayers will not bear fruit. But we feel happy that we have wished them ill. But Prophet not only dislikes such negative wishes, but advises them that if they convert their attitude to positive wishes, they will live with him in paradise. What a simple way to live in paradise with the Prophet! Still we human beings become inhuman and go on wishing bad to those whom we do not like.

Hypocracy

A hypocrate is a person who is hated, suspected, considered as unreliable and untrustworthy. They cause nuisance. Hypocracy has certain distinct characteristics. There are four significant characteristics as follows as narrated by the Prophet.

The taint of hypocracy will attach :

1. To the trustee who breaks the trust. A person who breaks the trust is a person who has lost faith;
2. To the speaker who tells untruths;
3. To the man who uses foul language when he is disagreement with others; and
4. To the maker of promises who fails to keep them.

Prophet further says that this taint will remain unless the wrong doer mends his ways.

Arrogance

According to the Holy Prophet, "a man who has as much as an iota of arrogance in his heart will not enter paradise". Hearing these words of the Prophet, a man asked, "what if a man likes to dress in good clothes and wear good shoes"? The Prophet said, "God himself possesses elegance. And he likes elegance. This has nothing to do with arrogance. A man is arrogant when he refuses to accept the truth and considers others to be inferior".

On the Day of Judgment, God will not even look at a man who, in a show of arrogance, lets his clothes sweep the ground.

False Evidence

The Holy Prophet said, "Giving of false evidence is like committing idolatry".

Many Muslims who face many charges including criminal charges in a court of law, have to swear in the name of God that they speak the truth. They touch the Holy *Quran* and say so. When they touch the Holy Book, they should naturally become nervous and avoid false utterances and give false evidence in favour or against somebody who is facing criminal charges. But shockingly they utter lies. They do not have the fear of Allah and Rasool. They may escape punishment in this world. But they are sure to face the horrors of Hell.

We have to learn from the Holy Prophet's life story and warning to human beings to avoid giving false evidence.

Education and Upbringing

One thousand four hundred years ago, the Holy Prophet laid particular emphasis on education to children. His words, "The best gift from a father to his child is education and upbringing". But we find utter failure in Muslim society, by and large, in respecting the Prophet's message. Education is very much neglected. Parents do not have value for education. Dropouts are causing a big alarm. Young children are dragged for work in workshops and agricultural activities. Parents value a small amount that these children can bring home. They have lack of futurity.

Girls' education suffers much more. They do not believe in giving better education to girls. They try to get them married much earlier hoping thereby that they get rid of the burden. They fail to realize that married daughters are constant source of headache for them because of the bad sons-in-law they have.

Prophet also lays down special significance on upbringing of children. Character building exercises should start from childhood. If children are not carefully watched, they may go astray and fall into the company of bad elements later on.

Suspicion and Envy

"Avoid falling under suspicion. For suspicion does the worst damage. Do not enquire into the lives of others. Do not pry.

"Do not exaggerate what others say. Bear each other no malice, and do not hurt each others' interests. And, by being brothers to each other become the servants of God."

"Save yourselves from envy. For envy eats up virtue as fire eats up wood."

But in reality we are violating all these golden words of the Prophet. Suspicion is the hallmark of our character. It amounts to character assassination. Stories are built on the movements of even good persons. Suspicion is aimed at causing mental and physical losses. This is very common at domestic level. Husband-wife relationship is damaged if either of the two suspects the character of the other. If the husband is close to another woman, wife gets doubts and always quarrels with her husband. If the husband suspects the wife, she is doomed. I remember a case of a young Muslim girl married to an autorickshaw driver. She had studied upto PUC and her husband had not even completed primary V standard. He got used to drinks. He was always suspecting her character. She was not allowed to stand at outside door of the house.

One day he came home suddenly. He saw his wife talking to her cousin. He got annoyed and went away. He returned after some time and beat his wife mercilessly. He had no patience to listen to her explanation. A few months later he married another girl and sent away his first wife.

People are generally prone to make all sorts of probe into the private lives of others. We develop more hatred and jealousy. We will not tolerate others coming up well in life. We fail to realize it is only God's will that prevails. Man cannot do or undo anything to anyone unless God wills. It is He who grants or withdraws. Why should we be jealous? Jealousy will kill our health. We suffer from mental disease.

Obey Law of the Land

"It is obligatory for a Muslim to pay heed to his ruler and obey him, whether he likes him or not, as long as the ruler does not order him to commit a sin. If he orders him to commit sin, then he is not to pay heed to him or obey him."

This message applies to Muslims both in Islamic countries and non-Islamic countries. The ruler may be individual or an institution. The individual could be a benevolent king or a dictator. Islam does not encourage dictatorship. Islam provides for a democratic institution where rulers are elected by the people. Even though kingship is better than dictatorship, the former's rule could be whimsical and autocratic. His rules could be just or cruel. But people are expected to follow. A dictator is an unwanted ruler. His rules can be still helpful to people. But if his rules are harsh, people may have to tolerate. But if the rulers are sinful, then people can reject. But in this event, they may have to face the consequences.

In non-Islamic countries, the situation is different. Such a country could be a Christian, Buddhist or Hindu. Muslims have to obey all the rules of the land. Most of the laws are common to all citizens. But where the laws are directly repugnant to Islamic rules and particularly observance amounts to commitment of sins, Muslims need not follow such laws. Of course, non-compliance may result in infliction of penalties and punishment. Then there will be a clash between the ruler and the ruled.

Wearing of *burqua* is encouraged in Islam to protect the modesty of woman. There is a law in parts of Europe which bans *burqua* and *naqaab* in public places. Non-use of *burqua* and *naqaab* does not amount to commitment of any sin. In India where 83 per cent of people are Hindus and the rest are Muslims, Xian's and others, there cannot be a law to ban *burqua* and *naqaab*! Nor there is any rule in Pakistan that all Muslims should wear *burqua*. But such a rule prevails in Saudi Arabia. Even non-Muslim women like Hindus have to wear when they appear in public. Hindu women have been following this rule saying that this is the law of the land. There is no question of any sin.

Good Teachers

"Verily, God Almighty, and his angels, and those who inhabit the heavens, even the ants in their holes and the fishes in their waters, bless the good teachers of mankind."

A good teacher is an asset to the Nation. The future of the young students lies in the hands of good teachers. A good teacher moulds the personality of the children. Early training on character building of the children is essential. Even when we are grown up and hold high positions in public life, we tend to remember our teachers, particularly in the primary and High Schools. We remember them with gratitude. Their teaching would definitely keep the student free from casteism and religious fanatism.

Prophet pays glorious tribute to good teachers and lays emphasis on appreciation of good teachers by angels, ants in their holes and fishes in the water.

Visiting the Sick

Prophet used to walk on the side of a road every morning. A Bedouin lady used to stand on the first floor and dump the contents loaded in a basket. This would fall on the head of the Prophet. He used to look up and leave the place without questioning her.

Later, for a couple of days this dumping of waste on his head was not there. The lady was missing. He made some enquiry. He came to know that the lady in question was sick. He traced her house and went there to enquire about into the health of the lady. She was shocked to see the Prophet sitting next to her. She put her head in shame. She cursed herself for dumping on his head. She asked the Prophet to forgive her.

This is how the Prophet behaved with a mischievous lady because she was sick.

Patience — Urination in Mosque

A Bedouin once urinated in the Prophet's mosque. People got up to punish him. The Prophet said, "leave him alone, and throw a bucket of water over his urine. You are here to make things easy, not to make things difficult".

This is a noble message of the Holy Prophet particularly to those who got upset when someone does a wrong. Urinating in the sacred premises of the mosque is a great sin, perhaps unpardonable. But the Prophet demonstrated by his action that we have to exercise great restraint and patience. Scolding or beating is very easy. But patience and forgiveness is more important. The wrong doer should be made to understand his wrong which he will not repeat again.

We have seen boys and even men beaten up if they urinate outside the mosque. We will not educate them not to repeat. Once they are made to understand, they will not repeat. Youngsters should particularly learn from the practical experience of the Prophet and spread the message.

Kindness

"Anyone who unjustly flogs his servant will be punished on the Day of Judgment."

"If you show kindness to your servant while employing him in some task, this will weigh heavily in your favour on the Day of Judgment. That will be your reward."

Maid servants in particular suffer a lot at the hands of women employers. All filthy and slanderous words are used. Sometimes they are beaten up. The hands are put on the burning stove. There are many cases of punishing the maid servants. Poor people come home for jobs. Providing a job is not the only help. But how we treat them is also equally important. Humanism should prevail. We should have the fear of Almighty Allah. Poor woman's curses will harm us and her good words will help us.

Rejoicing in the Misfortune of Others

"Do not rejoice in the misfortunes of your brother.

"For God may show him compassion, but create difficulties for you."

It is generally a common occurrence in the life-style of some who are bent upon taking revenge on those with whom they have differences. If someone is hated for some reason, he is not helpful when in good financial or official status, we all develop animosity towards him. We wait for his downfall. And when misfortune befalls on him, our tendency would be to celebrate his fate. We say "this fellow was very arrogant, very miserly, did not help me financially. Now what happened to him? God has punished him. The fellow deserves this". Thus saying we may try to insult him, humiliate him, show gestures at him.

But we have no moral authority to sit in judgment of God. On such occasions we should honestly share his feelings, console him, show sympathy to him. It is also possible that Almighty God may excuse him, restore his original status. He may show more compassion. In that case what happens to us for making unwanted comments? God may inflict punishment on us.

Retaliation

Retaliation is one of the weaknesses of human nature. Slightest provocation is not tolerated. "Tit for tat" is governing feature of human behaviour. But the Holy Prophet Muhammad has demonstrated through action that retaliation is not a solution to our problems. It leads to further aggravation of the strained relationship. The aggressor should be corrected through peaceful demonstration. He should on his own realize his fault and repent. If he surrenders because of fear or threat to his life, this is only temporary measure to get out of the immediate threat. It is only an external show. But in reality he still continues hatred and venomous attitude.

The Holy Prophet has demonstrated a simple and workable device which everyone can adopt in his life. A strong belief in Almighty Allah will solve the problem. Once he was resting alone under the shadow of a tree when Dasur, a hostile horseman, arrived by his side. He held his sword over Prophet meaning thereby that he had planned to kill the Prophet. Dasur asked the Prophet "Who will save you"? this was a sarcasting remark. Prophet raised his head, looked at him and said that "Allah" would save him. Though the word was straight and simple, it carried some magnetic power. Darus was awestruck. He became speechless. His arrogance of power disappeared. The hand that was holding the sword started trembling. He became nervous. The sword dropped.

The Holy Prophet picked it up and with all humbleness and humility at his command, he asked Darus "Who will save you now"? the horseman replied, "none". Prophet smiled and replied, "No, you are wrong. Allah will save you as he saved me, if you have belief in him". So saying the Prophet returned the sword and asked him to leave the place. Darus left the place and went ahead. After a few yards, he suddenly retracted and returned to the Prophet. He was a totally reformed person. He demonstrated signs of repentance and embraced Islam on his own.

The Holy Prophet has thus demonstrated that we can change the heart of any cruel person if we are honest and peaceful in our approach. Retaliation has no solution.

Repentance

"God extends His hand at night so that He may accept the repentance of those who indulge in wickedness during the day.

"God extends His hand during the day so that he may accept the repentance of those who indulge in wickedness at night.

"This will continue till the sun rises in the West."

"When a person repents, God's pleasure at this is even

greater than that of one who dismounts from his camel, loses it in the desert and then finds it again all of a sudden."

This message of the Holy Prophet throws light on the importance and significance of repentance in life. As humans we commit and sometimes repeat errors in life. But realization of our mistakes and then expressing regrets would ensure peace, harmony and brotherhood. The Prophet says that Allah would accept the repentance of a man even before the last breath. The words, "sorry", "regret" and "repent" have magical effect. Enmity for years would end instantly if the wrong doer utters any of these words.

But the devilish mentality of the human beings does not permit utterance of those words. Stubbornness in human nature has to be attacked first. Thousands of people may advice him to express "regret". But he may not. But the moment he realizes on his own and utters these words, there will be total transformation in the relationship between the two. But generally this positive attitude is a rare occurrence. Is it not our duty to remember the Holy Prophet and follow his message? If we do not, are we not guilty of sidelining his message? Are we not disrespecting him?

In Confidence

"When a man tells you something in confidence, you should not betray his trust."

In support to this dictate, the Holy Prophet proceeds further and offers an elaboration. He says, "A man without trust is a man without faith".

Every Muslim is bound to observe these words of the Holy Prophet. There is no laxity here. Whether a prince or a pauper, master or servant, father or offspring, husband or wife, everyone is bound to obey this command. But we find at the ground realities more breach than observance. Many battles are lost, many close relationships are broken, many great or small people have suffered because of breach of trust. Most trusted friends and relatives have betrayed the persons who trusted them. Mir Sadiqs are multiplied in number. As a Minister I have experienced this. By the time I sign some important documents, information is leaked whether about transfers, grants. I used to feel surprised. Information is leaked at some level for monitory considerations. Confidence is shattered. This is violation of the sayings of the Prophet. It means we disrespect the Prophet.

Secrecy

When there are three of you, one should not be left out while the other two share a secret, for this will cause his grief.

Everyday we come across such occasions. This is also the result of lack of manners. It could be that people are not aware of such behaviour. People should think of some method to overcome this malady. The left out person would be simply scratching his head as to why he was left out. This may wound his feelings.

Share Work at Home

According to Aishah, the Prophet used to cobble his shoes, stitch his clothes and do the kind of house work that is done in all homes. He was a human being just like anybody else. He used to milk his goat and do other Sunday works himself.

The general tendency of men at home is to avoid undertaking any work at home. It is true that they are generally the sole bread earners. When they go home, they want to relax. But the notion that they should not do any work at home as this is the work of the house lady is wrong. He can assist womenfolk by doing even small works. Prophet has shown the way by sharing domestic works. Why not we, ordinary mortals, follow his footsteps? False prestige serves no purpose.

There are also cases where both husband and wife are working and return home at the same time. It could be both are exhausted. If there are children, wife will have additional work. It means the burden of the lady is more. In such cases, if the husband extends a helping hand in sharing domestic works, this will be a big relief to the wife. But not many husbands do this. Should they not learn from the Prophet's life and practice?

Sharing Responsibility

During the battle of Badr, one camel was shared by three men, namely Abu Lubabah, Ali ibn Abi Talib and the Prophet. When it was Prophet's turn to walk, the other two would say to him, "mount the camel. We will walk in your place". The Prophet would reply, "neither of you is stronger than I am, nor am I less eager for rewards than you".

From this it becomes clear we should always share the responsibility. There is no question of some people performing duty and one person doing nothing. If it is question of sharing the burden everyone should be ready, whether he is a big man or a small man. But we do not follow this. May be we are not equipped with such noble guidance. But if we know what the Prophet has said and then do not follow his words, we are at fault and are perhaps punishable.

Bad Company

"One who walks with a tyrant, in the full knowledge that he is a tyrant, in order to strengthen him, is such as he has already left the fold of Islam."

Islam does not permit a person who knowingly moves in the company of a tyrant or terrorist or a rowdy element. Does he procure the services of such questionable person with the intention of harming others or protecting himself with their help? I know the case of a chairman of a famous social organization who used to have four rowdies employed by him for self protection. He is guilty of corruption, misuse of funds belonging to the public. The chairman should convince the public through assurances of a practical nature. By using such figures, he invites grave problems to himself.

There is a popular saying, "tell me your friends, I tell you what you are". Even good people turn out to be bad because of indulgence in bad company. Sometimes friends will have better control than parents in youthful days. Bad friends misguide, misdirect and misuse good boys. The Holy Prophet further says, "A man who helps his people for an unjust cause can be compared with a man who catches hold of the tail of a camel which is falling into a well".

It is not the mistake of the camel. But this man lacks sense in holding the tail of the camel. He is seeing how it is falling into the well. What shall we call such a person who knowingly firmly catches the tail? Likewise there are many bad friends who easily tempt their good and innocent friends to fall into their trap and get ruined themselves. The best course of preventive action is to avoid such friends who are not really well-wishers.

Prevention of Evil Action

"Whosoever of you see an evil action, let him change it with his hand; and if he is not able to do so, then with his tongue; and if he is not able to do so, then with his heart, for that is the minimum that is desirable from a believer."

It is a matter of common occurrence almost daily. A few youths start quarrelling on petty issues and later on this turns out to be a big issue, sometimes leading to group clashes or even communal clashes. People just stand as mute spectators. They do not realize that it is their responsibility as citizens to prevent any untoward events. Even if somebody is killing a person, we tend to stand as witnesses. But when taken to the court we simply plead our ignorance. Prophet has shown many ways in which conscious citizens can act and prevent criminal actions taking place right under their nose. Even in law, such behaviour is a crime, called abettor.

Economic Aspect

The Holy Prophet has laid down certain prescriptions to be followed by Muslims in matter relating to economic dealings. This is something like a blue print to be followed in matter relating to earnings, accumulation of wealth, excess of riches, acquisition of landed property, receiving, repayment and recovery of loan, payment of *zakat*, giving and receiving of bribe, etc. A true Muslim has to strictly follow these economic guidelines. These are not just optional, but are mandatory. A brief description of these issues is presented here.

Wealth in Islam

Communism does not permit an individual to own property which includes other forms of wealth. In its philosophy community owns the property. But Islam has absolutely no restrictions. Individuals can own property without limits and make other forms of wealth. But there are two conditions, namely means of making wealth should be justified. The means should be *halal* (permissible). Wealth earned out of corruption, black marketing, smuggling, lootings, etc., is not allowed. There is no limit.

Similarly, wealth should not be accumulated. It should be in circulation. A large number of poor should be benefited. Wealth should not be kept in the locker of any bank. How the wealth is used is also an important factor. Wealth should not be allowed to be misused.

Wealth after Death

"When a man dies, nothing lives on after him, except for three things; *Sadaqah jariyah*, knowledge which can benefit others, or virtuous offspring who will pray for him."

This is an advice or warning to those who accumulate wealth by all means. They are very reluctant to share the wealth with others, particularly the needy. Such miserly persons should know that when they die, nothing but two yards of white cloth will be on their body which is covered in the grave. Within a few days the white ants eat away the body leaving nothing but the skeletons. This state of affair should alert the rich people.

What do they carry with them after death? The good deeds and charitable exercise alone will help them for even until the Day of Judgment.

Excess of Richness

Once Prophet said, "they stand to lose". His companion asks, "to whom do you refer"? Then the Prophet replies, "To those with an excess of riches who just squander their wealth, heedless of the fact that they can be saved only if they spend generously for a good cause. And there are very few wealthy men of that ilk".

Wealth accumulated by foul means is a sort of *haram*. Its legality is questionable in courts of law. But Prophet has set a moral code for such persons. Since these wealthy people have not toiled hard to earn excessive wealth have no value for the wealth. The members of the family particularly women and youths are seen in wasting the wealth. They do not use it for the poor. They forget that a day would come when their treasure is empty and they are zero. The youths acquire all qualities of self-destruction. They resort to vicious life.

Acquiring Land by Tyranny

Greed for acquiring land by any means and at any cost is generally the present trend. Brothers and brothers land in dispute, lodge complaints in the police station. They file cases in courts. They resort to killing each other or hire *supari* killers. Land destroys the relationship between parents and sons. Sons harass parents for land. Sometimes they even go to the extent of wishing the early death of their parents. Finally they don't mind killing off the parents.

The Holy Prophet delivered his message 1400 years ago. He gave a stern warning about the consequences of acquiring land by tyrannical methods. He said, "A man who acquires a stretch of land by tyranny will be made to wear a yoke made of seven earths around his neck on the Day of Judgment".

Hoarding

"How evil is the man who hoards essential supplies! If God wills it that the prices of merchandise fall, that makes him unhappy. But if the prices rise, that makes him happy."

A merchant who hoards goods in order to raise their price is a sinner.

An honest and trustworthy merchant will be with the Prophets, the truthful and the martyrs.

When asked "which was the best kind of earning", Prophet replied, "That for which a man works with his hands and honest trading.

"It is not just for a man to sell his merchandise without disclosing its defects. It is proper for a vendor to tell the buyer of any defects of which he is aware.

"A trader who does not hoard essential supplies receives His sustenance, while the hoards of essential supplies are cursed.

"Allah will show compassion to those who show kindness while buying and selling, and recovering debts."

There are some markets primarily or mostly dominated by Muslim merchants. I have my own experiences. Their chief behavioural characteristic would hurt anybody. Their main behavioural characteristics are :

1. They are very rude, tough and harsh in their interaction with the customers.
2. The rates they quote are much higher than what is quoted elsewhere. What Islam says is that the seller should place himself in the place of a buyer and judge to himself whether what he is quoting is reasonable.
3. The sellers in general do not give adequate opportunities to the buyers to check the quality of the products. Whatever the sellers give, the buyers should accept.
4. Sometimes, they set up their own men as buyers. These buyers will accept the price with a small reduction. Then the seller tells the waiting customers, "see, how these buyers accepted. I offer at the same rate to you also". The buyers do fall a prey and pay at that rate.

Zakat

Zakat is a mandate for all those who are capable of paying a part of their income to the needy. The capable and eligible people have to pay at the rate of 2.50 per cent of their income to all poor Muslims.

"When you pay *zakat* (alms) you have done your duty as it is obligatory;

"But a person who amasses unlawful wealth and then makes gifts to the poor from it will have no spiritual reward for doing so.

"On the contrary, he will carry the burden of it with him into the next world".

"If a person to whom God has given wealth does not give *zakat* (alms), he will find that, on the Day of Judgment, his wealth will turn into a poisonous snake with two black sports on its head. It will be like a yoke around his neck. Then it will seize him by the jaws and declare, 'I am your wealth and I am your treasure'."

Bribe

"Those who take bribes and those who give bribes are cursed by God." This is the warning given to the corrupt people by the Holy Prophet.

Bribe or popularly called corruption is one of the serious social concerns today in the society. But what is the mandate of Islam? What is the message of Islam? Both the text of *Quran* and the words of the Prophet are crystal clear that corruption is the worst disease and one of the most serious crimes. It is a sin as well. Prophet says that both the giver and taker are sinners and in the eye of law also it is a crime. Whatever income a person has should be *halal.* One should sweat and earn. What are the means adopted to earn your income or wealth? If a person has accumulated huge wealth, he has to justify the means. Today we are caught in the web of corruption. Ministers, politicians, offices are known for bribes they take. No paper moves unless the hands are greased. Whatever amount is kept above the table is legal or *halal* and whatever is given below the table is *haram* or illegal.

Corruption surfaces because of lust for wealth. There are anti-corruption laws, administrative measures to avoid taking bribes. But they exist on paper, not found in action. Corruption is from bottom to top. Lokayukta has spread its net and we find everyday officers fall into the net. They face serious charges and consequential punishment. But corruption does not stop. Officers whose job is to catch others while taking bribe are also corrupt, atleast some. Ministers have enormous opportunities for corruption. They advance the plea of party fund, election expenses and so on. But all this does not help him to escape.

There are two ways of handling corruption menace. The first refers to legal force and the second refers to moral force. Muslim officers, politicians and ministers have to rely more on moral force. They should know that every rupee earned should be accounted before the Lord. A Muslim who gives bribe is an abettor. Rather he should be the first accused. There can be many supporting arguments. One can argue that without bribe the paper won't move a bit. Any delay in security relief from the government is detrimental to his needs. But this alibi will not come to his rescue. He is a sinner and a criminal as well.

Similar fate awaits the bribe taker. His income is *haram*. His family will be eating poisonous food. His whole family is tainted. The housewife is equally guilty of his sin and crime. A God fearing wife should reject such income and luxurious life. She should remain content with the meagre income through honest means. When Lokayukta publishes names of officers caught in the process of raids, the honour of the whole family suffers. Members of the family cannot raise their heads. How these people face the acid test which will be conducted on the Day of Judgment? Can they advance bribe there also? Do we ever think of Islamic prohibitions and consequences? Even small books have valuable information on bribe. We should realize that we have to face severe punishment these cannot be avoided.

There is an interesting story of a girl to be married. A God fearing mother asked the daughter, Asma, a rare question. "Asma, there are two proposals for your marriage. One boy is a high school teacher and he is from a good family. The other boy is a junior engineer in the Public Works Department and the background of the family is not transparent. What is your choice?" Asma replies, "Maa, I prefer a high school teacher because his income is *halal*. He will not be arrested due to corruption. But if I marry a junior engineer my future will be risky. His income has two elements, one is *halal* salary and other is *haram* income. One day or the other he is sure to be booked. Society may tease me because my husband is behind bars". Mother was very happy and blessed the daughter.

Muslim society is also responsible for spread of corruption. There are no preventive measures undertaken by religious and mundane leaders. Friday *khutbas* remain generally silent on corruption. There is absolutely no social boycott. There are no practical *fatwas*. Their money is accepted for building or renovating mosques and *dargahs*. If a Hindu wants to donate, mosque committee hesitates or if taken that money is used for other sundry purposes. If the Hindu donor comes to know, he will feel bad. Black money is acceptable. Money is accepted from smugglers.

Corruption in Muslim Society

It is a sad commentary on the refracted behaviour of a large number of *mutavallis* of mosques who indulge in receiving bribe for voting in elections to the wakf institutions. Election of office–bearers to some famous *dargah* committees provides concrete examples of the role of money. Candidates and voters are involved. Thousands of rupees will have to be shelled down by the candidates to the *mutavallis*. Further, corruption takes place in the election of office-bearers to the State Board of Wakf. This is the apex body in the State to protect and meaningful utilization of Wakf properties. Two representatives of *mutavallis* have to be elected. In the recent election, money played a big role. The amount paid ranges between one lakh to two and a half lakhs of rupees, as reported to me.

It is likely voters would have taken money from all contestants. When once the *mutavallis* have lost moral character, they go to any extent and adopt any means to acquire money. It is a shameful action. The candidates are also equally to be condemned. Where are the tenets of Islam?

Corruption for obtaining licences, clearance of papers in offices, for getting jobs and so on is very common. Muslim officers are generally tainted with corruption. Some Muslim IAS, IPS, KAS and other categories of administrative, police and technical are well versed and much experienced in receiving money. Lokayukta catches many Muslim officers too. Generally they escape punishment from the government by giving bribe to them. Politicians are generally no exception. Some Muslim politicians do take bribe. Exceptions are very marginal. Crores of rupees are minted. Multi stories buildings are raised. They are least bothered about their reputation.

Receiving as well as giving bribe is illegal and immoral. What is immoral is called in Urdu, *Haram*. What is legal and moral is *halal*. If a person who has received bribe, the act is illegal or *haram*. What do we call such a person whose action is *haram*? He is called a *harami*. I learn some Muslims did raise objection for using the word '*harami*'. I asked some people why these Muslims feel uncomfortable with the word '*harami*'. If spade is called a spade, why objections? I feel strongly if any Muslim found guilty of receiving *haram* amount raising objections for the word *harami*. The word *harami* refers to the giver and receiver of bribe.

Some Other '*Haram*' Type of Money

Any act that violates Islamic principles in making money, other than bribe, is also totally prohibited in Islam. There should be full justification for making wealth. There are many instances of encroaching Wakf land, transferring *khata* in the names of persons who are not *bona fide* owners of the Wakf land and also selling Wakf land. As a minister in-charge of Wakf, I could come across many such instances. In one district, a *mutavalli* of a reputed *Dargah* is said to have sold 8 acres of land belonging to the Wakf board. Government had to issue criminal notice to him. Many *sajjadas* of some *dargah* have also sold Wakf lands to their advantage.

Besides these *mutavallis* and *sajjadas*, there are many mundane people who have encroached Wakf properties in prime areas with lakhs of rupees. They have either sold the land directly or allowed formation of layouts and construction of houses. These people have made themselves quite rich.

Hundi is another method of collecting money from devotees who visit the dargahs. Their cash offerings are put in some tin or iron box sealed all around and also the hole through which money is put into the *hundi*. The Wakf board has certain norms and procedures for collection of cash from the *hundis*. As against this well set procedure, some Wakf officers, chairmen of committees and other vested interest would manage to open the *hundi* in the presence of the *mutavallis* and collect the available cash and carry it. When questioned by the *mutavallis*, they would only say that they take cash to the Wakf board and deposit in the bank as per procedures. But some *mutavallis* feel that the money goes to the personal account of the chairmen and others. I tried to get this verified. I got some truth in the allegations. I instructed the office to resort to a very strict procedure and nobody should have any doubt. There should be no room for alleging about misuse of *hundi* money.

Recovery of Loan : What the Prophet says

Not many humans are free from the dire need to resort to loan in life. From some it is essential for the very survival to take loan. For some it is needed for business, education, purchase of vehicles, house, site, and so on. It is not below the dignity of man. But the question of recovery is the problem. The Holy Prophet says, "one who makes sacrifices for the sake of God will have all his sins pardoned, except for his debts".

This message of the Prophet conveys the significance and importance of returning the debt. People tend to take loan because it is easily available. But when it is the question of repayment, the debtor feels that his backbone is breaking. In this connection also the Prophet says that the intention of taking loan is very important. If the intention is to meet the hard need, it is welcome. If there is malafide intention, it is bad.

The next important step is recovery of the debt. Here also Prophet lays emphasis on humanitarianism. Prophet quotes a case of a person who adopted this culture. He wishes all Muslims to adopt this.

"There was a man who used to give loans to poor people. When his associates had to go to them for recovery, he would urge them to be forgiving to those who were not able to pay back his loans with ease, believing that, in that way, perhaps God would show him forgiveness. When that man came face to face with the Almighty, he forgave him."

How far the followers of *Quran* and the words of Holy Prophet follow the culture laid down for recovery of loan can be illustrated by quoting a few examples. It can be best said that this is almost not followed. Non-repayment incurs the wrath of the lender. It is true that the loanees also try to evade repayment. They advance many reasons. Some of them may be true and some false. The lender is not bothered or bound to listen to the reasons. He is bent upon recovery. There may be written agreement or only verbal agreement.

Written agreement may take the parties to the courts which may drag considerable time. But recovery is almost certain. But verbal agreement will generally lad to heated argument, intervention of outsiders. This could be a smooth affair or tough affair. The Islamic prescription is very simple. The Holy Prophet has clearly said that the debt has to be repaid sooner or later. There should not be any force in recovery. "One who makes sacrifices for the sake of God will have all his sins pardoned except for his debts."

But in reality the situation is quite different. There are some debtors who take loan with the intention of repaying the amount. But for certain genuine reasons, they cannot repay. We have to be quite considerate with them. There are some who take loan with the intention of not paying back. We should get back the amount. But the Prophet has said that, the steps adopted shall not be harsh. Sometimes the debtors are so cunning and evasive that other than harsh steps nothing else is practical. How to reconcile between what the Prophet has advocated and the reality needs. It is true Prophet's words shall be respected and obliged. One such harsh method adopted in recovery is mentioned here.

Maqbool unnissa Begum has six children. Husband has two wives. She is the senior wife. Husband has totally neglected her and her six children, four daughters and two sons. The eldest is a daughter, Azra Khanum. She is a graduate. Maqbool is in the habit of resorting to loan quite often. She is also known for evading repayment. For her second daughter's marriage she took rupees forty thousand loan from one Farida Banu. Maqbool spent money like water. She crossed her capacity to repay the loan amount. She had no regular source. She would take loan from a few persons and repay earlier money lenders. But in the case of Farida Banu, it was very difficult. Farida is a bulky woman known for tough methods for recovery. She gave some time for repayment. Once she told her, "see Maqbool, I am a bit lenient with you because you have four daughters. You start repayment in instalments", but Maqbool continued to dodge. Farida lost her patience.

One day she brought two rough men and took away furniture meant to be given to the daughter. Second time she beat Maqbool mercilessly. Third time she tackled Azra Khanum. She started shouting at the top of her voice outside the house. Men and women gathered on the road. They could easily hear all the filthy words of Farida. She caught hold of Azra and said, "if your mother cannot repay the loan, let her pledge you with me. I will sell your body and recover the loan amount. Meanwhile, you come home and sleep with my husband". People outside were feeling very uncomfortable. But they were helpless because Farida is a notorious lady. Her vocabulary would scare any decent person.

All that Maqbool could do was to appeal to Farida for a last chance. She took three month's time. She got her son married and took lot of dowry amount from the father of the girl. Her son is a qualified technician and there was no problem in getting good amount. She changed the house to a distant place. She repaid the loan amount.

Who should be blamed in this case? Farida adopted too harsh methods which negate Prophet's words. Maqbool also negated Prophet's words in dodging repayment. The very intention of Maqbool was to dodge repayment. She is a habitual offender.

Zina

Islam is dead against illicit sexual relationship with any woman. This is called *zina*, a dreaded sin in man's life. Most severe punishment will be inflicted in the world hereafter. Every Muslim male is aware of this. Perhaps *zina* is mentioned only in Islam.

But what about fear of *zina* in practical life? Though it cannot be said, that such cases are in abundance, it cannot be ruled out that *zina* is not practiced. There is no statistical figure available. I do not think that any research or survey has been done on this personal and sensitive issue. However, it is also not ruled out that *zina* is totally absent. Sporadic information is available to show that *zina* prevails, though not in a big way.

Prostitution

Prostitution is an age old profession which prevails throughout the world. Islam prohibits prostitution on moral and health grounds. Men involved in prostitution get ruined financially also. The family becomes instable. Both men and women are involved. Prostitution has no class, caste, race and religious barriers. Muslim women are in large number. They are generally from poor families. There are many ways in which they get involved. When once they are caught in the profession, very rarely they leave the profession. There are many names associated with this profession. There are call-girls, street-girls and so on. Sometimes even educated girls are also involved in this profession. Some take to this profession for very survival and some for more comforts. Some women are involved without the knowledge of their husbands and some with their knowledge.

Young Muslim girls ranging from the age of 13 years and some women beyond 30 years are found. There are women in *burqua* waiting for the customers in certain known places. Women are in hotels and sometimes women are taken to hotels. Many Muslim girls are also found in bars.

Many Muslim countries have prostitutes. In Indonesia I came across some Muslim women trying to take tourists to certain hotels where arrangements are available for entertaining them. Iran, Egypt, Pakistan, Malaysia and some other Muslim countries have allowed this profession to thrive. The question is how these Muslim countries are allowing. Perhaps Malaysia excels others. It is really a matter of shame.

Alcoholism

Islam is perhaps the only religion in the world which has totally banned alcoholic drinks in any form. The reasons are multiple. Health is ruined. Heart attack is not avoidable. Family is ruined. Wealth gets melted. Respect in the society is lost. Property is lost. Liquor shops for the poor and clubs for the rich are common. It is a shame that Muslims violate the Islamic mandate. Many Muslim countries have allowed liquor consumption for non-Muslim foreigners. Local Muslims also take advantage, but very stealthily.

We do not find any serious attempts made by Muslim leaders to stop this. On the other hand, the society tolerates. Where is the respect for Islamic principles? Illicit liquor manufacturers are generally Muslims. Wine shops are also opened by Muslims. When questioned, they said, "we only sell, but we do not drink". They hardly realize that selling liquor or wine is also prohibited in Islam. If liquor is available in the shops, then only people go to the liquor shops.

Elite Muslims who go to clubs as well as low class Muslims are on par so far as liquor is concerned. Not many elite Muslims drink. But even the small number is adequate to damage the spirit of Islam. But the low class Muslims are ruined. Families are ruined. Many rape cases surface. It is a disgrace to Islam and Muslim society. As said above, Muslims are also involved in illicit liquor making business. There is a place called *Ambajidargah*, where the entire population consists of Muslims. The whole village is involved in illicit liquor business. They do not allow outsiders to enter the village. Once I happened to visit this village. I was not allowed. With much difficulty I could go inside. A distant relative was residing in the village. Through her I entered the village.

I was not allowed simply because I would know their business. I saw a number of vehicles loaded with illicit liquor barrels. People were minting money. This village was notoriously known for illicit liquor business. The business people used to tip the excise as well as police officials. It was a roaring business for all.

I asked one Moulana as to what steps he took to prevent this. He said, "I am from Bihar. I am paid well. People have told me not to open my mouth about liquor. I am waiting for a chance to leave the village at the earliest. They do not allow me to leave because they are afraid I might tell outsiders. They have taken a pledge from me. I am helpless. I know that I am doing sin".

Woman, another held; Ganja seized

A 60-year old woman said to be drug peddler and her friend were arrested in Bangalore for allegedly selling *ganja*. The CCB police arrested Begum Jaan Nurulla of Cottonpet and Munna Shah (30) of Singayyanapalya and seized *ganja* valued at Rs. 50,000 and Rs. 1,030 in cash from them. The police said Begum Jaan Nurulla's entire family was in the business. Her four sons are lodged in Bangalore Central Prison. The woman was arrested on the same charge in 2007 and the case is pending trial.

Extravagance

One extreme form of arrogance is extravagance in life. Allah has permitted humans to lead a happy life, thereby enjoying certain facilities in life. Of course, these facilities are a dream to certain sections of society. Allah has bestowed some privileges on some people denied to others. He alone knows why he has favoured some and denied to others. W cannot sit in judgment over His decision. We should simply welcome His actions.

But what Allah has granted has to be judiciously utilized. In the process of utilization, one has to be free from arrogance. The tendency to display one's wealth to create one's superiority is hated by Allah. What is legitimate, what is normal is most welcome. But what is abnormal is most hated by Him. We have seen or heard of some people who were very rich once and later on became paupers. This wealth is gone. Their palatial houses are replaced by ordinary houses. Their children are struggling hand to mouth. I had some relatives in Bangarpet they were very rich, rather floating in wealth. Marriages were on unbelievable grand scale. Display of jewellery meant for their daughters and grand-daughters would create jealousy. Rather it was a show of vulgar luxury. They would invite relatives and friends to see this display of wealth. The road was named as Abdul Ali road. The spacious house in which the joint family of five brothers lived with their families was called Abdul Ali Manzil.

A few important incidents will be brought to the notice of the readers. The niece of the Patriarch of the family was married to a rich person from Tamil Nadu, Jamal Khan. He was a leather merchant. As time passed on and the elders had passed away, this Jamal Khan became a painter, earning daily wages. One Nasir Humayun, one of the nephews somehow managed to obtain MA degree in Economics. He got a job in Mysore University. He had to report as lecturer in Kolar, nearby place. He showed the appointment order to the patriarch. His face became red. He took the order copy, tore it into pieces and burnt saying, "I made a mistake in allowing you to study. Today you want to bring disgrace to our family by becoming a slave of the government. What salary you get per month is not even one day's wager we give to our workers. You are a stupid. Don't entertain such ideas. In course of time Nasir Humayun had to struggle hand to mouth. He used to take loans for survival. This is the reward he got from his uncle.

Some of the grand-children are drivers and conductors. When some of them come to us for help, we shed tears. This is a warning to many arrogant rich people. There is a fine story about the arrogance of a rich person in Islamic literature. It is worth mentioning this here to create proper sense and fear. There was a very rich person. He was an embodiment of arrogance and extravagance. He was a good host only for the rich. He had scant respect for the poor. Beggars had to collect remains of delicious food in the drain or gutter. Once a *fakir* stood in front of the door and went on pleading for food. None cared for him. But he would not retreat. The rich man came out and rebuked the *fakir*, "You are worse than dog. If we shout it will run away". But you have no shame. You are adamant. If you stay any more, I will let loose my dog which would tear you into pieces". Yet, the *fakir* was unmoved. Then the rich man showered on him all types of harsh words and brought the dog. The *fakir* got scared. He told the rich man, "God will not spare you. You will repent one day. Your wealth becomes your poison". The rich man laughed and closed the door.

Time passed on. One day a *fakir* appeared at the gate and asked for help. The rich man came out and talked to the *fakir* coolly and politely and gave some help with a smile on his face. The *fakir* was nervous and in tears. The rich man understood this and said, "Look here, I was the *fakir* who appeared before you for help. But you were very rude and arrogant. You were very rich and extravagant. But yet, you did not help a deserving poor. But today God has helped me, shown his grace and has made me humble and prudent in spending money. This is a lesson for all. Tables are turned. You are now what I was earlier. I am now what you were earlier. Remember wealth is transitory. Arrogance kills us. Extravagance destroys our wealth". The *fakir* cried and apologized.

Let us see how the Holy Prophet reacted to a few situations where extravagance was noticed. Once the Prophet was sitting in the shade of Kabah. He saw one Abu Dharr al-Ghiffari coming to him. Prophet said, "They stand to lose". Abu Dharr asked who he was referring to, "To those with an excess of riches who just squander their wealth, heedless of the fact that they can be saved only if they spend generously for a good cause. And there are very few wealthy men of that ilk."

Another occasion of Prophet's warning to reckless spending of wealth by conducting luxurious life is his advice to Maudh bin Jabal who was appointed as Governor of Yemen. Prophet told him, "abstain from luxuries, for those who live luxurious lives are no servants of God". We see how the members of the families of the rich lead a luxurious life. The womenfolk are the culprits. They are mainly responsible for squandering wealth by spending money recklessly. Their jewellery, dress and style of life would cause havoc. Children are not far behind. In a short period wealth is exhausted.

Islam is not against worldly things as such. What is normally permitted is not prohibited, nor it is allowed to go waste. God has been gracious to grant wealth to some. This is for proper utilization. If this is followed, wealth remains in tact. If you have excess riches, use this to feed the poor, to educate the poor, to allow the poor start some small scale industries or employ them by starting industries. God gets pleased and grants more. But if the God's gift is misused in luxurious ways, God's grace will disappear.

Desire has no limit. Desire is natural. To kill desire is to kill self. But wise methods should be employed. Prophet says, "Wise is he who controls his desires and prepares for the life which starts after death. And cast-down is he who lives for the love of this world and has false expectations from God".

Marriage meal or meal served at a social function throws better light on extravagance. Everyone naturally expects delicious food on such occasions. Reasonable expenditure is permissible. But many affordable people cross the limit. A marriage meal includes mutton biryani, varieties of fried chicken, fish, varieties of costly sweets, bread, etc. Today a plate of such meal will cost around Rs. 300. The gathering will be more than one thousand. Greed is so much that as soon as the biryani and fried chicken dishes are kept on the table, everyone tries to grab as much as possible for the fear of not getting his choice mutton or chicken pieces. Everyone wants leg piece of chicken. Sometimes uncultured behaviour is observed. Finally, significant portion of biryani is left over in the plate and this will be dumped in the gutter or on the road thereby inviting crows and dogs. Ugly scenes are witnessed. What a shame; what a waste! If the rich take proper care of wasteful expenditure, quite a few mass marriages can be arranged and thereby earn the grace of Almighty God.

Such extravagant expenditure has two side effects. First, the ruination of families of this nature is not far off. There is no point in repenting later on. It can only serve as a warning to others who can be prevented from falling victims to this vivacious happening. Secondly, it has tremendous effect on the poor. While the rich can afford to spend luxuriously, the poor cannot. They struggle for survival. But human nature is not immune to such temptations. Not mindful of their own limitations, the poor become mad and endeavour to step into the shoes of the rich. Their children and womenfolk bring pressure on the males to provide them with such facilities, at least to some extent. The male members have to beg. borrow or steel. They are forced to adopt all possible dubious methods to reach the goal. If they resort to loan, they will invite grave consequences as their repayment capacity is poor.

Islam provides easy solutions "stretch your legs according

to the length of the bed". Happiness lies not in wealth, but in contentment. We have to adjust ourselves to realities. Simple life brings solace. Manage families within the limits of your own abilities. Do not try to lead your life on borrowed strength. How long can we live with the support of ventilation. When once the ventilation is withdrawn, life is out. Islam does not rule out a comfortable life. What is legitimate, what is possible within our reach need not be sacrificed. Finally, the message of Islam is just to avoid extravagance which brings nothing but misery at the end.

Tongue

Tongue has lot of importance and significance in human social life. We do not realize all this. A person who is deaf and dumb knows this because he cannot speak, let alone hearing. The dignity of a person is also neglected through tongue. It is a means of communication in human society. What a person speaks and how he speaks would reflect as his personality. Divine grace is attached to it when a person speaks soft and uses good words. Divine curse is also attached to a person who was harsh and abusive language. It is also said tongue speaks of the quality and status of the family. Tongue is used to read the Holy *Quran* and *Hadith*. Daily prayers are offered by using the tongue. One abusive word will kill the bond of relationship between two individuals. One sweet and dignified world would bring harmonious relationship between two warring friends.

Islam has given recognition to the tongue. A man pleads God to give a tongue that speaks the truth. This is stressed by the Holy Prophet: He says that there are four characteristics which together make a person a complete hypocrite. The taint of hypocrisy will attach to the trustee who breaks his trust, to speaker who tells untruths, to the maker of promises who fails to keep them and to the man who uses foul language when in disagreement with others. It is also said that it is not proper to tell lies either in serious or in light vein. Neither it is proper to make promises to one's children and then not fulfil them.

Tongue should not be used to hurt the feelings of others. The Prophet once asked his listeners if they knew what slander was. People could not answer. Then he explained that slander meant speaking of one's brother in a manner that was hurtful to him. Prophet also expresses his mind to indicate that tongue should not be used in a manner that would amount to backbiting.

There is another reference to the importance of tongue given by the Prophet. A person once said to the Prophet, "O messenger of God, a certain women is said to offer *salat* (prayers), observe fasts and give alms generously, but she hurts her neighbours by the way she speaks". The Prophet replied, "She will go to Hell". Then the man said, "O messenger of God, a certain other woman says fewer prayers, keeps fewer fasts voluntarily and offers little in the way of alms. She only gives a few pieces of cheese. But she never hurts her neighbours with her tongue". The Prophet replied, "She will enter Paradise".

Thus the sanctity of tongue upheld and propagated by the Holy Prophet should also be borne by all followers of Islam. But the question is "do we follow in our day to day life?" The answer is by and large negative. Let us throw light on the practical aspect of the sanctity of tongue at different stages and levels in life. Calling a person in singular is not to be encouraged and tolerated. It is very common that parents call their children in singular. Wives are called in singular. Elders call youngsters in singular. Common words used are "*tou aa*, (you come) *aa re, aa ge* (come) *jaa re* (go) *karti hai, karta hai* (do). This is not a very serious example. Serious words are '*suvvar ka baacha* (child of a pig), *tu ek kutta hai* (you are a dog), *haramzaade* (bastard), *chinal ka beta* (son of a prostitute). Using such words or phrases is a shame and speaks low of the quality of the person. But the society has been tolerating and thereby indirectly encouraging. Perhaps this is due to lack of education and culture. I do not say that this is practised only in Muslim society. But Muslims are particularly mandated to follow dignity and decency in life. When Islam specifically prohibits such language, Muslims are supposed to follow this. It is also observed that some husbands when in high tamper use the word '*chinal*', thereby meaning prostitute, even wives are observed so. They fail to realize at the spur of the moment that their wives are no exception. This amounts to character assassination. How can a woman from a decent family pocket such insulting and humiliating words? But they are helpless as they are not bold enough to counter their husbands, ferocious animals. The personal life of the Holy Prophet should be a mirror through which the followers of Islam should understand how to respect their wives.

Uttering lies tantamount to a sin. Under no circumstances should a Muslim speak falsehood. He should face the realities and speak the truth. Sacred tongue should not be polluted. It is not necessary to pen down what one promises. A simple word is enough. People definitely repose faith and trust in his words. Promise once made cannot be broken at any cost and in any form. This is the strength of Islam. A *momin* is always expected to stand by his words. The present day politicians in Muslim society are also generally known for false utterances.

For some people tongue has no value. They speak whatever they would like to. They make all sorts of rosy promises and for them heaven is the limit. It is like drinking water for them, so easy and so unmindful. For some people it is very difficult to speak the truth. Self glorification is common. Taking oath in the name of Allah, Prophet, parents and even their own children is a practice to confirm what they speak is true. More than this, promising in the name of the Holy *Quran* is also in practice. They have absolutely no fear of God. There are many Bou Tibbs as dramatized by Oliver Goldsmith. While living in huts, some people boast of the luxury of a palace. In marriage alliances this type of false utterances are common. Either of parties try to dupe the other. Politicians are well known for such faults. I have seen quite a few politicians who have absolutely no command over their tongue.

In the courts also some Muslims touch the Holy *Quran* and say, "I speak the truth and nothing but truth". When they utter so, their conscience, if any, would certainly be pricked. Where is the fear of Allah and Rasool? Even some Hajis use foul and false words. A Haji is a reformed person. His words are final and people repose faith in his words. This is not so today among some Hajis. It is really a sad reflection of deviation for Islamic culture. Character assassination to condemn a person is also very common. Many false adjectives are attributed to them just to damage the reputation of some people not in the good books of these people.

Thus, tongue which has sanctity in Islam is today polluted. Speaking truth is unwanted, is a laborious process and has negative effect. We tend to look to the present day, not to the world hereafter. We forget that we have to prepare ourselves to gain entry into the paradise promised by Allah. But the satan has control over our tongue. And we have to pay heavily for this.

Interest, Wealth and Poverty

Credit system is a necessary social evil. In the process of managing affairs of the government it becomes often inevitable to take loan from some source. Similarly, in the family affairs too taking loan either for the marriage of daughters, or a festival or even routine family management resorting to loan becomes unavoidable. All religious scriptures too make a mention of loan. Resorting to loan is not a sin. But the element of interest that is associated with loan is a subject matter of controversy. Normally those who have surplus money lend some money to others who are in need of financial assistance. There are some issues which are essential to judge whether loan is desirable or not. These are :

1. *Purpose* : The purpose for which loan is taken decides the character of loan. It could be for productive purpose or simply for consumption or non-productive purpose. If loan is for productive purpose, it is welcome because it helps a person to augment his income through business. Loan for education is also productive as it enables the person to get better education which enables him to earn well later on. But loan for non-productive purposes is generally suicidal. Loan amount is spent. But there is no source to earn and repay. Loan for marriages is un-productive.
2. *Source* : From where loan is obtained? This is also a deciding factor in one's life. Loan from the government is no problem because government loan

gives loan for productive purposes only. Similarly, loan from credit co-operative societies is also welcome. Loan from professional money lenders leads to loss of jewellery or something like this which is pledged. But loan from private lenders is dangerous as they are generally reckless and inhuman in the process of collection of loan.

3. *Interest* : It is the element of interest that is invariably associated with loan which decides the fate of the individual. A person who has no capacity to repay the loan as well as interest amount is doomed forever. He loses everything in life. He may lose his property, jewellery, and finally his honour. Sometimes the amount of interest if accumulated may be more than the principal amount of loan. In such case the loanee cannot pay the interest amount itself, let alone the principal amount. It is for this reason that Islam does not encourage the element of interest. It does not encourage the practice of taking loan. But has not put any total ban. This is so because there are various reasons which compel a person to resort to loan. Islamic principles are exemplary if followed strictly. Individuals develop the tendency of taking as much loan as possible. Because loan amount is easily available, one forgets his limits and needs. One does not bother about the consequences of loan with interest. Reckless loan ruins him forever. So, Islam issues adequate cautious to prevent him from getting ruined. The money lender is more accountable and responsible. If one has more than his requirements, one is encouraged to help others who are in dire necessity of loan. It is his moral responsibility.

Wealth

Islam has no bar on wealth. There is no limit for the extent of wealth. But two significant conditions are associated with acquisition of wealth. One has to justify the means adopted to acquire wealth. Means should justify the ends. Acquisition of wealth by resorting to illegal and immoral means is totally prohibited. It is *haram*. Black-marketing, smuggling, looting, robbing, deceitful methods, etc., are the means prohibited.

The second element relates to utilization of wealth. Islamic principles say that wealth should not be locked. It should be in circulation so that a large number of poors in particular are benefited. Their economic conditions could improve thereby. Thus, the rich can contribute a lot to the enrichment of the poor. They need not dole out for nothing at all. Charity, if meaningful and absolutely essential, is permissible. Otherwise, it kills the spirit of self-effort to come up in life. Any help should be like seed money so that anybody can take advantage of this and pool other resources and enable himself to come up in life.

The other way to help the poor is to give interest free loan. The rich can afford to take an element of risk while giving interest free loan. Even a small financial help can boost the morale of petty trades. If vegetable vendor need money to purchase vegetables in the wholesale market and then sell in their own localities they have to take loan and repay with abnormal interest. In the wholesale market, the seller will give, say, rupees one thousand for purchase in his shop. But while giving one thousand, he will deduct rupees two hundred by way of interest and gives rupees eight hundred only. The buyer will be happy because he is sure of purchasing commodities of his choice in the shop. The merchant is happy because he gets rupees two hundred by giving just rupees eight hundred in one day and he also gets the benefit of selling his goods without much effort. In a sense he exploits the poor vegetable vendor.

It is in this context that the rich can play their role effectively. The same amount of rupees eight hundred can be given by him without interest and get the money back in the evening. This is a big help to a poor vegetable vendor. This is the spirit of Islam. This is the duty of the wealthy people.

They can also help small industrialists to improve their trade so that a large number of poor can get employment. They can also set up charitable hospitals or clinics for helping the poor. The question is what happens to the wealthy if they go spending like this. This wealth will melt soon. Therefore, they should give some importance to trade and industries of their own so that they go on getting huge profit which can be utilized for helping the poor. If a few wealthy people can help the poor with their resources and start a joint venture on a co-operative basis, wonders can be achieved.

But unfortunately such a situation is not right now seen. Many rich are selfish, individualistic and heartless. There are instances of the rich exploiting the poor. They show least concern to the poor. Their children do not bother about the society. They want to enjoy. They are brought up in exclusiveness. They do not know what poverty is, what sufferance is. They become arrogant. They lack basic values in life. They are not taught the basics of Islamic philosophy of life. They squander their wealth. It is here we find a great gap between the spirit and letter of Islam and the cultural behaviour of Muslims. They should be made to know that if they do not correct their habits and culture, they will be doomed fast. Allah's curses will visit them.

Zakat and Other Type of Help to the Poor

Zakat is compulsory in Islam. All those who are capable of giving Zakat are morally bound to give *zakat* in kind or cash to only those who are in need. This is one way for the rich to use their wealth in the larger benefit of the society. The Holy Prophet made alms giving on Idul-fitr an obligatory act. Giving food to the poor is also a type of *zakat*. It was meant to atone for any absurdity or immodesty that may have been committed during fasting in the month of Ramadan. Even otherwise, help to the poor can be given during any part of the year.

But *zakat* can be given and God's reward for this is possible only when the *zakat* given is out of wealth acquired through lawful means. If through unlawful means, there will be no spiritual reward. On the contrary, he will face odds. He will be carrying the burden of it with him into the next world. If a person who is duty bound to give *zakat*, but fails to do so, will find on the Day of Judgment his wealth turns into a poisonous snake with two black spots on its head. It will be like a yoke around his neck. Then it will seize him by the jaws and declare, "I am your wealth, I am your treasure." This is the warning given by the Holy Prophet.

This is the essence of *zakat* in Islam. But the actual reality is different. Today there is wider publicity for *zakat*. The *zakat* giver desires, not all, name and fame. He thinks of titles and awards. We find a large number of Muslims who are in the queue for giving *zakat* out of their illegally acquired wealth. The famous Haji Mastan was well-known for giving *zakat*, feeding and sheltering the poor. Footpath sleepers in Mumbai received lot of comforts. His was household name. But he acquired wealth through unlawful means like black-marketing, smuggling, etc. Even now there are many rich people and politicians who are involved in illegal activities in the process of making wealth. They help a large number of Hajis. What is significant is that the Muslim society accepts this and does not make hue and cry. A small amount contributed by the honest person is hundred times better than huge contribution made by a dishonest person.

Recovery of Loan Amount

It is universally well-known that recovery of loan is a herculean task. Normally no person who has taken loan would happily return the amount in time and without being demanded. There may be genuine reasons for non-payment of loan in time. There are instances where non-payment is intentional without justifiable reasons. What about the lender? It all depends partly on his attitude. No doubt he has to get back his amount as per the written or verbal agreement. But it is always a human problem. A lender may be a professional or a non-professional. For a professional, getting this is a source of livelihood. Until he gets back his lent amount, he may not be in a position to run his trade and maintain his family too. It is well settled that a lender of this category collects some amount over and above the principal amount. This principal amount may be called interest or a goodwill help or it could be an element of profit or non-profit. Generally it is interest.

Since interest is strictly prohibited in Islam, lenders try to employ tricks of trade to avoid public criticism. He is cursed by the society. His social status is lowered. His public image is damaged. But what about his intention, whether his intention is *bona fide* or *mala fide*? Can he deceive his conscience and hoodwink Almighty Allah. What about morality? Is morality above legality? Should a person be afraid of legality more than morality? Will he remember that violation of law results in punishment in this world itself? Punishment for violation of morality is a deferred punishment in the other world. The confirmed belief is that "Allah is all merciful and forgives all sins if a person repents even at the last minute of his life". But the same person forgets that Allah will excuse all sins excepting non-payment of debt.

How many creditors are prepared to forgo the loan amount? Why should they be blamed if they try to get back the loan? A good hearted and God-fearing person may show some mercy and give additional time for repayment. He may also forgo the extra income from the loan. But he may not let go his principal loan. He will take steps to recover the amount. Should he be soft or hard in his attempts to recover? The Holy Prophet has expressed his mind on this issue. He does not want harsh steps for recovery. The creditor has to be soft. The Holy Prophet has expressed his views. There was a man who used to give loans to poor people. When his assistant had to go to them to recover the loan, he would urge him to be forgiving to those who were not able to pay back his loan with ease, believing that way, perhaps God would show him forgiveness. When that man came face to face with the Almighty, He forgave him.

This message of the Holy Prophet is not known to many. But even then not all knowledgeable persons follow this. We read in newspapers that the money lenders harass the loanees, assault them and kill them in a fitness of anger. I know one instance where a lady money lender created havoc. This middle aged Muslim lad had lent a few lakhs of rupees to another Muslim lady who needed money for the marriage expenses of her daughter. The lady Muneera, was avarious. Since money was easily available, she did not bother to think whether she is capable of returning the amount. She took three times the amount she needed to purchase minimum furniture and utensils to be given to the bridegroom's party.

She easily and lavishly spent the whole amount not only for the purpose for which she took loan, but also for throwing a gala marriage party. Many months were over. There was no sign of preparation for return of the loan. I used to caution her. But it had no effect. The money lender, Salma, visited the house a number of times for return of loan. Muneera was giving lame excuses. But one day Salma became furious in dealing with Muneera. She beat Muneera, started shouting, using bad language. People started collecting on the road. Muneer's daughter Fouzia, a college student appeared there. Salma started abusing Fouzia. Finally she went to the extent of saying, "you come home and give company to my husband until the loan amount along with interest amount is repaid. Fouzia was taken aback. She was in tears.

Muneera is a sinner. Salma is equally a sinner. Both have offended Islamic mandate. The Holy Prophet's message is that the debtor has to clear the debt. God forgives all sins, but will not forgive a debtor. Salma has violated Holy Prophet's message. She should have exercised restraint and patience. Both could have appeared before the *Jamaat* for a decision binding on both.

III
Burqua System

Col. Muammara Gaddafi, appealing to his population to fight the Western coalition's decision to stop his troops from killing the rebels in his land, played the Islamic card. His speeches called their action a modern Christian Crusade against Islam. Col. Gaddafi is not known as the most pious of Muslims. Neither was Saddam Hussein, or for that matter, Muhammad Ali Jinnah. But then that's politics ! I don't know what Col. Gaddafi does in tent. He may piously pray five times a day, refrain from drinks and stick to *halal* food, but I do read in the press that his sons have — how shall one put this? — tastes and pastimes which can't be characterized as strictly Islamic. These pastimes are well publicized — shooting, yachting and clubbing with financiers and supporters of Israel. I couldn't care less, but what would Iranian President Mahmoud Ahmadinejad say?

Col. Gaddafi's daughter Aisha recently appeared on TV. She had covered her head, but wasn't in full *burqua.* I have never seen or heard a public speech by a person in full *burqua* and would, I admit, be interested to. I have, so far, found that the expression and facial rhetoric of orators and speakers convey to me very much of the intent and meaning of their words. Look, for instance, at footage of Hitler and the sly, ducking expression between trades. The burquaed rhetorician would be to me like Big Sister making pronouncements, I don't suppose looking for a website of the Iranian Parliament will satisfy my curiosity by offering me a speaker in such full array. I suppose they have women in their Parliament. But I don't know how they are dressed — though one does hear of what happens at secret Tehran parties.

This is the week in which the French police have been called upon to act on the new French anti-*burqua* law. It's not a law that common sense should support. Obviously a gang of men entering a bank wearing balaclavas and robes which could conceal machine-guns should be immediately challenged by the local constabulary. For the same reasons the anti-*burqua* law should only be applied in parallel or identical circumstances; three *burqua-nasheens* urgently entering a bank with a getaway car driven by another hidden one waiting a few feet away at the curb? I don't think so. Send for Inspector Poirot! But in general, *burquas*, *hijabs* and *niqabs* should not be the business of the state. Personally, I operate the Groucho Marx principle which states that he wouldn't want to belong to any club that would accept him as a member. Similarly, I don't wish to see the face of anyone who, for some religious belief, doesn't want to show it to me. I really can do without.

I am though fascinated to know what fundamentalist Islamic girls' schools do for group photographs. Does the photo of the Class of 2010 and 2009 all row after sitting and standing row in their black *burquas* look exactly like the class of 2011? Are they all smiling when the photographer says "say 'cheese'?" perhaps we shall never know. Very many Muslim societies and millions of Muslims, including some very learned and respected ones, don't accept that Islam enjoins women to be covered from head to foot. Nevertheless what people wear in the land of liberty, equality and fraternity is, with notable exceptions such as the balaclava in the bank or the birthday suit in the High Street, none of France President Nicolas Sarkozy's business.

Neither is what Col. Gaddafi chooses to wear any of mine. I am free to wonder why he wants to look like a circus clown parodying a Ruritanian general with medals which look like they were bought wholesale from Mumbai's or Marrakech's *chor* bazaar? It certainly isn't a form of dress sanctioned by Islam, so perhaps he is following Idi Amin's tasteful example? Apart from the bad taste, he also behaves badly in public. In the late 1980s, working in British TV, I sent a crew down to Zimbabwe to cover the Commonwealth conference and get an interview with Prime Minister Rajiv Gandhi. Robert Mugabe, who was not then known as a murdering swine or usurper, had invited as a special guest to the conference his friend Col. Gaddafi.

Darcus Howe (Trinidadian British and a writer and broadcaster by profession), the producer and interviewer of my TV crew, told me the story. The delegates were assembled in a public hall. The traffic in Harare had been strictly restricted with police and Army roadblocks in control. The rule was that no armaments should be allowed past the roadblocks and into the hall. Col. Gaddafi arrived, dressed in his clown's outfit, with a large contingent of female soldiers carrying machine guns and other weapons. The Zimbabwean police stopped them and there was an argument and a consequent delay to the proceedings. Col. Gaddafi wasn't personally stopped and he entered the hall to applause, got onto the stage, was welcomed and looked a bit disconcerted. One of the male generals came hurrying down the aisle and climbed onto the stage and was immediately berated in Arabic by the good Colonel. Where the hell were his female bodyguards? He had arranged and expected to make an entrance into this congregation flanked by them! The general muttered his excuse. They had been detained by the Zimbabweans.

In front of that international delegation, Col. Gaddafi slapped with an open palm and shouted at him. The flunkey general slunk off holding his smarting cheek. In a few minutes the female Libyan bodyguards walked into the hall carrying their sub-machine guns and rallying in pantomime array to flank their leader. Mr. Mugabe's police had been induced somehow to change their minds and make an exception for the Libyan delegation. Darcus subsequently interviewed Rajiv. The interview ranged over very many topics and when they were off camera Rajiv chatted with Darcus who asked him what he thought of Col. Gaddafi and the previous day's performance. "He's mad isn't he?" was Rajiv's response.

Europe Frets over *Burqua*

An immigrant's obligation to the society he has left and duty to the country that provides him with a home clash in the furore over *burquas*. The controversy suggests that Europe is a sea of billowing black veils. Actually, it's the alien symbol that outrages public imagination, not the fact. Only a few thousands out of a million Muslim women in Britain are veiled. The French estimate it at between 400 and 2000. *Burquas* are hardly ever seen. Ironically, when you do spot one, it probably drapes an European Muslim's wife, a convert who is more zealous than a born Muslim. Class distinction is the third irony. Humbler Arab tourists in London may be veiled but not the wives of Arab kings and presidents. Nor sheikhas and sultanas from the Gulf. They flaunt Parisian haute couture without even the wisp of veil. The biggest irony is Europe's insistence on forbidding something that the Islamic world considers the antiquated and irrelevant relic of pre-Islamic times. Syria recently banned *burquas*. Egypt, Turkey and Tunisia have imposed restrictions even on wearing the *niqab* or *hijab*, as the headscarf is called.

The excitement is in Europe. Though only France and Belgium have actually banned *burquas* (Italy is reportedly planning to follow them), opinion polls indicate that grassroots level sentiment is remarkably similar in all 27 European Union countries. They are against allowing Muslim women to be shrouded in black from head to toe. Even in Britain where Damian Green, the immigration minister, says there is no question of forbidding the *burqua* for the wives and daughters of 2.4 million Muslims, 67 per cent of the population would welcome a ban. President Nicolas Sarkozy's law enjoys the robust support of more than 80 per cent of French citizens. The figures for Germans and Spaniards who want a similar ban are 62 and 59 per cent respectively. A possibly quite irrational fear of Muslim influence helps to explain this sentiment. Europe, with 13 million Muslims, feels threatened by immigrants not only from North Africa but from Islamic countries as far away as Bangladesh. An internet posting is headed, "Germany, Wake Up! Muslims are Taking Over, And You're Asleep at the Wheel" ! Germany's four or five million Muslims are guest workers from Turkey. France's six million or more Muslims and the million or so in Spain are from the Maghreb. Historical memory buttresses contemporary conditions. Moors ruled large parts of Spain for centuries. Albania and Bosnia-Herzegovina are reminders that the Balkans were part of the Ottoman empire whose armies swept up to Vienna.

Un-British: Britain does not share those memories. Moreover, the British fought for religious freedom whereas the French Revolution exalted the non-religious state. Damian Green thus thinks a legal restriction on a personal religious symbol would be "rather unBritish" and contrary to the conventions of a "tolerant and mutually respectful society". But a Conservative member of parliament, Philip Hollobone, is preparing a private member's Bill to compensate for what he calls the government's failure to uphold the public interest. Though threatened with legal action for discrimination under Britain's Equality Act, Hollobone refuses to meet female constituents in *burquas*. He calls it commonsense. "If you want to engage in normal, daily, interactive dialogue with your fellow human beings, you can only really do this properly by seeing each other's face." He calls the *burqua* "the religious equivalent of going around with a paper bag over your head with two holes for the eyes". He is not alone even among politicians. Jack Straw, the former labour justice minister, also asked his constituents in the heavily Asianised Lancashire town of Blackburn to uncover their faces if they came to see him. He can't recall a single occasion when the lady concerned refused to lift her veil.

The *burqua* provokes intense debate with Imran Khan, the former cricketer and now Chairman of Pakistan's Tehreeke-Insaf party, warning that any attempt to ban it could radicalize Muslims and undermine the British way of life. Many British Muslims fear they have been stereotyped as terrorists since the 2005 London bombing that killed 52 people. Their resentment feeds on opposition to British foreign policy, particularly the war on terror and invasions of Iraq and Afghanistan. Surveys show that 40 per cent want *Shariat* law in certain areas (which would mean geographical ghettoisation) while one out of five sympathises with the feelings and emotions of suicide bombers. These positions are not surprising considering that 60 per cent of Britain's more than 1,500 mosques follow the Deobandi school. Community leaders like Sadiq Khan, a

Labour MP involved with the official task force set up after the London bombings, regrets that "vast number of Muslims feel disengaged and alienated from mainstream British society". Yet, according to Farooq Murad, head of Britain's Muslim Council, Britain is the most welcoming country in Europe for Muslims. Immigrants are economic refugees. What no one mentions is their obligation to assimilate with the host society. Those who feel strongly about cultural totems like turbans, dreadlocks or *burquas* should not leave the country where they are treated as normal.

Muslim Clerics Condemn *Burqua* Ban in France

Condemning the ban imposed on *burqua* in France, Muslim leaders and clerics said the 'undemocratic' move violates basic human rights and appealed to the government to raise the issue with the European nation. "The veil is an integral part of our religion. Banning it is against the freedom of religion. . . . The French Government's move is undemocratic and against secularism", said a statement issued by prominent Islamic seminary Darul Uloom Deoband. The joint statement was signed by Darul Uloom's acting Vice-Chancellor Maulana Abul Kasmi Banarsi and Deputy Vice-Chancellor Abdul Khalique Madrasi. The clerics also appealed to the government to raise the issue with the French Government and press it to withdraw the ban. France on April 11 became the first country in Europe to implement a ban on the wearing of full face coverings, including the Islamic *niqab*.

Niqab or *burqua* is full face covering, whereas veil is the traditional head covering. Maulana Abdul Hameed Noamani, an Islamic scholar and a senior member of Jamiat-Ulema-e-Hind said, "The ban is against basic human rights. Only a very small minority wear *burqua* . . . . There was no need for such legislation". "Everyone should be allowed to follow his religious values", he said. Maulana Afroz Mujtaba, a senior cleric, said, "The ban on *burqua* was uncalled for. Everyone has a right to wear a cloth of his or her choice, why such discrimination against minorities in Europe"?

Muslims with a population of 175 millions are the largest minority community in India. In 2009, a Muslim girl was not allowed by her college in Karnataka to attend classes wearing a *burquas*. The college and the girl later reached a compromise. “In a democratic and secular set-up, people have every right to practice the religion of their choice. Such a move (ban on *burqua*) will only strengthen extremist group in their propaganda against western countries”, said Maulana Asghar Abbas, a Delhi-based cleric. “The European countries should avoid steps which could help the radical groups”, he added.

French Ban on *Niqab* faces Muslim Resistance

The controversial ban on the *niqab* that covers a *burqua*-wearing woman’s face, came into effect in France, with Belgium and the Netherlands considering a similar step. In the United Kingdom, though, opinion appears to be more against the French government’s decision than in favour. In defiance, Kenza Drider, a 32-year old French mother of four, intends to leave her home in Avignon by wearing a *niqab*. She may not be arrested but could be fined. Under the new law, French citizens are forbidden to cover their faces in public places. While the wording of the legislation is unspecific, there’s little doubt it targets Muslim women. “I’ll be going about my business in my full veil as I have for the last 12 years and nothing and nobody is going to stop me”, said Drider, a French woman of Moroccan origin. But if she sets foot on Avignon’s railway station to take a train to Paris, she risks fine of 150 euros. A repeat offence would pack her off to a “citizenship course”. An estimated 350 to 2,000 women wear *niqabs* in France. The new rule will not impact foreigners.

Drider’s defiance has made her a bit of a celebrity. “I never thought I’d see the day when France, my France, the country I was born in and I love, the country of liberty, egality, fraternity, would do something that so obviously violates people’s freedom”, she said. “If women want to go around half-naked, I don’t object. But why should I not be allowed to cover up?” parliamentarians and feminists in France, though, have argued that the full veil is a symbol of male oppression and that *niqab*-wearing women are bullied into it by their husbands. In the UK, the three main political parties, Conservative, Labour and Liberal Democrats, are thus far opposed to the French order. But it's suspected that a section of Conservatives silently support Sarkozy on the ban.

Protests in France over *Burqua* Ban

The women, part of a demonstration that erupted in front of Notre Dame cathedral here, were detained for taking part in an unauthorized protest rather than for wearing their veils. But, in theory at least, French officials can now slap fines on Muslim women who refuse orders to expose their faces when in public. "Today was not about arresting people because of wearing the veil. It was for not having respected the requirement to declare a demonstration", said police spokesman Alexis Marsan. Two women in *niqabs*, a woman wearing an Islamic headscarf that did not cover her face and a protest organizer were arrested, Marsan said. Separately, businessman and activist Rachid Nekkaz said he and a woman friend of his wearing the *niqab* were arrested by the police in front of President Nicolas Sarkozy's Elysee Palace.

"We wanted to be fined for wearing the *niqab*, but the police didn't want to issue a fine", said Nekkaz, who has promised to auction off a two-million-euro property to start a fund to pay off fines for veil-wearers. One of those arrested in front of Notre Dame was 32-year old Kenza Drider from the Southern city of Avignon, who was due to appear on television and has become a symbol of France's tiny community of *niqab* wearers. "This law infringes my European rights, I cannot but defend them, that is to say my freedom to come and go and my religious freedom", Drider told reporters as she boarded a train for Paris before the protest.

Many French police fear the law will be impossible to enforce, since they have not been empowered to use force to remove head coverings, and could face resistance in already tense immigrant districts. "The law will be infinitely difficult to enforce, and will be infinitely rarely enforced", said Manuel Roux, deputy head of a union representing local police chiefs. "It's not for the police to demonstrate zeal", he said, predicting that when patrol officers meet veiled women, they will simply try to explain the law to them and to persuade them to remove their face covering. "If they refuse, that's when things get really complicated. We have no power to force them", he said. "I can't begin to imagine we are going to pay any attention to a veiled woman in a sensitive area, where men are proud." The law came into effect at an already fraught moment in relations between the state and France's Muslim minority, with Sarkozy accused of stigmatizing Islam to win back votes from a resurgent far right.

***Burqua* Ban: Is it a Progressive Act ?**

The French decision to ban the use of the *burqua* by women in public has met with an interesting range of reactions. There are those who find the action culturally intolerant and smacking of the Islamophobic undercurrent that seems to be running through the developed world. Then there are others who see this as an affirmative step that pushes back against what they see as the tendency to pander to the interests of various minorities in the name of diversity and multiculturalism. And of course, there are still others who are torn between wanting to respect the right of all cultures, particularly those marginalized by the mainstream, and fighting the battle for gender equality. The banning of the *burqua* creates a schism between two liberal concerns and makes it difficult for the set of people to take a clear view.

It is an interesting, one which marks an inflection point in the attitude of the developed world towards the idea of tolerance towards other cultures. For years now, the tide has been turning against immigration with more and more countries tightening their laws and taking active measures to stem the influx of people from other countries. The debate about outsourcing in the US, too, reveals the ease with which countries that stood on pulpits and lectured to the world about the virtues of the free market backtrack when their interests are placed on the line. And of course, the post 9/11 world, liberal and otherwise, looks upon Islam in particular with deep suspicion, and this apparently legitimate need for caution has given force to a latent unease about the changing character of their own cultures in the wake of the relentless waves of immigration.

The fault line has been established between culturally neutral and universally applicable liberal values and countries that are culturally 'loaded'. An asymmetrical relationship gets established between modern universalist ideas and "cultures", one where local cultures need to be patronized in the name of respect. Liberal notions are seen to stand outside culture instead of being seen as being apart of another kind of culture, which is what they are. The *burqua* debate tends to be seen as a conflict between modernity and Islam whereas it is perhaps more accurately described as one between two different cultures, both with their own set of constructed assumptions.

It is important to recognize that the uncritical acceptance of a certain view of modernity as being absolute, universally applicable and inevitable is inherently flawed. Take the example of arranged marriage for instance. To the modern mindset this is an anachronistic institution, rooted in repression and one that must inevitably give way to what we call a love marriage in India. The Western mode of marriage is seen to be the right one, and something that the rest of the world must be converted to at some stage. And yet, it is hardly that simple. Firstly, the Western model is by itself flawed, in that it is still rooted in gender inequality (even now only the man can propose marriage) and offers little practical hope of durability. More importantly, in a culture like India which has opened up to change, the arranged marriage has evolved so as to take care of contemporary needs and continues to thrive. Increasingly, there are people choosing this mode out of their own free will.

Even when the world seems to be embracing more modern notions of political organisation, it does not follow that it is equally keen to embrace other modern ideas. The brutal molestation of CNN reporter Lara Logan at the hands of a pro-democracy Egyptian mob is a reminder of the complexity of change. It is likely that democracy when it does come to the Middle East will look different from its cousins elsewhere, just as freedom in the political area will not necessarily lead to emancipation in another.

What seems to be happening is that with the reduction in the power distance between the developed world and others, the idea of liberal tolerance has taken a knock. The gap between professed ideals and primitive instincts is no longer sustainable and we can see a resurgence of shriller voices emerge in many parts of the world. The US is a good example of the nature of political discourse in today's times, for the debate there is being framed by people like Sarah Palin, Donald Trump, and an assorted bunch of fringe lunatics preaching a dangerously simple-minded form of mainstream hate. And in a wider sense, when it came to the crunch, the West's liberal pretensions have collapsed quickly and dramatically, as is evident from Guantanamo and selective attacks on unfriendly regimes. The fact that the US celebrates Barack Obama because he is the first black President after over 200 years of independence and alleged equality is a telling commentary of the reality when it comes to tolerance and fairness. And even now, he is plagued by accusations of being Muslim, as if it were some sort of crime.

The trust is that every culture will find its own trajectory of evolution. It is likely that the change will happen non-linearly, with movement taking place both forward and backward. The attempt to force change from the outside using external yardsticks of an absolute nature are unlikely to succeed, although they too will play a role in determining the pace and the nature of change. The banning of the *burqua* is a French reaction, not a modern one and is rooted in a set of cultural assumptions and not anything universal and absolute. The French have a right to safeguard what they see as their own way of life in their own way but, unpalatable as it might be to some, their actions are not fundamentally different from the say the Saudi ban on women driving. Both are primitive responses aimed at protecting a way of life and both take refuge in high-minded ideologies. What we call modern is, at one level, just another culture or; put another way, just another tradition peculiar to some cultures.

France's *Burqua* Debate Stokes Passion in North Africa

A French proposal to ban full face veils has stoked debate in Europe and also provoked strong reactions across the

Mediterranean in North Africa, where many of France's Muslims trace their origins. Former French colonies Algeria, Morocco and Tunisia are still tied to France by history, language and migration, so their views on the *burqua* issue could have a direct influence on how Muslims inside France react to a ban. People in North Africa are split between those who see the proposed ban – a version of which has already been approved by Belgium's lower house of parliament – as an attack on Islam, and those who applaud Europe for defending secular values.

What is shared though by at least some people on each side of the argument is a concern that talk of a ban could be exploited by unscrupulous politicians and ratchet up tension between the authorities in Europe and Muslim communities. "I am against this form of dress . . . . but we should not enact laws against it", Khadija Riyadi, President of Morocco's leading independent human rights groups, AMDH, said. "The right wing in France will take advantage of this law during elections when they should be addressing the situation of Muslims in France and trying to help them shrug off joblessness, poverty and racism", she said. The *burqua* issue has, in France and other countries, become the focus for a debate about Islam and European society.

Belgium's lower house of Parliament approved a bill to ban wearing the full Islamic face veil in public, though it still needs to pass the upper house. France, home to the European Union's largest Muslim minority, is planning to debate a draft law to ban all face veils in public. Influential politicians in Austria and the Netherlands have also advocated a ban. For some people in North Africa, those discussions are evidence of a racist push to evict Muslims from Europe. "It is not just a campaign but a war against our people in Europe", said Sheikh Abdelfetah Zeraoui, a cleric in Algeria who belongs to the traditional Salafist strain of Islam. "We will urge our decision makers to apply reciprocity for European women entering into Algeria. They should be wearing the Muslim veil. Otherwise we won't let them come to Algeria."

Just as in Europe, women in North Africa who wear full face veils — known as the *niqab* or *burqua* — are a small minority. Many women wear the *hijab*, which covers the head but leaves the face exposed, while a sizeable minority go uncovered. Fatima Bougttaya, 32 comes from the working class neighbourhood of Sale, near Rabat, and wears a full *burqua* that covers her from head to toe, with only her hands exposed. "It is just a racist decision to destroy Islam", she said, when asked about the proposed French ban. "Why do they not make a law against women who exhibit their bodies in public and in front of cameras?" North Africa plays a role in helping form Muslim opinion in Europe because many people of North African origin regularly travel back to the region and the mosques they attend abroad are often run by clerics trained in Algeria, Morocco or Tunisia. Secular-minded people in North Africa sympathise with European moves to ban the face veil, seeing an echo of their own concerns that hard-line Islamists in their countries are becoming too powerful.

Belgium Bans wearing of *Burqua* in Public

Belgium became Europe's first country to vote for a ban on the full Islamic veil or *burqua*, sparking dismay on Friday among Muslims and warnings of a dangerous precedent with France set to follow suit. The Bill, which also draw fire from human rights group Amnesty International, will not enter force for weeks and may have to be re-examined if early elections are called as Belgium battles a political crisis. "We're the first country to spring the locks that have made a good number of women slaves, and we hope to be followed by France, Switzerland, Italy, and the Netherlands; countries that think," said Liberal deputy Denis Ducarme. In the lower house of the federal Parliament, 136 deputies supported a nationwide ban on clothes or veils that do not allow the wearer to be fully identified, including the full-face *niqab* and *burqua*. There were two abstentions. No one voted against.

The ban will be imposed in streets, public gardens and sports grounds or buildings "meant for public use or to provide services" to the public, according to the text of the Bill. People who ignore it could face a fine of $ 20-34 and/or a jail sentence of up to seven days. All governing parties and the opposition agreed on the move — most for security reasons linked to the fact that people cannot be recognized while wearing the clothing. In *Le Soir* newspaper, Michael Privot, an Islamic scholar, said Belgium "now joins Iran and Saudi Arabia in that exclusive but unenviable rare club of countries to impose a dress code in the public domain." He said the three cite "the protection of dignity, or even the freedom, of women to justify the unjustifiable; the restriction of individual freedoms of some of our citizens".

"The vice-president of the Muslim executive of Belgium, Isabelle Praile, warned the vote could set a dangerous precedent and pave the way for a crackdown on other symbols of religious expression such as Sikh turbans. "Given the acute crisis which our government is facing, this move to kill our liberties, which will deprive dozens of women of their fundamental rights, is totally over the top and driven by ideology", she said.

Purdah Nasheen takes the Plunge

Begum Shehnaz Sidrat, president of Bazm-e-Khawateen which is a 75-year old outfit for Muslim women empowerment, filed her nomination for Lucknow seat with a premonition of a stinging *fatwa* from city clerics weighing on her mind. The "objectionably bold step" had already drawn dark threats from Muslim Majlis and half a dozen minority leaders some of whom personally made calls to make Sidrat realize her station in life. Politics, she was told, was not for a *purdah nasheen* (veiled woman) and as an office bearer of the reputed Bazm-e-Khawateen, she was expected to confine herself to social causes only.

Half the battle is already won. It has been nearly a week and the *maulvis* are quiet, says a relieved Sidrat who, incidentally, could be the only candidate representing a Muslim women's body. Facing holy wrath is a lot tougher than taking on the links of Nafisa Ali or Rita Bahuguna Joshi, she adds, half seriously. Moreover, with prominent Muslim women's organisations in UP like All-India Muslim women movement and All-India Women Personal Law Board seconding her candidature, the 50-year old has added a few inches to her stature.

Not that she has done anything to defy the class. Sidrat, a post-graduate in political science and former student council president of Moradabad Degree College where she was the lone girl student at the time, observes *hijab* (*purdah*) albeit with a few practical alterations. Instead of the shuttle cock *burqua*, she has designed a *burqua* coat – a somber grey coat like a doctor's apron – and "as Islam does not demand covering the face but only hair", her henna-tinged locks are tamed under a severely wrapped *dupatta*.

Due to her position in Bazm, Sidrat is a well-known face among the Muslim lower socio-economic segment as well as the middle class. She also has her lines ready. Muslim women and their issues don't figure in any political party's agenda, she says. Issues like illiteracy, health and evil practices like triple *talaq* find no solution. "Even a woman chief minister Mayawati chose a man as a successor", she notes. Winning or losing, she says, is immaterial. What matters is to make a point. "Let them see that even a woman in *hijab* has the courage to join public life and the commitment to do her best if chosen."

Burqua **row in Bhatkal College Festers**

It seems as if controversy over the *burqua* refuses to go away from Karnataka's coastal areas. While colleges in Mangalore and Bantwal grappled with similar problems, this time some students at the Government College at Bhatkal who objected to the right of fellow students to attend colleges in the *burqua*. The row which started a week back, remains unresolved despite the intervention of J.D. Naik, Bhatkal MLA, and the president of the betterment committee.

Some students, who objected to some girls wearing a *burqua* to college, have been demanding the introduction of a uniform dress code. The college betterment committee, which held a meeting a few days ago, resolved to maintain *status quo* till the principal seeks a clarification from the Commissioner of Collegiate Education. The committee had warned of action against students who tried to create disturbance.

A few students have been attending the college wearing

saffron clothes with vermillion on their foreheads since Friday. Some girls too attended the college wearing saffron colour veils on Saturday. "Why should we not do so when a few students were allowed to attend the college wearing *burqua*?" Some said. Naik told *Express* that guidelines have been sought from the government. Reacting to the students attending college in saffron clothes, he said he has asked the principal to take action. Meanwhile, principal R.I. Khan said that the controversy would be resolved early.

Headscarf Row : Principal Suspended

The Principal of Believers' Church English Medium School at Gurupuram, who issued a transfer certificate to a Muslim girl student allegedly for wearing a headscarf to school, has been placed under suspension by the school management. However, the parents of the student have refused to accept the suspension and have threatened to move court if the Principal was not sacked.

Believer's Church Kerala Secretary Fr. Williams informed the decision to suspend the Principal at a meeting convened to sort out the issue here on Friday by District Collector P. Venugopal. Fr. Williams said the church authorities did not know about the issue of the transfer certificate and that they were not informed about it at any stage. The Principal's act, they said, had questioned the very credibility of the church, he said. Talking to reporters after the meeting, Fr. Williams said there were several Muslim students in various schools run by the Believer's Church, and nowhere did any such rule banning headscarves exist.

Separate Enquiry : Apart from suspending the Principal, Mary Jessintha, the Education Committee of the church was conducting a separate inquiry and, if need be, further punitive action would be initiated. The church would also cooperate with any probe by the government and had in fact demanded that an officer of IG rank should conduct an inquiry, he added. However, Nazir Musaliar, father of the student, said the Principal's act had questioned religious customs and that a mere suspension was not enough. "She should be sacked, a criminal case should be booked against her and she should be jailed. If they do not do it, we will file a case in the court and see that she gets apt punishment", he told reporters.

Mr. Nazir also said he did not intend to send his daughter to the same school, though the school management had agreed to take her back. He wanted to send her to another CBSE school in Mannancherry. The Collector had allowed some time to take a decision, he said. Mr. Venugopal, meanwhile, said he preferred the student to return to the same school. But since the parents were not of the same opinion, he would help them to secure admission in the school of their choice, he said. The Principal, Ms. Jessintha, did not participate in the meeting.

Woman, who did not wear *purdah* and headscarf, alleges threat to life

The Kerala High Court, on Thursday, ordered police protection for Ryhana R. Kazi (22) of Kasaragad who complained of receiving threats to her life for not wearing the *purdah* and headscarf. A Division Bench directed the Superintendent of Police, the Circle Inspector and the Sub-Inspector, Kasaragad, to provide protection to her parents and siblings also. The orders will remain in force for three weeks.

Threatening calls: The woman said in a writ petition that her neighbours and distant relatives had been insisting that she wear the *purdah* and the scarf on her return from Chennai after graduating in aeronautical engineering. She had been resisting the intrusion into her personal freedom. She alleged that she had received threatening calls from persons claiming to be Popular Front of India (PFI) activists after her plight was published in the media.

Ryhana said she received a threatening letter from one of her neighbours, Muhammad Kavungoli. The neighbours had started levelling false allegations against her, she alleged. Ryhana said that though she had lodged a complaint with the police, no action had been taken. She had lodged a complaint with the State Women's Commission also. The petitioner said that if she was not granted police protection to prevent "the illegal intervention in the name of religion" to place restrictions on her personal freedom, it would cause prejudice and hardship to her and her family.

Pak Women prefer *Hijab* to *Burqua*

Young girls in jeans and T-shirts roam freely in the up market Zamzama Road of Pakistan's largest city that houses many fashion boutiques and cafes. So do many women clad in the traditional salwaar-kameez, though they cover their head with a *Hijab*. Women in *burquas*, however, are not a regular sight in this cosmopolitan port city.

"Wearing a *hijab* or a *burqua* or not covering your head at all is just a matter of choice. If a woman wants to wear the *hijab* – and not the *burqua* — it's because she has been brought up by a steady dose of modernity", Aamna Haider Isani, a senior fashion journalist, said. "You will see a lot of single women, single mothers, and all types of working women here. Many corporates are giving Pakistani women an opportunity to change the perceptions of people around the globe who think Pakistan is a conservative country", she added.

This correspondent, to her surprise, found a lot of women from various walks of life choosing to just cover their head. "You will be surprised to know that it was only the Prophet's wife who was supposed to wear a *burqua* so that she could be identified, but then some fanatics forced it on women to protect them from the glare of the public eye", Huma Adnan, a fashion designer, explained.

"Islam preaches that a woman should be well covered so that she doesn't attract unnecessary male attention, and the reason why she has to cover her head is because hair is considered to be an attraction for men", she added. During private parties, a lot of women don elegant dresses, evening wear and off-shoulder gowns, but skin-show is limited. The majority of women here shy away from showing their legs, arms and back — the idea is elegant dressing. An average woman in Karachi covers her head and dresses in a salwar-kameez and heads off to work.

France approves Ban on Face Veils

France's lower house of Parliament overwhelmingly approved a ban on *burqua*-like Islamic veils on Tuesday, a move that is popular among French voters despite serious concerns from Muslim groups and human rights advocates. There were 336 votes for the bill and just one against it at the National Assembly. Most members of the main opposition group, the Socialist Party, refused to participate in the vote — though they support a ban, they have differences with President Nicolas Sarkozy's conservatives over some aspects of it.

The ban of face-covering veils will go in September to the Senate, where it also is likely to pass. Its biggest hurdle will likely come after that, when France's constitutional watchdog scrutinizes it. Some legal scholars say there is a chance it could be deemed unconstitutional. The main body representing French Muslims says face-covering veils are not required by Islam and not suitable in France, but it worries that the law will stigmatise Muslims in general. While ordinary head scarves are common, only about 1,900 women in France are believed to wear face-covering veils. Champions of the bill say they oppress women.

Woman told to remove *Burqua*

A British court asked a Muslim woman to remove *burqua* to show her facial expression while testifying against her husband in a physical abuse case. Georgina Richards, 36, who is eight-month pregnant, reluctantly agreed when magistrates said they might not accept her evidence if they could not see her "facial expressions", according to *Daily Mail*. The case at Leicester Magistrates Court was held up for over an hour on Thursday while magistrates agreed to hear her evidence from behind a screen. Richards gave evidence against her ex-partner Ismail Mangera, 30.

Shiv Sena demands *Burqua* Ban

"If the *burqua* is to be used to steal children, then we demand that it be banned as per law", an editorial in party mouthpiece

Saamna said. Referring to France risking the wrath of the Islamic world by banning the *burqua* and other full-body robes worn by some Muslim women, the editorial said the French President took a "revolutionary step" to ban the *burqua*. "When *burqua* was banned in Turkey by Kemal Pasha, Islam did not come in between. Why only is it so in India", it said.

The Shiv Sena, particularly its newly appointed Yuva Sena chief Aditya Thackeray, is facing flak over forcing Mumbai University to drop Rohinton Mistry's book *Such a Long Journey* for alleged derogatory references to Maharashtra and Marati Manoos. However, Mistry has voiced dismay over Mumbai University providing "deluxe service *via* express delivery" in quickly dropping his Booker Prize nominated book from the college syllabus. "A political party demanded a change in syllabus and Mumbai University provided deluxe service *via* express delivery making the book disappear the very next day. Mumbai University has come perilously close to institutionalizing the ugly notion of self-censorship," Mistry, who is based in Canada, said.

Meanwhile, Maharashtra Chief Minister Ashok Chavan has endorsed the University's decision. Chavan, who in the past stood against Shiv Sena's attempts to indulge in moral policing, said: "Whatever language is used in the book is highly abusive". A delighted Shiv Sena spokesman Sanjay Raut said: "If the Chief Minister of the State is also with us, you have to understand that we are right". Nevertheless, Chavan said his stand should not be seen as an endorsement of Sena's cultural and moral policing. The Chief Minister said these were his personal views and that he would not like to interfere in the affairs of Mumbai University "I had not gone through the entire book. Whatever paras were shown to me, I read that, the language is highly abusive. Do we expect our students to go through such books and use them in the educational curriculum", Chavan told reporters. Chavan also said he found the language in certain portions of the book "highly objectionable". "There is objectionable language in Rohinton Mistry's book as well and we wouldn't approve his book for students", he said.

Oz: *Burqua* Ban Plan Vetoed

A bill to ban *burqua* in Australia's most populous state New South Wales on Thursday fell through as centrist and leftist legislators condemned it as racist. The bill had been moved by the leader of the rightist Christian Democratic Party Fred Nile, who had called for banning *burqua* citing security reasons and to what he called "set women free from domination of males". The legislation had been moved apparently to keep up with the trend in Europe where nations like France and Belgium are heading to ban the *burqua*. Mr. Nile's bill was defeated in the state's Upper House by 26 to 3 votes, with members opposing saying that such a step would spread fear and hatred in the country.

The legislation was moved following a nationwide heated debate sparked earlier this month by conservative legislators who called for a ban on the *burqua*, claiming it was emerging as the "preferred disguise of bandits and ne'er-do-wells". These comments were apparently prompted by the use of *burqua* in a daring armed robbery in Sydney. But Prime Minister Kevin Rudd made it clear that enforcing such a ban was not a state policy. Mr. Nile's Full-face Coverings Prohibition Bill was modelled on legislation passed in Belgium. He said concealment of a person's face — male or female — for any purpose, including terrorism, anarchism or discrimination against women, should be banned.

New Turn in French *Niqab* Ban Row

The controversy in France surrounding an imminent ban on the wearing of the *burqua*, the *niqab* or other full face coverings suddenly took a dramatic turn when a young woman revealed she had been fined €22 by the police for driving while wearing a *niqab*.

The 31-year old woman, a French national, said she had been wearing the *niqab* for the past nine years and had never had either an accident or a problem with the police. She said she had committed no crime and planned to challenge the fine and sue the government for harassment. Nothing in France's traffic regulations prevents a person from driving whilst wearing a must. The police imposed the fine claiming that her *niqab* "reduced her field of vision".

The government immediately waded into the controversy making the situation infinitely worse. Interior Minister Brice Hortefeux alleged that the woman's husband was polygamous and suggested he should be stripped of his French nationality acquired in 1999 following his marriage to a French woman. Mr. Hortefeux asked the Minister for Immigration and National identity to examine the case and determine whether or not the woman's husband had four wives and twelve children and had radical Islamist views as alleged. The Minister charged that each of the four wives independently claimed child support payments from the state. The government also indicated it could usher in a law banning the *burqua* in a matter of weeks by using article 49.3 of the Constitution which allows bypassing a parliamentary debate in order to legislate by ordinance.

Far from getting across-the-border approval, the proposed law has sharply divided France. The opposition Socialists, Greens and other leftists as well as members of the ruling UMP party have said such a ban would be impracticable and would cover the government with ridicule once it was struck down by the *Conseil d'etat*, the country's administrative court or the Constitutional Council which could declare it unconstitutional. But Prime Minister Francois Fillion said he was "prepared to take such a risk" while deciding to opt for a total ban.

"We supposedly live in a country which respects human rights. Why are members of the special police forces allowed to drive wearing hoods in that case"? asked the woman's lawyer. It is doubtful if the Interior Minister will succeed in revoking the French nationality of this woman's husband. French nationality is not easily obtained but once granted, it cannot be easily taken away either.

The Ban on the *Niqab* is an Assault on Women

Nicolas Sarkozy's decision to put forward a bill banning Muslim women from wearing the *niqab* in France's public spaces is a broadside against a global religion. And if that wasn't enough Belgium, the Netherlands and Denmark are all planning the very same bill. There is no love lost between this column and organized religion, but an assault on choice is an assault on the very intellectual liberalism that has made Europe the greatest continent on the planet.

Even before the September 11 attacks, Islam was being derided from all quarters, even though its fundamental segment comprises a mere fraction of its believers. Post. 9.11 and George W. Bush's "crusade", Islamophobia became the new black, and the legions swelled. Even in India, where we have a large Muslim population, non-Muslims tend to straddle the fine line between vehement opposition to the religion and fearful avoidance of those belonging to it. It is stunningly unfair to Islam's history and those that choose to follow its teachings.

The world seems to have forgotten the rich history of the caliphates of the Rashidun, the Umayyads and the Abbasids, where freedom of religion was not only allowed but actively promoted; where the arts and sciences flourished, and the age of discovery left Europe, in its wake. The caliphates' mark on history is an indelible one. Many leading historians believe that it was the destruction of the Abbasid caliphate by the Mongols that directly led to the Dark Ages.

For a religion so rich in intellect and culture to be so maligned speaks volumes of the state of our world. Religion, by its very nature is war-like. It can only survive by destroying its competitors, and let's face it.

But apart from all this, the proposed ban on the *niqab* is also an attack on women. Most of France's 2000-odd *niqab* wearers are French women who have converted to Islam, and choose to wear the garb. Is Sarkozy saying that these women have chosen wrong? Or that their choices do not fit into the lattice of a country increasingly adept at telling its citizens what it can and cannot do? Sarkozy has not learned from the mistakes he made that led up to and stoked the 2005 Paris riots. Where others wish to bring minorities into the fold using reason and incentive, he uses fear and the "law".

If women in France cannot wear the *niqab* in public places, then they should also ban motorcyclists from wearing full face helmets, and in the dead of winter, ban the balaclavas and face-smothering scarves. The UK, which also mulled a similar bill a few years ago, thanks to the always entertaining Jack Straw, is quite content to allow *imams* to spout anti-British fury from loudspeakers; it's fine that a very few Muslim men take to the streets demanding the Britain follow the rule of *Shariat* law. But heaven forbid a woman should choose to wear a *niqab*; that simply will not do. India has its scars, but atleast in our metropolises, Muslim women can wear what they choose. We must keep it that way. If we are going to keep religion going, then we have a duty to make sure that all of them are given the same rights. It's a hard journey, and one that may be intellectually futile. But if it's a journey we must make, then let's make sure it is made en *masse*.

Panipat to Paris : Muslim Women and the Veil

In 1947 my mother and other women of the family decided to shed the *burqua*. Our family comes from Panipat, which was at the time a flourishing district of Punjab with a large population of Muslims. The distinguishing feature of this erudite, Sufi-dominated town was the primacy of women. Our homes were known by the name of the woman of the house; for example, Bi Maimuna Ki Haveli (much later I was pleasantly surprised to see in Marrakesh the same formulation: Riad dar Maimuna). The decision of these Panipat women to remove the veil was accepted and respected by the men of my family. They were agents of their own fate. When several of these women reached Pakistan (per force they had to migrate), they did not revert to the veil. They were not asked to wear them or remove them, either by the state or their families.

Sixty-three years later, on July 13, 2010, France's Lower House of Parliament voted to ban the wearing of face covering veils in public places. The vote was passed 336 to 1, with the Left parties abstaining. In its report, the French Parliamentary Committee said that requiring women to cover their faces was against the French Republican principles of secularism and equality and deemed such practice as a "symbol of the repression of women and of extremist fundamentalism".

What is the link between Panipat and France on the issue

of Muslim women and *burqua*? France is the classic upholder of human rights. I, as many of my generation, grew up on stories of the French Revolution, the Storming of the Bastille, "Liberty Equality, Fraternity", Montesquieu', Robespierre, Louis XVI, Marie Antoinette, and the ubiquitous guillotine. Panipat was the place where caravans of Sufi scholars migrated to from Afghanistan and Iran to spread their teachings among a populace which was ready and willing to learn. Many schools of Islamic jurisprudence flourished there; people openly debated religion and followed their own maslak, each according to his or her light. Today, Panipat is a flourishing town where all the obvious signs of development hit you in the face. But the very fact for which it was distinctive has become its greatest bane; its neglect of gender issues gave it one of the lowest sex ratios in the country.

IV
Status of Women

Mazharuddin Siddiqi in his book *Women in Islam* says, "The position of women under Islam has been the subject of repeated controversy among educated Muslims ever since they came under the impact of western civilization. It is still a live issue capable of generating heat and passion.

"Islam is not a rigid framework of laws and institutions, but a set of principles capable of fresh application in changing social conditions.

An American writer, Mary R. Beard, sums up three divergent viewpoints on the subject of women's place in society in her book, *Women as a Force in History*. She says, there are three views about women's status :

1. Can be solved by complete equality with men, and this can only be established under communism.
2. A second view is that women must find her greatest happiness and contribution most to the states by limiting her ambitions to domesticity and still more narrowly to child bearing. This is the view of fascism.
3. The third view is that women should have the right to choose her way of life even to the point of self centred interests. This is the ideology of democracy.

Another glaring area where woman is ill treated is where the husband deals with his wife. Islam provides an enviable position to woman as a wife. Perhaps in no other religion wife enjoys the status as in Islam. The Prophet has emphasized time and again the way in which a wife has to be treated. He made his followers to behave most humanely towards their wives:

"Consent with them (i.e., the wives) in kindness, for if you hate them it may happen that ye hate a thing wherein Allah hath placed much good." "The best of you are those who behave best to their wives." "A good Muslim must not hate his wife, and if he be displeased with one bad quality in her, then let him be pleased with one that is good", said the Holy Prophet Muhammad. Prophet said, "woman is the queen of her house". In Islam woman is an independent personality. She can enter into business, make any contract or testament in her own name. She is entitled to inherit as mother, wife, sister, daughter — a thing unknown in any other religion, civilization or legislation. She is given liberty to choose her husband. It is not lawful for a guardian to force an adult virgin into marriage. None, not even the father nor the sovereign can lawfully contract woman in marriage who is an adult and of sound mind without her permission, whether she is a virgin or not. She can own wealth in her name.

Pierre Crabbites in his article, "Things Muhammad did for women", observes:

> "The Muslim women is a driving force which was fashioned by Muhammad's mastermind. Muhammad fourteen hundred years ago, assured to the mothers, wives and daughters of Islam a rank and dignity not yet generally assured to women by the laws of the West."

But how far Muslims follow all these Islamic injunctions is a relevant question. This is examined in brief with reference to religious freedom and equality.

Women, Freedom and Equality

There are three schools of thought which throw light on woman's right to freedom and equality. It is better to examine these views before understanding the views contained in Islamic scriptures. Communism stands for complete equality with men. Both are born equals and both should live as equals. A second view is that woman should limit her freedom and equality to find her greatest happiness and contribute most to the state by limiting her ambitions to domesticity and still more narrowly to child-bearing. This would enable growth in population to secure the state against overcrowded neighbours. This is the view of Fascism. The third view is that woman has every right to protect herself, her liberty, her own interest and in short her own way of life. This is the view of those who strongly believe in democracy.

The history of development of all these schools of thought has enough evidence to the fact that woman's role was inevitable in these movements. These teachings have nothing to do with woman's status in Islam. There was no political necessity to enlist the support of women. Islam treated the question of equality between men and women on the basis of human nature. Islam promulgated the doctrine of human equality, including sex equality, in a comprehensive verse which negates all inequalities due to sex, race, colours, nationality, caste or tribe. Female children were downgraded. Birth of female child was a bad omen, disgrace, problematic before Islam. Prophet discarded such negative views. The Holy Prphet said, "If a daughter is born to a person and he brings her up, gives her a good education and trains her in the arts of life, I shall myself stand between him and hell-fire".

In religious duties, the *Quran* recognizes no distinction between men and women. Their obligations toward God and man are similar in many respects and, therefore, their position and status in the eyes of God are also not dissimilar. Women have equal rights to offer prayers, education and public affairs.

But generally Muslim society is still dominated by men who always try to put down women. A woman's rightful place is kitchen. She has to give birth to child and bring them up. They have no right to education beyond a lower level. They have no right to appear in public life. They cannot accept jobs outside their homes. They cannot go to mosque to offer prayers. They cannot enter the *dargah* as men do. They cannot sing in public. They cannot mix with men. They cannot become public leaders. They cannot be ministers, judges, lawyers. They should do business. They should not act in films. They should always be in *burqua*. They should not apply lipsticks and nail polish. There is no end to such social restrictions which ultimately reduce women to the status of slaves.

But we have to examine which restrictions are totally against Islamic principles and which are not. Where Islam has imposed total ban nothing can be done to undo what has been done in accordance with Holy Prophet's views. He was always pragmatic and proactive. No one can take away what Prophet has bestowed upon women. And similarly, no concession and right should be given to women when all this is denied by the Holy Prophet.

The rights and restrictions should be common to all Muslim women throughout the world. How can one country has one set of rules and some other country a different set of rules. Whether it is a Muslim/Islamic country or a non-Muslim country, Islamic culture should remain the same. But we find contradictions and conflicts, meaning thereby that we have deviated from Islam. A brief reference is made to what Islam permits and how Muslims prevent.

1. Women's Right to Education

The Holy Prophet laid great emphasis on education. "Go as far as China to acquire knowledge", is his message to Muslims. The best gift of the father to the children is providing education and upbringing. While stressing emphasis on education, Prophet made it abundantly clear that even girls should be educated. There should be no discrimination between boys and girls in matters of quality and extent of education. But by and large parents have their own mental frame, particularly from the lower-middle and lower classes. The general trend is to provide education for girls upto primary level. High school education is very professional and technical education is out of mind. Even if girls are interested, parents, particularly grand-mothers will create hurdles with their traditional mind set-up.

Thus, a large number of Muslims are denying education to girls who form 50 per cent of the total population as a result of which Muslim society suffers. This block should be removed. Poverty is the reason quoted by the parents. But it is not so. It is the poverty of mind that causes damages.

2. Women's Right to Employment

Islam is a dynamic and progressive religion. It allows adoption to current societal requirements. Of course, woman's modesty and safety should be safeguarded. There could be exclusive banks for women, schools and colleges for girls. But nothing should prevent women from taking up jobs elsewhere too. Women were used in wars during the early period of Islam. There are female doctors, judges, legislators, prime ministers and ministers, receptionists, top officers in Islamic countries today. Why then some hardcore male members raise load voice against women in employment market and public life? We have to keep in mind the rights and freedom enjoyed by women in the days of the Prophet and the social situation in several Muslim countries in the world. I have visited nine Muslim countries and studied the prevailing socio-economic conditions of Muslim women. Women are coming up fast. Why Indian Muslim leaders are not showing magnanimity in promoting the cause of employment among Muslim girls. Some Muslims feel that employment for girls is not to be encouraged because they become bad. This is a wrong notion. Employment helps to improve the girls. An employed girl is an asset to the family, community, society and the nation.

3. Women's Right to Offer Namaaz (Prayer) in Mosque

One of the most controversial issues facing the Muslim community today is the conflict of interest between the orthodox Muslim men and liberal Muslim women, over women's right and freedom to offer *namaaz* in the mosque. There are four ways in which women can offer *namaaz*, namely *namaaz* at home, *namaaz* in separate mosques for women, *namaaz* in the same mosque where women offer in the ground floor, and women and men can offer in the same floor by having a screen in between men and women or even keeping a reasonable distance between them.

But till recently men were very conservative and would not budge an inch. They would just ask women to offer *namaaz* at home. Entry of women to a mosque was totally banned. However, there are mosques which have been open to women for the last 60-70 years. These are located in educated Muslim *mohallas*. Women elsewhere did not demand for their right to offer *namaaz* in the mosque. Now some educated Muslim women who are activists have thrown a challenge to men. They insist upon their freedom. Men oppose. All India Muslim Women Personal Law Board was set up by a few leading women activists to deal with the problems of women. There was good response from Lucknow, Chennai and Kerala. Other States lag behind. But they are sure to catch up soon.

These women leaders have told male leaders that women should be allowed to offer prayers in the same mosque. They can also offer congregational prayers in Idgah Maidan on Ramadan and Bakrid special prayers. If not allowed, they would construct separate mosques for women. Men are puzzled. Some women even think of approaching court on the ground that there is sexual injustice, discrimination and inquality. The simple question is, "why men take away from women what Islam has given"? If women were encouraged by the Holy Prophet to go to mosque to offer prayers daily and also offer congregational prayers, why male members go against the Holy Prophet himself? Are not men and women allowed to offer prayers in the Holy mosques in Mecca and Madina? How can there be different treatment to women in a country like India?

There is no objection to separate women from men while offering prayers in the same mosque. Neither women desire joint prayers. But total denial is unjustified. Religious leaders and others who perform Haj and Umra do not learn a lesson and change their rigid attitudes. It is really unfortunate. Why should these religions be attacked aggressively by women. Religious leaders should be respected by all. But they should also realize the situation. What is prohibited in Islam should not be allowed. But what is permitted cannot be denied.

I am presenting here three cases of women taking bold steps to offer prayers in the mosques. In the first case, Muslim women of Mangalore took the lead to offer prayers in the mosque. The second case relates to Muslim women of Lucknow where Shaista Amber played a notable role in paving way for Muslim women to offer prayers along with men. The third case is reported from Shillong in Meghalaya.

One significant feature emerging from women in mosques is that these women have not rebelled against the male religious leaders. They have just asserted their rights granted in the Holy *Quran* and encouraged by the Holy Prophet. If we are forced to offer our answer to the question, "who is at fault", the simple and honest reply is "male religious leaders". While they are suppressing what Islam has granted, women are just exposing the fact that Islam is for gender equality in all matters excepting in such matters where nature plays its role. While one group is sidelining the Prophet, the other group brings Prophet to limelight as the champion of woman's cause. While one group is violating constitutionally guaranteed sex-equality, the other group is asserting its right to exploit Constitutional Rights – Fundamental Rights. Let us see what we learn from these three case-studies.

Women offer Namaz at Mangalore Masjid, Create History

For these 15 Muslim women – as much as for the entire Muslim community – this Eid-ul-Fitr would be etched in history. In a path-breaking event, these 15 women were allowed to offer *namaz* in a mosque on Eid-ul-Fitr in Mangalore on Friday on the directions of Karnataka High Court. Mangalore, along with Kerala, celebrated Eid on Friday. History was created, when Noor Masjid opened its doors to the women, following the court's orders to offer *namaz* in the mosque.

The women had earlier petitioned the court seeking to be allowed to offer *namaz* in the mosque after being repeatedly denied the right to offer prayers to celebrate Eid-ul-Fitr. The Noor Masjid managing committee is headed by Sunnis and they had opposed entry of women into the Masjid. But the Salafis – a sect in Islam – had argued that they wanted the women to be allowed to pray inside the mosque on Eid-ul-Fitr.

The High Court in its order delivered to the Masjid committee directed it to allow the 15 women to pray, citing their names. But when a few women who were not mentioned in the list sent by the High Court also wanted to offer prayers, the Masjid committee disallowed them. The copy of the Court order was also sent to the Mangalore South Police Station. The Mangalore South Police Inspector, Ramakrishna told DNA that "we have carried out the order of the High Court to the last letter and allowed the 15 original petitioners to offer prayers at Noor Masjid.

Women, Men Pray Together at Mosque

The first day of the Holy Month of Ramzan, witnessed, for the first time, Muslim women offering prayers along with men folk at a Sunni mosque in the walled city Lucknow. The joint prayer by Muslim men and women comes close on the heels of a woman donning the mantle of "quazi" and solemnising the marriage of a Muslim couple in the city recently. "The joint prayers, which would be held throughout the month of Ramzan, was organised at the initiative of the All India Muslim Women Personal Law Board (AIMWPLB)," Chairperson Shaista Amber told the *Deccan Herald*.

Known for her progressive views, Ms Amber lambasted the Muslim clergy saying the women were not allowed by them to hold prayers in the mosques. She said the joint prayers would continue throughout the month of Ramzan. "It is the first step towards bringing about a revolution against narrow-minded self-proclaimed religious leaders, who think they are custodians of Islam", the AIMWPLB chairperson said. Muslim women usually hold prayers within the confines of their homes, as they are not permitted to pray in mosques.

At some mosques special closed enclosures were made to enable women to offer prayers. The AIMWPLB had recently decided to establish special mosques for women only for offering *namaz* (prayers). The mosques would act as centres for imparting social education among Muslim women so that they could improve their social status within the community. Just as *maulanas* and *imams* deliver sermons after prayers, women priests would also address the Muslim women after the *namaz*, Ms Amber said. The new initiative of the Board has met with serious objections from Muslim clerics. Taking strong exception to the development, All India Muslim Personal Law Board member and senior Sunni cleric Maulana Khalid Rasheed Firangimahali said there would be problems if women were allowed to offer *namaz* along with men-folk at mosques. "Women can offer *namaz*, but they have been barred owing to certain practical difficulties", he told.

Another cleric Maulana Fazlur Rehman Waizi Nadvi also voiced his opposition to such a move saying it could pose problems to women themselves. Ms Amber, however, rejected the objections claiming that women used to offer *namaz* during Prophet Muhammad's time. Amber had recently come out with a new "*shariat nikahnama*" granting several special rights to women and making registration of marriages compulsory.

Mosque Doors Open for Women

The call to *Ramzan* prayers may have never been more special for the women of Meghalaya as the State became the first in the region to allow them into mosques to worship alongside men. As *Ramzan's* special *azan* was heard in Shillong, groups of women wearing head-scarves filled into the Idgah Masjid in the Laban area of the city, a sight the North-East has never seen before. The mosque, built by the Shillong Muslim Union (SMU), divides the male and female prayer areas with a curtain. The first Friday it opened, roughly 50 women, young and old students, joined the congregation. Many said they were acutely aware of the significance of having a mixed congregation in the mosque.

"It was a distant dream for us, but we achieved it. So long, women were given status of a mother and daughter. But they also should be given the right to pray", SMU general secretary and legislator Saidullah Norgrum said. But according to S.M. Haque, President of the Shillong Mahila Majlish, it may take a little while for all the city's Muslim women to understand, appreciate and take advantage of the chance to pray in congregation. Haque said some women were still shying away from coming, but "we are trying to make them understand."

SMU executive member Noor Nongrum said it was a blow for equal rights. "Women should be treated on par with men. We have tried it through this endeavour and we are proud." Many believe the mosque's inclusiveness is a sign that Muslims are re-examining the gap between accepted practice and Quranic text. Nongrum said it was wrong to say Muslim women are not allowed inside mosques. Neither the *Quran*, nor the *Hadith* or saying of the Prophet, restrict women from mosques, she said. "Men and women enjoy equal rights everywhere in the world and we tried to bridge the gap between the sexes in the region", Nongrom said. Haque of the Mahila Majlish said it was one of the best Ramzan gifts ever. "We have been trying for this for a long time and we are now thankful to Almighty Allah for allowing us to offer prayers in the mosque, which is like a Ramzan gift to us."

Women Qazi

Perhaps there is no mention of women *qazi* to perform *nikah* till now in any literature in India. But recently history was created in Lucknow where for the first time a Muslim lady priest donned the mantle of 'qazi' and performed the *nikah*. A separate *nikahnama* was prepared and this is aid to be more in favour of women. I personally feel *nikahnama* should be broad based so as to include certain essential guarantees for women.

Anyway, reaction of men towards women qazis is not positive. But they are helpless because this is not prohibited in Islam. When Islam ensures gender equality, performance of Nikah by woman *qazi* is a part and parcel of this broad vision of Islam.

Women Imam

A woman can also be a *Imam* and lead the congregational prayer when only women are present. Women are well trained to take up this role and their competency cannot be questioned even by men. In China many women are trained to become *imams*. It is only in India that Muslim women are far behind the Muslim women in Islamic/Muslim countries.

However, Indian Muslim women are far better than Hindu women who were not allowed to read Hindu religious scriptures till recently. Even now they cannot become priests in Hindu temples and also they cannot take the lead in religious matters.

I am presenting here the first case of woman *qazi* solemnizing a marriage in Lucknow.

Woman Qazi solemnizes Marriage

In what could be considered to be a great leap forward towards women empowerment and gender equality in the Muslim community, a Muslim lady priest donned the mantle of "qazi" and solemnized the marriage of a Muslim couple at a function here. Although there is no restriction on women solemnizing marriages in Islam, only male priests performed this function traditionally and women priests doing this work are not heard of. While the bride, Naeesh Hasan, has been in the forefront of the fight for women rights in the Muslim community, the groom is a doctor of philosophy (PhD) from Aligarh Muslim University (AMU) and is associated with a social organization.

The marriage is also an example of Shia-Sunni unity. While the priest Sayeeda Ahmed is a Shia Muslim, the couple belongs to the Sunni sect. That the ceremony was completely dominated by the women was evident from the fact that the four witnesses to the marriage were also women. The brain behind the marriage and State convener of the Indian Muslim Women Andolan, Naaz Raza, told the *Deccan Herald* that very little had been done to really empower the womenfolk.

"While people talk of empowering the women, little has been done when it comes to implementing the principles", she said. Raza said the *nikahnama* prepared by her organization gave more powers to women but at the same time it adheres to the *shariat* (Islamic laws). "This is the first marriage in accordance with the new *nikahnama*", she said. The priest Sayeeda Ahmed is currently a member of the Central Planning Commission. Raza said the marriage would be an example to be followed by women coming to the forefront to assert their rights. An elated groom Imran Naeem said that the marriage would serve as an example for other Muslim couples. "It is to be seen how the society views the marriage and the change", he said. Muslim religious scholars, however, differ on women donning the mantle of *qazi*.

Dress Code, Perfume, etc.

Islamic dress code is Allah's boon especially for a Muslim woman which not only safeguards her modesty and chastity, but also brightens her *akhirah* (the life-hereafter). Coverage of the entire body of a woman with an outer garment is a shield against the lustful eyes of a man falling on the sensitive parts of the woman and this may lead to sexual desire. This outer garment is called Islamic *jilbab*. A woman should not appear before any man who falls under the category of prohibited men. "*Haya* and *iman* are attached together, if one of them gets separated, the other separates with it", says the Holy Prophet.

Islamic dress has wider scope. Barring face and hands, the remaining parts of the body of a woman should be strictly covered. According to the Prophet a woman has to observe veiling even in front of a blind man. No doubt he cannot see a woman. When a woman asked the Prophet said, "Are you also blind? Do you not see him?" contrary to our practice of not allowing the bride and groom to see each other's face and hands, Islam permits this in connection with a marriage proposal. But this liberty should be within limits. Islam does not permit western culture of dating and wooing.

When a Muslim woman has to consult a male doctor, she need not observe veiling. Hand shaking with a woman or a man as the case may be is not at all allowed. Wearing wig to change the look is not allowed. Men and women should not wear the dress of opposite sex. Similarly, wearing tight and thin clothes is prohibited as both attract men who instantly develop sexual desire. Men get attracted with the beauty of such women.

Women are not allowed to apply nail polish and lipstick. There is a more scientific reason than religious in this case. Generally people quote *wazhu* as the reason as water does not touch that part of the body. But the real reason is that nail polish and lipstick have chemical elements which would affect the health.

Use of Perfume

Once a woman had applied perfume and was walking on the road. Abu Hurairah, Prophet's companion, saw this woman. He asked her, "Are you heading for the mosque"? "Yes" was the answer. "Have you used perfume for this purpose?" "Yes" was the answer. Then he advised her, "go back to your home and wash it off". He made it clear that Allah does not accept her prayer. If a woman is outside her home, perfume should not be used as it attracts the attention of men.

Clothes and Jewels

Prophet said, "whosoever wears a dress for conspicuous display in this world, Allah will give him to wear a dress of shame on the Day of Resurrection, then it will be put on fire".

Even to this day, many Muslim men and women are guilty of violation of this serious mandate of the Prophet. Men and women when come out are seen in their best of dress, most fashionable. Ladies display jewellery on their person. Hands are full of golden bangles, ears are full of jewellery. The affluent section does this and the middle class people are affected by this.

Silk clothe is a sign of luxury and show of affluence. Men are not allowed to wear this. Similarly, men are not allowed to wear jewellery since it is meant for women. Further, wearing jewellery by men is a sign of arrogance. Generally we find that these restrictions are followed by Muslims. There are some exceptions, perhaps arising out of ignorance.

But in reality today we find that many of these directions, suggestions of the Holy Prophet are virtually mutilated. In a sense there appears to be a sort of disregard to Prophet. The question is why Muslims are not strictly following the directions of the Prophet. There are purely Islamic countries and there are countries like India where Islamic rule is absent. Muslims form a minority group. Strict adherence to Islamic code may be desirable but not practical. Conversions from the Hindu religion to Islam may be one of the reasons as to why strict Islamic code is missing.

But what about Islamic/Muslim countries where strict adherence is mixing? In some countries like Iran, Egypt, Malaysia headscarf is used. *Naqab* (covering face) which is not mentioned in Islamic dress code is followed. *Naqab* poses many practical problems in day to day life. Application of lip stick, nail polish, lack of outer garment and shaking of hands with men are all observed. Political leaders are the best example. Such women even share the public platform with *moulanas*. Tight dress and thin clothes are used by many girls from affluent families. The vulgar western culture is welcomed and practised. Parents allow their daughters to parade in somewhat partial nudity under the label "westernization, modernity, progress . . . ."

Wigs

Use of wigs by both men and women is prohibited in Islam. This is so particularly when offering prayers. A woman asked the Holy Prophet, "I have a daughter who has just married. She suffered from measles and resultantly lost her hairs, can she wear a wig"? The Prophet replied in the negative. "Allah curses the one who makes the wigs and the one who wears them."

It means 1400 years ago the then society was using wigs. But despite prohibition of wigs by the Prophet, some men and women use wigs as they feel uncomfortable without hair. This prohibition is generally not known to Muslims. Perhaps they do not use wigs as a violation of the message of the Prophet. But I cannot say whether those who use wigs are prepared to discontinue its use. This is to be tested. Since the number of users is so insignificant, it is not a nuisance to the Muslim society.

But when it comes to a question of practice, it is a different story. Many of our women have utterly failed to follow these restrictions. They appear in public with attractive dress, jewellery and cosmetics. This happens in mixed gatherings too. Men and women shake hands. At higher levels, this has become common. Muslim women in high positions do shake hands with men holding similar positions. When Hina Rabbani Khar, External Affairs Minister of Pakistan visited India, China and USA she wore no *burqua*. She had applied cosmetics. She shook hands with her counterparts and other high dignitaries. Late Benazir Bhutto, Hasina Sheikh and Khalida Zia were found violating all these Islamic restrictions. Even religious leaders mix with them and share dais.

Touching of women is also forbidden, except in cases of grave emergency endangering life or health. A tradition says "If a person touches a woman with whom he has no legitimate relation, his hands will be burnt on the Day of Judgement". Once a group of women came to the Prophet with the intention of embracing Islam and asked him to extend his hand, he said, "I do not shake hands with women".

Can we blame all these women? No doubt they are deviants. They are sinners from Islamic point of view. How do we judge their behaviour? Islam has not allowed exceptions. What is true in the case of an ordinary Muslim woman should also be true in the case of high profile women. But circumstances of a modern society are different. At the same time, Islamic principles hold good for all times to come. How to reconciliate with these two diotrically opposite views? I am not competent to express my views. I am confused. Let great Islamic scholars decide this issue. But I feel guilty that along with many, I am also a sinner because I do shake hands with women and girls without any foul intention in public functions. In this changed world shaking hands with women becomes a dire necessity. Thus committing sin in this way should make us be ready to have our hands burnt on the Day of Judgment.

Effects of Modernization

The effects of modernization are so severe that even some Muslim countries which are known for conservative attitudes have begun to change. Can we expect women in Saudi Arabia drive cars? Can we expect women pilots in this country? A few years ago, absolutely no. But today this is happening. Islam does not permit a male to sit before women and talk. But this is allowed by the society today. Shaikhs of Saudi Arabia do have dialogue with women Ambassadors and High Commissioners. How to react to these fundamental changes which are totally un-Islamic?

In Iran, Kuwait and other Muslim countries we find women lawyers, judges, ministers and so on. Kuwait has gone far ahead in modernization. There is more western culture than Islamic culture. I was attending one international conference in Brazil. There was a cultural programme at the end. This included one dance programme. I was surprised to find a few Kurdish young Muslim girls dancing.

All this is prohibited in Islam. But barring dance, I think other changes have become inevitable in modern society. While dancing should be condemned, mixing in working place has to be tolerated. This is compulsion, which cannot be avoided. *Prima facie* this is barred in Islamic culture and indefinitely punishable. But we cannot go against the modern current. We have to be realistic. There is a need to have a fresh look into the Islamic prohibitions and divide all this into two categories namely, (1) Any relaxation leading to sin and (2) relaxation not resulting in sin.

Religious leaders of different countries should have comprehensive discussion with open mind to provide fresh guidelines from practical point of view. But the basic structure of Islamic character should not be altered. What is a sin cannot be negotiated. There cannot be any compromise on this issue. But what is not a sin can be negotiated and a settlement could be reached. It means tolerable deviation and intolerable deviation. Let there be no class of interest between Islamic scholars and intellectuals. This is a tough exercise, but very much needed. Finally, there should be nothing against *Quran* and the Holy Prophet.

Marriage and Divorce

The Holy Prophet stresses the importance of marriage. He says "it is necessary for you to marry, because marriage is the most powerful shield against the allurements of sight and the protection of your private parts; if one of you cannot afford it, let him fast because fasting weakens the sexual impulse". A tradition of Islam as reported by Anas is, "When a man has got married, he has made his religion half perfect. Then let him fear Allah for the remaining half".

Many eminent sociologists have stressed the importance of marriage which is a major social institution. Dr. Westermark, a well known sociologist says in his book, "The Future of Marriage in Western Civilization", that there are three essential elements in every normal marriage. There are (1) the gratification of the sexual impulse; (2) the relation between husband and wife; and (3) procreation of children. Christianity looks upon marriage as if it were a necessary evil. But Islam regards it as a most sacred institution and makes it incumbent on every Muslim man and woman to lead a married life.

There are certain guidelines, limitations and prohibitions in Islam in following the institution of marriage. Marriage is a contract, not a sacrament as in the Hindu society. Both the parties have right to enter into a mutually agreeable contract between two parties. If the terms and conditions are not fulfilled, this marriage agreement may be cancelled. Let us see what Islam stipulates and what Muslims do.

Right to Choose

One of the most essential factors of a happy marriage is the right of free choice by either party. The Holy Prophet insisted on a number of occasions that a person wishing to marry a woman should have a look at her before finally consenting to marriage. Thus Abu Hurairah reports. A man came to the Prophet and said, "I intend to marry a woman of the Ansar". He said, "Have a look at her, because sometimes there is something defective in the eyes of Ansar". Jabir reports that the Prophet said: "When one of you seeks a woman in marriage and then if he is able to have a look at one he wishes to marry, let him do so'. Mughira reports: I sought a woman in marriage. The Holy Prophet asked if I had seen her. "No", said I. He said: "then look at her, because it is more proper that love should be cemented between you".

It is also agreed by many Islamic jurists that this right to have a look at the prospective partner is equally eligible for the member of the female sex. Of course, there is a slight disagreement be among various scholars about prior permission of the bride to see her.

There is also another important factor. Since marriage in Islam is a contract, permission of the girl is needed. Marriage cannot be forced on her. If she just remains silent, that is her consent. I quote two instances among many, to prove the point how serious and firm was the Holy Prophet in insisting upon the consent of the girl. A virgin grown-up girl came to the Prophet of Allah and narrated that her father had given her in marriage to a person whom she disliked. The Prophet gave her option. She could accept or reject.

In another case, a father of the girl gave her in marriage, after she became a widow. She disliked the husband and came to the Prophet. He annulled the marriage.

Now let us find out how far our Muslim brothers are following the decisions of the very Holy Prophet. First of all, the boy and the girl have no voice in selection of their partners in India, for example. The parents of the boys and girls select their partners and force them to marry. Almost total freedom is denied. Whether the girl is ugly or the boy is ugly it is immaterial. If the boy and girl resist the suggestion they are condemned. They are cursed. They get branded as rebels, notorious, disobedient.

Very rarely boys and girls are allowed to see each other before selection is finalized. The tradition is so bad and had that they see each other after *nikah* is performed. About 40 years ago the custom was that after *nikah* the bride and bridegroom would be made to sit opposite to each other. A thin curtain would separate them. A small mirror would be kept below the curtain. Then the bride and bridegroom should see each other through the mirror. Even though this strange custom is not observed today, the fact remains that they are not allowed to see each other before *nikah*. It is also possible for the educated and employed girls to meet and see each other. But wooing or dating is almost not found barring some exceptions.

In Islamic countries, it is the Islamic culture that prevails. I went to Egypt and tried to find out their customs. They follow Islamic methods. Boys and girls meet and decide. They inform the parents who agree without any reservation. In rare cases, parents may suggest their views. But it is left to the sons and daughters to heed to the parent's choice or not. In any case, parents do not insist on their choice.

Selection of Girls

What should be the qualities of a girl to be married in Islam? The Holy Prophet has laid down certain guidelines of great significance. He gives four guidelines for a man to marry a woman.

1. Wealth
2. Lineage
3. Beauty
4. Faith

1. Wealth

According to the Prophet, the first-three qualities are purely temporary. They are all externally attractive forces to mislead. A girl from a wealthy family is likely to have developed arrogance, least respect for the elderly persons in the family of the in-laws, may lack adjustability to the new family's economic conditions, lack of co-operation and so on. Wealth itself is an evasive temptation. Therefore, it is better to avoid girl from wealthy background.

2. Lineage (Khandan)

This is also a misleading force. What to do with the past glory of the lineage? Grand-father and great grand-father might have been very resourceful, respectable. But what is the social status of the present generation? So, it is better to avoid dependence on the lineage.

3. Beauty

Beauty of the girl is the most dangerous force in ruination of the groom. What devilish mentality is behind beauty. Beauty is tempting. It may overcome all hidden evils in a man's behaviour. Beauty *perse* is dangerous and transitory. It may last for a few years. Gradually beauty fades, particularly after the delivery of three or four children.

4. Faith

This is what makes the boy happy in life. A slave girl who has faith in Islamic traditions and culture can give everlasting peace and keep the husband and the family smiling for long. A faithful girl can be trusted. She is liked by God and the Prophet. Therefore, Prophet recommends marrying a girl, even if she is black, if she has unquestionable faith in the basics of Islam.

But generally the present Muslim society does not care for all these precious qualities recommended by the Holy Prophet. When the parents of the boys go in search of girls, the enquiry centres around land, bank balance, gold, lineage, etc. Education receives least attention. No information is sought for about the girls and their parent's religiosity-prayer and fast, charitable nature, helping nature, etc. Then comes the most important question about dowry, marriage meal, quality and quantity of gold, furnitures, utensils, etc. The entire relationship between the girls and boys people rests on these un-Islamic expectations. Are not these people deviants from Islamic point of view? Are they not disrespecting Holy Prophet's words of advice for a blissful life?

Polygamy

One of the most controversial social concerns is the question of plural marriages which could mean a man taking more than one wife. This social system is called polygamy and a woman taking more than one husband, this is called polyandry. Islam has totally prohibited polyandry. Perhaps at no point of time we can find evidence of this in Muslim society. This practice prevailed in the Hindu society till recently, though not in general. This system is legally banned.

So, what remains is the question of polygamy. Muslims are attacked on this ground. Researchers have proved that the right of the male to take more than one wife is legally permitted, but in practice rarely prevails. Muslim society does not encourage this. But if someone takes a second wife, he is not condemned or looked down. The society accepts this. But why then there is so much of uproar? The problem arises not because of plural marriage, but because of whimsical behaviour of man who violates the basic terms and conditions laid down in Islam. The Holy Prophet was seized of the consequences of plural marriages. So a few conditions should necessarily be fulfilled. What Islam desires and what a Muslim does? It is here the greatness or lofty ideals of Islam stand and pettiness of a Muslim is exposed. The Holy *Quran* says:

> "And if we fear that ye will not deal fairly with the orphans, marry of the women who seem good to you, two or three or four; and if ye fear that ye cannot do justice (to marry) then one (only) or the captives that your right hand possess. Thus it is more likely that ye will not do injustice."

It is evident from this that Islam does not enjoin polygamy, but only sanctions it to meet the exigencies of time. Some men, however limited the number is, have uncontrollable weakness for excess of sexual appetite. They become restless and indulge in illegal and immoral activities. They resort to prostitution, rape and so on. It is better such people marry again. Such cases should be ignored. Let us not make a mountain out of a mole.

Dr. Annie Besant said, "there is pretended monogamy in the West, but there is really polygamy without responsibility; the 'mistress' is cast off when the man is weary of her and sinks gradually to be the 'woman of the street' for the first lover has no responsibility for her future and she is a hundred times worse off than the sheltered wife and mother in the polygamous home. When we see thousands of miserable women who crowd the streets of western towns during the nights, we must surely feel that it does not lie in western mouths to reproach Islam for its polygamy. It is better for a woman, more respectable for a woman, to live in Islamic polygamy united to one man only, with the legitimate child in her arms surrounded with respect, than to be reduced, cast out on the streets perhaps with an illegitimate child outside the pale of law — unsheltered and uncared for, to become a victim of any possessor by, night after night, rendered incapable of motherhood, despised by all".

Dr. Billy Graham, the world famous Evangelist says, "Christianity cannot compromise on the question of polygamy. If present day Christianity cannot do so, it is its own detriment. Islam has permitted polygamy as a solution to social-ills and has allowed a certain degree of latitude to human nature but only within the strictly defined framework of the law. Christian countries make a great show of monogamy, but actually they practise polygamy. No one is unaware of the part mistresses play in western society. In this respect, Islam is a fundamentally honest religion, and permits a Muslim to marry a second wife".

But this permission is not a license. Islam has laid down certain essential conditions which should be fulfilled for a second marriage. These are:

1. There should be justifiable reasons. It is not for seeking sexual pleasure. It cannot also be for *post facto* sanction, "First sex, then marriage". Prophet makes it clear that the second wife cannot be taken at fancy.
2. Consent of the first wife is inevitable. This consent should be free from force, threat or inducement.
3. The man should have capacity, both physical and financial to treat all the wives equally. Prophet says, "A man who has two wives, but does not give them equal treatment, will find "half his body lost on the Day of Judgment".

In some Muslim countries like Pakistan and Egypt, the man should make application to a designed committee and the committee should give permission after due process of enquiry.

But in spite of all these restrictions and conditions, undesirable polygamy cases are found. A few cases are presented here:

Ayub and Habib: Marriage with Brother-in-law

Marriage with sister's husband is prohibited in Islam. But there are quite a few instances of such marriages. How the society tolerates such marriages? How the *Jamaat* permits? How the *Kazi* solemnizes such a *nikah* by using the *Nikahnama*? It is generally said that "wife's sister is half wife". Many parents do not allow the sister to come into close contacts with the brother-in-law. I know few such cases. One case is presented here.

Rahmat and Ayub were living happily as model couple. Rahmat had some health problem and got admitted to a hospital. She had to be in the hospital more than a month. She requested her younger sister to be in the house and manage the household affair. Within a short period she fell in love with her brother-in-law. It led to sexual relationship between Ayub and Habib. Rahmat's illness continued for four months. She was happy that her sister was taking care of her husband.

It was soon confirmed that Habib conceived. Ayub and Habib decided to get married. They convinced a *kazi* who agreed to perform *nikah* at home. He managed to get two witnesses. Of course, he was paid well. Rahmat was discharged from the hospital and returned home. Slowly she found out that her sister has become pregnant. Sister explained to her all that happened. Rahmat was unhappy, but tolerated. She knew her health would never permit her husband to have sexual gratification from her. She told her sister that she would not mistake her. Both the sisters stayed in the same house. After six months she died. Habib lived with her husband now.

Naazneen's Case

Whatever may be the background such marriage is not allowed. There is one more case which is highly ridiculous. A certain gentleman, Haji Wahab, aged around 65 years, doing very good hotel business in Bangalore had to face the ignomy of facing a second marriage and consequences. Since he was a rich person, he had employed three girls to work at home. One girl, Nazneen, was just around ten years when she was employed. She had no father. Nazneen used to stay in the house of Haji Wahab, her employer. He had three married daughters. They were all between 30 to 35 years of age.

Wahab sab's wife had died few years ago. Nazneen used to stay at home. At nights she used to massage the legs of Wahab sab before he could sleep. Slowly Nazneen used to sleep in the same room. One night he woke up the girl to get a glass of drinking water. Now she was fifteen years old. She was very beautiful. He got attracted. He asked to sleep on the cot next to him. This went on for some time. One night he pulled her and asked her to sleep very close to her. He lost control and indulged in sexual activities. She conceived. No attempts were made to abort her. He made up his mind to face the consequences. The issue became public. People started grumbling.

He arranged for *nikah*. All formalities were observed. One *kazi* was summoned with *nikahnama*. In the presence of a few employees of his shop, *nikah* was solemnized. Then his daughters were informed. Slowly the news was made public. People were not happy, not because he married again, but because of the age difference and the way in which he married her. But nothing could be done. The young girl became pregnant. If he had not married her, she would have been in greater trouble. Girl's parents were annoyed in the beginning. They wanted to lodge a complaint in the police station. The police inspector, a Hindu gentleman, advised the mother of the girl that it is better to reconcile with the reality and accept the marriage. There was nothing illegal as Islam has not prescribed marriage age in absolute terms. So ended this episode. Nazneen is leading a happy life as a rich man's wife. She could also help her poor parents.

Ameena's Case

I know the case of a person taking a second wife without the knowledge of the first wife. Khaleel married a Hindu girl after converting her to Islam. She had two children. She had one friend, Zarina who used to visit the house very frequently. She was also a graduate. Khaleel's first wife's name was Ameena. Ameena used to take Zarina to movies and also to resorts along with her husband. She had full confidence in both. Whenever Ameena used to go to her mother's house, Zarina would manage the house. She was a widow. She was young and beautiful. Slowly they developed intimacy. They started loving each other.

Once Ameena went to her mother's place for her first delivery. She had to stay there for three months. Zarina agreed to take up the responsibility of the house. Khaleel started sexual relationship with Zarina. After repeated sex with Zarina, Khaleel was feeling guilty, not because he had deceived his wife, but because of the fact that he had performed Haj two times. He decided to marry her. One day he took her by flight from Bangalore to Coimbatore. He had made all arrangements for *nikah*. His trusted friends helped him. *Kazi* performed *nikah* in a hotel room. His friends were witnesses. But there was no *nikahnama* record. *Nikah* was performed orally. *Kazi* had been paid well. He returned with his bride by the evening flight.

Zarina was happy. Khaleel was a rich businessman. By the time Ameena returned home, Khaleel had taken a good house for his second wife. He had given her all facilities including finance. Ameena returned home. Zarina used to help Ameena and the child. Zarina was made a partner in the business. Ameena and Zarina became friendlier.

This is a typical case of a man who ditched his first wife. There was no question of taking consent. *Nikahnama* was not used. Everything was cooked up. Khaleel is a two-time Haji. He managed to marry Zarina only to cover up his sin by having illicit relationship with her. Khaleel cannot escape from his sin at any cost. Being a Haji he had violated all principles of Islam.

Other Cases

There are many cases of taking second wife breaking the conditions laid down in Islam. I had been to Egypt. I took up a small study on marriage and divorce system. One gentleman who knows English told me that second marriage without fulfilling all the conditions laid down in Islam results in severe punishment. In spite of this, some people take second wife. When caught, they would simply say that the girl in question was just a friend.

Arabs generally take wives up to four. But they provide

them with all facilities and ensure equality. Each wife is kept in a separate house. But not all Muslims elsewhere can afford to do this.

Procedure for *Nikah*

Nikah in Islam has a set procedure to be observed. No option is allowed. There are instances of *nikah* celebrated privately in the presence of a handful of friends including two witnesses and a guardian. This cannot be dismissed altogether though Islamic procedure of *nikah* being solemnized in the presence of gathering of public consisting of friends and relatives is missing. The bridegroom has to commit himself to the marriage. That is his consent should be pronounced three times loudly so that the gathering hears his consent and then he has to sign in the *nikahnama*. *Kazi* has a significant role to play. He takes bride's consent too in writing.

When this is the case, how can there be *nikah* by phone. What the bride and the bridegroom say is not heard. It is not known. All the procedures indicated above are missing. Should not the religious leaders declare such marriages as null and void? I present a very interesting case of Shoaib Malik, former captain of cricket team of Pakistan who married Sania Mirza, the darling of tennis fans all over the world. It is said he had got married to another girl earlier. But he rejects that marriage was a phone *nikah*.

Phone *Nikah* not valid, I was duped, says Shoaib

Former Pakistani cricket captain Shoaib Malik flew into Hyderabad early on Saturday. Shoaib 28, is in the City of Pearls for his marriage with Indian tennis star Sania Mirza. However, the groom was greeted on arrival by allegations of already being married to another girl. While the Siddiqui family — who claims their daughter Maha, also known as Ayesha, was married to Shoaib — took their story to TV, the Pakistani Cricketer appeared stumped at the news. He believed those questions had been answered in a legal notice to M.A. Siddiqui two years ago. There had been little talk on the matter — until news of his marriage to Sania broke.

However, once the scores were made known, Shoaib took on the allegations with an unwavering calm. In an exclusive interview with the *Sunday Times*, he told the story. He made it clear that a telephone *nikah* is not valid under Muslim law, and he had been cheated. Excerpts.

When did you meet Ayesha Siddiqui for the first time?

This relationship was started on the telephone, in the year 2001. I was in Sharjah at that time, with the Pakistani cricket team. She telephoned me, introduced herself as Ayesha, and told me that she was a fan of mine who lived in Saudi Arabia. That's how we got talking.

When then did you meet Ayesha Siddiqui?

As we started talking more and more, Ayesha sent me some photographs, which she said were of herself. I haven't met the girl in the photographs, not to this day.

Can you explain that?

When I returned to Pakistan after the Sharjah tournament, I showed my parents the photographs Ayesha had sent me. I told them that I liked this girl. We spoke every single day. I kept pushing her to meet me, but she resisted it. She said we will meet at our *shaadi*.

Who is the girl in the photographs?

I thought it was Ayesha Siddiqui, the girl I was talking to, but now I honestly don't know.

You were talking every day to a girl you were interested in. Didn't you want to meet her?

Of course, I did. In 2002 (I can't remember the exact date) I came to Hyderabad with the sole intention of meeting Ayesha. Just before I left Pakistan, she called me and told me she had to rush to Saudi Arabia on urgent work. She told me that her cousins Reema and Maha Apa (meaning older sister) would take me around. I then asked her cousins and parents where she was, and they said that in the past year she had put on a lot of weight because of which she didn't want to meet me. I told them that I had photographs of her, and that she looked fine, but they said the photographs were of a year ago. A year or so later, I travelled to Hyderabad. Again, I was met by Reema and Maha Apa. Ayesha gave me the same excuse, saying she hadn't lost the weight she had put on because of which she didn't want to meet me.

What was your reaction? Were you all right with not meeting her?

I wanted to support her. I want to understand her situation. So before Pakistan's tour of India (2005), I told my brother-in-law that we should visit India, meet the girl, and formalize the relationship. My brother-in-law, Imran Zaffer, had to come to New Delhi on work. He called Ayesha and told her he would be coming to Hyderabad. The day before he was to come here, she called and told him that she had to leave for the United States on urgent work. My brother-in-law wasn't very happy, but since his tickets were already booked, he came to Hyderabad. She had told him she would leave her cellphone with her cousin Maha.

Then I got here for the tour. In a game in Hyderabad, the day before the Pakistani cricket team was invited to the Siddiqui house for dinner, I won the "Man of the Match" award. When I collected the award, I said that it is good that this happened in my wife's city.

Inter-religious Marriages

Islam permits inter-religious marriages between Muslim boys and Christian and Jewish girls. In such cases conversion of the girls is not needed since Christianity and Judaism are based on revealed books and their prophets are the prophets of Muslims too. But a Muslim girl cannot marry a Christian or Jewish boy. Quite often the Christian and Jewish youths have very critically questioned this restriction as very unfair, illegal and irrational.

But if a Muslim boy marries a Hindu girl, she should get herself converted to Islam before marriage. Without conversion such marriage is not permitted. Even the courts have upheld this view. Recently Allahabad High Court held that a non-Muslim girl must convert to marry a Muslim. Highlights of this case are given here.

Non-Muslim Girl must Convert to Marry a Muslim: HC

In a judgment with far-reaching implications, the Allahabad High Court has ruled that a non-Muslim bride must convert to Islam to marry a Muslim. Failing that, the matrimony with a Muslim man would be void as it would contradict Islamic dicta and tenets of Holy *Quran*, the court said. The ruling by a division Bench comprising Justice Vinod Prasad and Rajesh Chandra, came on a writ petition filed by Dilbar Habib Siddiqui. The petitioner had sought quashing of an FIR registered against him under sections 323, 366 and 363 of IPC with Naini PS, Allahabad and prayed the court not interfere in his peaceful matrimonial life with Khushboo Jaiswal.

The judges directed a speedy probe into the marriage of Siddiqui and ordered the cops to separate Khushboo Jaiswal who was lodged in Nari Niketan, and hand her over to her parents. The primary question for adjudication was on whether the FIR could be quashed or not. A perusal of the contents of the FIR indicated that Khushboo Jaiswal was alleged to have been abducted by the petitioner three months prior to its lodging. However, the petitioner had succeeded in preventing the FIR from being registered.

"In our above conclusion we are fortified by the fact that in the affidavit and application filed by Khusboo herself subsequent to her alleged contract marriage, she has described herself as Khushboo and not by any Islamic name. As Khushboo, she could not have contracted marriage according to Muslim customs. In those referred documents she has addressed herself as Khushboo Jaiswal daughter of Rajesh Jaiswal", the verdict said. "Thus, what is conspicuously clear unerringly without any ambiguity is that Khushboo Jaiswal never converted and embraced Islam and, therefore, her marital tie with the petitioner Dilbar Habib

Siddiqui is a void marriage since the same is contrary to Islamic dicta and tenets of Holy *Quran*", the court ruled.

But conversion without conviction is not allowed in Islam. Just because a Hindu girl is pretty or falls in love, a Muslim cannot marry her. But such marriages are very common. Film actor Kishore Kumar brother of famous actor Ashok Kumar married Madhubala. Her mother put a condition for the marriage. She asked Kishore Kumar to get converted to Islam. He obliged and married. After her death, he went back to Hinduism. Recently a Hindu IAS officer got converted to Islam and married a Muslim girl who is also an IAS officer. Both are in Karnataka. Legally such marriages are permissible, but not according to Islamic principles. Muslim society tolerates such conversions. The religious and Muslim society is up against a Muslim girl marrying a non-Muslim boy without his conversion or a Muslim boy marrying a Hindu girl without her conversion. But there are many such marriages. Husbands remain Muslims, wives remain Hindus. Islam does not permit this. Muslim society just murmers. If the Hindu boy comes from a powerful family, Muslims keep quiet. But if the boy hails from a lower class or even middle class, Muslim parents will not take this easy. They try to avoid before marriage or even after marriage within the legal limits or crossing the limits. They even result in "honour killing" methods.

Neither the law of the land nor Islam permits this type of vandalism or hooliganism. Killing is not allowed. It is a crime against the society and a sin against the religion. This situation also prevails in Indian Muslim society. Barring this exception, such inhuman and illegal practice do not permit in any Muslim country.

Special Marriage Act

Special Marriage Act permits inter-religious marriages without conversion. The man and woman can have a common religion or different religions. But there are many conditions to be filled before marriage is celebrated. This is a sort of government sponsored marriage where the priest is the designated officer. Marriage hall is the office of the officer. There is no *nikah* as prescribed. But it is also a registered marriage. Age of the man and woman should be as prescribed by law. Neither of them should have a living spouse. One month's notice should be given.

But Islam does not recognize such marriages. The relationship is sinful. Their offsprings too have no Islamic connections. Though there is no open protest, such marriages are not tolerated.

Registration of Marriages

Unlike a Hindu marriage, marriage in Islam is registered. The document is called *nikahnama*. But the Government of India wants all marriages, irrespective of religious background, to be registered legally according to set procedure. While the Hindus have unanimously accepted, there is vertical division among Muslims. Some Muslims and some Muslim groups consider this to be a sort of interference. I do not agree with this on two grounds. First, in Islamic countries like Egypt, every Muslim has to get the marriage – *nikah* — registered in a designated office within ten days from the date of *nikah*. Or else, *nikah* is deemed to have been declared null and void.

The second ground is that Islam desires every Muslim should follow the law of the land, unless it is against Islam and as such leads to commitment of a sin. Muslims who live in India have to follow the law of the country that every marriage has to be registered as said earlier.

Let not Muslim leaders of India insult Islamic stand keeping something else in mind.

Marriage Age

The age at marriage is not found in Islamic scripture for boys or girls, whereas, the government has prescribed age right now at 18 for girls and 21 years for boys. Every Indian whether he is a Muslim or Hindu or Christian is bound to follow this legal prescription. Muslims have to claim exemption from operation of this rule. This is Islamic to follow the age prescribed by the government. It is no sin or violation of Islamic prescription. Some Muslim organizations try to mislead the people. This has to be countered.

Divorce

Islam never regarded marriage as a sacrament, indissoluble except under extraordinary conditions. Divorce is the necessary corollary of the freedom given to men and women to choose their partners. The American authors of *Male and Female* makes the sensible remark: "With freedom to choose goes the right to change men's mind . . . . the spouse who clings to such a marriage is committing one of the worst acts in the American list of sins, limiting the freedom of another person, exploiting and taking advantage of someone else's past and impulse, freezing a past mistake into a present prison'. The idea that there is something essentially and inherently immoral in divorce was bequeathed to the world by Christianity and Hinduism.

Roman Catholic doctrine — a consummated Christian marriage is a sacrament and must as such remain valid forever. It represents the union between Christ and the church, and is consequently as indissoluble as that union. The Roman Catholic doctrine of indissolubility of marriage except by death was never accepted by Protestant reformers. They all agreed that adultery should be recognized as a ground for divorce and malicious desertion also. French law is like Islamic law — divorce is easy. But Islam has introduced checks and balances. Prophet has said though divorce is allowed, Islam does not regard it as desirable. "The most repugnant of things made lawful in the sight of God is divorce." Another tradition says, "marry but do not divorce, because God does not like men and women who relish variety in sexual pleasure."

Whether divorce is good or bad is debatable? This is a vital issue in human relationship. It is not desirable to keep the unwilling souls together by force. Marriage is not merely for sexual gratification. If this is so, one need not marry and be bound by rules and procedures. Marriage is a sacred pact. It is a union of hearts and souls, and must always remain intact and secure. The word "divorce" should be dropped for the vocabulary of human society. A wife and a husband should know that nothing except death can separate them for each other. This is the view of Catholic Church which is not prepared for any change. It is generally so in Catholic Italy and Spain. But even here voices for official declaration of divorce are strongly heard today. Many people enter into illicit sexual relationship because of lack of provision for divorce.

This was the attitude of the Hindu society till recently. Once tied can never be untied. Marriage is a sacrament. The relationship lasts even after death. Therefore, a widow can never remarry as she is supposed to have her husband forever. If she remarries, it amounts to bigamous marriage punishable under law. But unlike the catholic society, Hindu society is surrendering to the compulsion of divorce now.

The situation is different in Islamic society. The provision for divorce was enshrined in the Holy *Quran* ever since it was revealed and came to earth. It means it was prevalent more than 1400 years, whereas Christians and Hindus are struggling to have recourse to divorce now. It clearly indicates how progressive and rational was Islam 1500 years ago. In Islam marriage is a civil contract with clear terms and conditions. There is specific provision for coming out of this civil contact either mutually agreed solution or either of the couple resorting this course as against the wish of the other. But though Islam guarantees equality between man and woman, woman seems to be less equal when it comes to divorce. She can divorce, but the method is slightly different. It is called *talaq* when husband takes the initiative for permanent separation and *Khula* when the wife takes the initiative for divorce.

There are two controversial issues stemming from the Islamic provision for divorce. The intention and prescription of divorce in Islam and the intention and prescription of the present day Muslim society are poles apart. Islamic views and procedures are *bona fide*, whereas in general the views and procedures of the Muslim society are malafide. The second issue relates to the form of divorce by men and women. Talaq is the name given to the divorce made by the man and *khula* is the name of divorce given by woman. Though *khula* and *talaq* mean the same, namely divorce, there is a question often raised. That is, do *talaq* and *khula* have the same force? Are they equal? *Prima facie* it may look like that. But in practice it is not so. There is lack of equality even though according to the spirit of Islam there should be no differentiation. As observed or commonly understood, man can divorce his wife whimsically without the consent or knowledge of the wife, whereas, wife cannot divorce her husband without his consent. Normally husband does not give consent. One of the reasons for not giving consent is the fact that he has to forgo the dower amount (*meher*). It is also possible that he wants to harass his wife. A little more explanation is perhaps needed as this topic is very important to remove the possible misconception in the society.

The problem we observe in today's Muslim society is lack of the spirit of Islam when it has afforded an opportunity of seeking separation from each other when union becomes a mirage unbearable. Divorce is not the first resort. It is the last resort. It should be based on strong grounds. It cannot be whimsical. It cannot be just to derive sexual gratification of varieties by divorcing one wife for taking another wife. How many present day Muslims are aware of warning and advice given by the Holy Prophet? Let me quote one instance that happened during the Prophet's time. In *Kitab al Kafi*, (one of the most authoritative collections of *Hadith* in both *usul* (principles of faith) as well as *fiqh* (jurisprudence) compiled by Abu Jafar Muhammad ibn Yaqub ibn Ishaq al-Kulayni during the lifetime of the twelfth Imam it is narrated:

> The Prophet went to a man and enquired, "What did you do about your wife"?
> He said, "I divorced her".
> The Prophet asked, "Did you see anything objectionable in her".
> He replied, "No, I did not see anything objectionable in her".
> The matter stopped here, and that man married again.
> The Prophet asked him, "Did you marry another wife"?
> He said, "Yes".
> After some time the Prophet again went to that man and asked him: "What did you do about your wife"?
> He said: "I divorced her".

The Prophet asked him: "Did you see anything evil in her"?
He said: "I did not see anything evil in her either".
The matter closed again here, and that man married for the third time. The Prophet asked him, "Have you taken another wife"?
He said, "Yes, O' Messenger of Allah"!
A considerable time passed and the Holy Prophet went to him and asked: "What did you do to your wife you married"?
He said: "I divorced her also".
The Prophet asked him: "Did you see anything evil in her"?
He said: "No, I did not see anything evil in her either".
The Prophet said: "Allah considers as His enemy and damns the man who relishes changing wives one after the other, and the woman who delights in changing husbands one after the other".
The Prophet was informed that Abu Ayyub al-Ansari was determined to divorce Umm Ayyub, his wife. The Prophet personally knew Umm Ayyub, and knew also that the divorce of Abu Ayyub was not grounded in any genuine cause. He said: "Verily, the divorce of Umm Ayyub is a great sin".
The Prophet also said: "Jibra'il (Gabriel) so much commended the cause of the woman, and so counselled me as to give me the impression that, except in the clear case of adultery, the wife does not deserve to be divorced."

Imam (Ja'far) as-Sadiq quoted the Holy Prophet as saying: "To God no house is dearer than the house where there is the union of marriage, and no house exists which deserves His wrath more than that in which the union of marriage is broken by divorce." Imam as-Sadiq then said that the word *talaq* (divorce) occurs repeatedly in the *Qur'an*, and that the details of the matter of divorce have been honoured with the attention of the Holy *Qur'an*. The reason for this is that God is an enemy of separation.

Tabarsi in Makarimu 'l-akhlaq (Noble Deeds of Morality)

quoted from the Prophet: “Get married, but do not divorce because the throne of Allah shudders when there is divorce.”

Imam as-Sadiq said: “No lawful thing is the object of so much wrath and hate in the eyes of Allah as divorce is. Allah considers the man who repeatedly divorces as His enemy”.

This thing is not especially found in traditions from Shi’ite sources. The Sunnis have also quoted similar traditions. In the Kitab as-Sunam, Abu Dawud quotes from the Holy Prophet that Allah declared lawful nothing so abominable to Him as divorce.

Mawlavi (Jalalu’d-Din Rumi) in his well-known story of Musa (Moses) and the shepherd alluded to the same tradition of the Prophet when he said:

> “As far as possible do not step into separation,
> For the most detestable thing to me is divorce.”

In spite of all these references, today we notice even educated and highly placed Muslims lack patience and resort to divorce very easily. Where does the remedy lie? Do we show respect and reverence to the Holy Prophet in practice? Lack of patience and consequences drives many to the extreme steps. How many are aware of the fact that hasty divorce followed by repentance and alter desire to rejoin the spouse would create a nasty situation? The ex-husband has to see that his ex-wife is remarried to someone who sleeps with her one night and has sex and thereafter he has to divorce her. This woman has to remarry the former husband. What happens if trusted man who marries the ex-wife develops liking for the woman and does not divorce her? Legally he is safe, but morally he fails because it is a question of breach of trust.

Further, there is a controversy on the methodology for divorce. There are two extreme views on three pronouncements, whether at a single sitting or three sittings with a gap of one month in between. Many jurists hold the views that three pronouncements at a single sitting is enough for effecting divorce. But some other jurists reject this view. One month’s interval between each pronouncement is essential. It provides reasonable opportunities to see if it is possible for reconciliation. Elders and friends can intervene and patch up. This procedure avoids hasty and harsh decision of the husband in a fit of anger or emotion.

Prophet was not in favour of three pronouncements at a single sitting. There is a tradition that Abdulla Ibn Umar divorced his wife when she was having her monthly period. His father reported this matter to the Prophet who became very angry and ordered that Abdulla should revoke his divorce and wait until his wife is clean, after which he is free to do as he liked. Another tradition is still more clear. Prophet advised Ibn Umar, "you adopted a wrong method. The right one is that you should wait for *tuhas* (period of cleanliness) and then pronounce a divorce during one *tuhas* and another during the second. During the third *tuhas* you should decide finally either you retain your wife or to divorce her".

Thabit b. Qais whose two wives sought divorce, one of them, Jamilah b. Abi Salul disliked his features. She came to the Prophet and complained, "O Prophet, nothing can bring him together with me. I lifted my face covering to see him coming along with a few other men. I notice he is the blackest, the most short-statured and the ugliest of them".

Jamilah, "you see Prophet, how beautiful I am, but Thabit is an ugly man".

Prophet, "Will you give him back the orchard he gave you", she replied, "yes, and also more, if he wants". Prophet said do not give more and ordered Thabit to accept the orchard and divorce her.

Islam protects the interest of woman too. She is not denied her right to divorce the husband. There are two options for a woman. A woman can take the initiative and try for mutual agreement for separation. This is called *khula*. The second alternative is to move the court. Even here, woman is morally bound to be careful in exercising decision. However, her right is not curtailed. Once a woman came to the Prophet and sought his permission to divorce her husband who was very ugly as against her beauty. Prophet allowed her request. There are quite a few such cases. These women succeed in getting permission to get separated by pronouncing *khula*.

But in spite of all these traditions, Muslim society today is witnessing conflicts and contradictions, totally disregarding

Islamic prescriptions. Divorces at will, fancy, pleasure, and so on are very common. While men enjoy their freedom, women are deprived of this. The words of the Holy Prophet have no bearing on Muslim society. Women stand to suffer. There are husbands who ditch their wives, harass them day and night. Wife's life is made miserable. The husbands do not want to divorce them nor agree to give the *khula* sought for by the wives without divorcing them, wife cannot take the second husband without giving divorce (*khula*) to the husband. Though Islam provides social equality to woman, this remains only on paper. Almost nothing is done by religious leaders to ensure the legitimate rights of women as granted in Islam and as propagated by the Holy Prophet.

Divorce through Letter

Salma, a resident of Shahnapur in Uttar Pradesh had an affair with Muhammad Tayab and married him 2007. The relationship was healthy and enjoyable. But later on it became sour. They had frequent differences and quarrels. Life became miserable. Meanwhile Tayab secured a job in Gulf country. This was an opportunity to get rid of Salma. Salma insisted she too would accompany him. But he gave many excuses and promises. She became helpless. Tayab blamed his wife. He held her responsible for implicating his family members in false cases. He had decided to leave her forever. He had taken two signatures as witnesses. She came to know about all this.

Her parents approached Mufti Ehsan Sahib, a senior cleric of Deoband for a *fatwa*. He said that it all depend upon the intention. It is very crucial. All this surfaced only when she received a letter indicating his intention to divorce her under triple *talaq* weapon. Mufti Sahib examined the letter signed by the husband with two witnesses. Mufti Sahib finally expressed his opinion that the *talaq* was valid since the intention was not malafide.

The point for consideration is whether *talaq* pronounced in three quick successions is valid. This is a debatable issue. In my opinion, this was a fraud exercised by the husband. The wife is just duped. This is definitely an un-Islamic stand. What the Holy Prophet has said about the procedure for *talaq*, what the *moulanas* do? This analysis exposes the divided opinion of the *moulanas*. The procedure laid down in Islam for divorce cannot be compromised. Let there be three *talaqs* separately with a gap of one month each time. This would also allow the parties to try for reconciliation.

Man divorces Wife by Text Message

A Saudi man has snapped nuptial ties with his wife by sending an SMS. The man was in Iraq when he set the legal precedent by sending the SMS, informing his wife that she was no longer his spouse, and followed up with phone calls to his two relatives, confirming the split, the Arab News reported.

Asma, the Victim of Irresponsible Husband

One more instance of mental torture being faced by a young educated and beautiful girl is presented here. Asma got married against her consent when she was just in pre-university college. She was around 17 years. Her father is employed in government service. The bridegroom was her cousin and a qualified engineer. He got a job in USA. He told his bride he would take her to USA at the earliest. No one suspected him as she is his cousin. The mothers of both are sisters.

A few years rolled. There was no word from the husband. Asma's mother met her sister several times. But no proper information was available. Meanwhile Asma joined a degree course and then completed her post graduation. It means five years were over yet no trace of husband was available. Suspicion grew very strong. Finally it was learnt that he got married to another girl and he took her to USA by manipulating all relevant documents for taking her to USA. Asma's aunt, her mother-in-law was dodging. Asma's parents tried hard to get the address of the boy. But it was not possible. Parents of the boy would simply say that they are also trying to get the address, but yet to succeed.

Asma's parents now lost hopes. The boy has not even divorced her. She cannot marry anyone else as this becomes illegal. Asma joined some college. She is now a lecturer. Of course, economically she can stand on her own. But, for a young girl, money is not everything. She has all natural desires of having her own family. How long can she stay with the parents? After all, what wrong she has done to receive this punishment? How can her own aunt kill the future of this young girl? I am related to her. Hence, I am also very keen in finding some solution to solve her problem at the earliest.

Asma's parents have realized that it is not worthwhile waiting any longer. Asma is also not keen as her husband has already got married to another girl. All that is required is either divorce from the husband or *khula* from her side. The husband is not prepared to give divorce perhaps because of the American law on marriage and divorce. If the government comes to know about his having two wives he will not only lose the job, but also other punishment since he has suppressed the vital information about his marital status. He has a fear that Asma's parents or Asma herself will inform the US Government about his affair. Therefore, his address is not available. His parents also dodge.

Asma cannot send *khula* because of want of her husband's address. I told the parents, "you please give me some information about the boy, I will write to the Indian Embassy in USA. That office can easily furnish the details about the boy. Somehow, Asma's father is not cooperating. Mother is helpless. The real sufferer is Asma.

Where are Islamic principles governing marriage and divorce? Whose responsibility it is to safeguard the interest of young girls like Asma who become the victims of the husbands? The *jamaat* has also failed. Allah's fear is lost. Rasool's words are neglected. There may be many more Asmas either suffering or in the pipe to suffer tomorrow. Some solution should be found.

Divorce allowed by the *Jamaat*

There has been a custom of approaching the mosque committee for settlement of the differences between the husband and wife. One form of settlement is divorce. After hearing both the parties the committee tries for reconciliation. If this is not possible, then divorce is allowed.

According to the custom this is binding on both. Otherwise, the committee may impose social boycott.

But sometimes dangerous consequences may be in store for one of the parties, particularly the woman in question. There are cases where women get the nod of the committee for divorce. But the husband is not happy. She gets married to another person. Then the former husband moves the court against the decision of the committee. The court sets aside the committee's decision. Then it means her marriage with the previous husband remains intact. What about the new husband? She will have in theory two husbands. Court does not recognize the second husband. The second marriage either deemed to have been cancelled or both should voluntarily divorce each other. There may be many other consequences of adverse nature. This is not a healthy situation.

Who has to be held responsible for such an awkward situation? It is the *Jamaat*. It has no legal power. It is a clash between the committee and the court. Court order supersedes *Jamaat's* decision. Therefore, *Jamaat* has to be held responsible. Law should prohibit *Jamaat* from acting against the law, Muhammadan Law. It should not be allowed to usurp the powers of the court.

Conditions for Divorce in Islam

1. Option of puberty;
2. No economic sustenance;
3. Change of religion;
4. Impotence;
5. Infectious disease;
6. Wilful desertion; and
7. Disappearance of the husband.

Divorce Rate on Increase

Divorce rate viewed from the global perspective is on the increase. No community is an exception. The major reason for divorce is the vulnerability of the present marriage system. Marriage has almost lost its stability. The deep rooted love springing from the bottom of the heart between husband and wife has dried. Moral and social values are eroded. Materialism has overtaken spiritualism. The greatness of Islam which allowed divorce only as a last resort has been misused. Instead craze for divorce has increased. Influence of western society has almost destroyed the values and culture of Islam. Neither agents of social control nor self control are in operation.

Religious leaders have also failed to assert their rights to control and minimize the reckless increase in divorce rate. Divorcees should not be easily allowed to remarry unless a thorough post mortem enquiry is conducted by a competent authority. In other words, both preventive and curative steps should be undertaken in time. The question is, who has to bell the cat?

Dower and Dowry

Dower is the consideration for the marriage to be payable by the husband to the wife in cash or kind any time after *nikah*. Whereas, dowry is the cash or property demanded by the bridegroom or his people from the bride people in consideration of the marriage. This is a demand not allowed in Islam as well as in law.

We have to make a distinction between dower and dowry. Dower (*mehar*) is stipulated in Islam. It is compulsory. The form and quantum are left to the individuals. Prophet recommends dower amount should be simple and easy to pay any time after *nikah*. It is mandatory. It is a sin if not paid. It remains a debt even after death. If the wife excuses the dower in her life time, it is alright. Otherwise, the burden continues and can be recovered out of the income or property of the husband.

Payment of the dower is not uniform. Conscious husband pays. But in majority cases it is not paid. This is based on my survey. It is not to say that intentionally this is not paid. It is generally unpaid out of ignorance. However, non-payment remains a debt and man faces the wrath of Allah. But without mentioning and agreeing to pay dower, marriage is incomplete. The *kazi* cannot complete and get the signature of the bride and bridegroom.

Dowry

Dowry is unknown to Islam. Dowry is an evil practice that was introduced and is today widely practised by the Hindus. Whether educated or not, rich or poor, whether Ministers, legislators, officers or judges, this evil system is well nourished in the Hindu society. In contrast, Muslim society is totally free. Marriage expenses are met by the bridegroom. He pays dower to his bride. While marriage is a financial burden to the bridegroom among Muslims, it is the opposite among the Hindus. Girls' parents have to bear not only the marriage expenses, but also payment of cash, giving jewellery, furnitures, landed property and so on. Parents are totally crippled by the time their daughters are married. Some parents commit suicide. They take heavy loan. When they cannot repay they commit suicide. Some girls remain unmarried. Dowry is taken at the time of marriage and also later on. Wife-beating, harassment are all common. There is no end to the lust for dowry. There is a law which prevents both giving and receiving dowry which term is defined in the Act. This is also applicable to Muslims who cannot claim exemption on the ground of personal law.

Though dowry system was originated in the Hindu society and it is widely followed by the Hindus, unfortunately Muslims have become victims of the draconian law. This is a totally un-Islamic custom. If there is anything good in the Hindu society which is not found in Muslim society, there is no harm in copying unless it affects Islamic thoughts. But dowry system is outside the pale of Islam. Why Muslims have copied this? Barring rare exceptions, Muslims have fallen prey to this vivacious practice. Hundreds and thousands of Muslim families have witnessed broken families. A large number of young married girls are harassed, beaten up and killed by the heartless husbands, their mothers and sisters. Whether rich or poor, this demand has spread among all.

What is painful is the mute role of social workers, community leaders, law-makers and above all religious leaders. Islam is disgraced, humiliated and virtually deserted. We still take pride that we are followers of Islam. I say boldly that these people are no longer Muslims. They are deviants.

Even the All-India Muslim Personal Law Board has not initiated any concrete steps to put down dowry harassment. *Nikahnama* should have a reference to the dowry issue. Both the parties should declare in writing and sign that they have neither received dowry nor given dowry. Why this is not done? I had made this suggestion 25-30 years ago when there were heated debates and discussions on Common Civil Code. Muslims know by and large to shout at the government if there is any possibility of making an administrative order and legal provision affecting the *Shariat*. But why not the same group provide some alternative solution to address the problem and provide relief to the sufferers? We find generally that those who speak loudly against dowry are the same people who take dowry silently. This attitude is nothing but contradiction and hypocracy.

Two instances of dowry harassment are very interesting. A top Muslim officer Abdul Wajid agreed to give a new costly car to the groom besides other items. The groom and his people arrived at the marriage place. Ghani sab was restless as the car had not arrived. He went on reminding Abdul Wajid. Finally, it was found out that the car had not reached Bangalore as it was booked in the then Madras city. Ghani's face became red. He started shouting. The groom was a probationary officer. He was helpless. Wajid tried to convince Ghani by showing relevant documents. Ghani would not listen. He told his son that there was no option but to retreat. Wajid and his people were in tears. Ghani threatened that he would take legal action for breach of trust. But he was advised by some lawyers present there that he himself would face consequences of violating Anti Dowry Act. This silenced Ghani.

Some elderly people interfered and told Ghani that he was going against the spirit and letter of the Holy Prophet who always stood for simple marriages. This episode took ugly turn. Ghani had three daughters to be married. He had to face similar music when the parties who come forward to marry his daughters demanded much more than what he had demanded from Abdul Wajid a few years ago.

The second case relates to the marriage of the daughter of a rich and respectable textile businessman in Bangalore. He was one Iqbal. The boy was Haneef, son of a timber merchant, Saifulla. Saifulla demanded heavy dowry. Iqbal agreed as the boy was well educated and handsome. It was to be a grand function. As the day of the marriage approached, Saifulla started demanding new items. Iqbal was getting fed up. But he controlled himself.

The day of marriage approached. All the invitees were seated. But the bridegroom and his father sat in a room attached to the pandal. Iqbal became a bit suspicious. He went to Saifulla and informed that the *Kazi* had arrived. The bridegroom had to be seated on the dais. Saifulla said, "you had promised to offer a bungalow, but till now you have not obliged. Iqbal said that he would register it in a week's time as he could not get some documents for execution of the sale deed. But for half an hour there were arguments. Finally Saifulla desired a demand draft for one crore or a cash of one crore and then only he would allow his son to go the dais. Iqbal lost his temper. He protested after his repeated appeals failed. Then Iqbal told him that he can take back his son.

Iqbal announced whatever happened. Some people wanted to assault Saifulla. But Iqbal prevailed over them. He requested the invitees to wait for another half an hour. He asked one of the sales boys, Yakub to get ready to marry his daughter. He announced this. People were surprised. He called for the boy's parents. He sent his car to fetch them. They were informed. They were speechless. In forty minutes bridegroom was ready. Kazisab solemnized the *nikah*. Grand marriage meal was served. Yakub was made the manager-cum-partner of his roaring business.

All appreciated the way in which Iqbal conducted himself and his decision to give his daughter to one of his employees. People used to quote this episode for many years. This had happened about 30 years ago.

It is unfortunate that this un-Islamic culture of dowry prevails without symptoms of its disappearance. Vice-Chancellors, legislators, parliamentarians and top officers have also become victims or sometimes perpetrators.

When this is the case, an attempt was made by the people of Puttur to end this social menace. This attempt proved to be successful. If Puttur people succeed, why not people elsewhere. A brief report of the success of Puttur people in Dakshin Kannada is presented here.

Dowry takers face *Jamaat* ban

"Dowry is a huge problem in our community. Many of our men give up their education to go to the Gulf and make money to pay the dowry of their sisters and daughters. They spend their entire lives saving up for the dowry. Some have even lost all their belongings in the process. It is time to put an end to this evil", says Mr. Bashir.

Burdened by the demands of dowry for decades, people of the Shekhamale *Jamaat* in Puttur Dakshina Kannada, have decided to put a full stop to the practice and bring back the smiles into their lives. Around 90 families of the *jamaat* in Puttur vowed to not accept or ask for dowry at a meeting headed by honorary *Jamaat* president K.P. Ahmed Haji, in the town. So firm was the *jamaat* on its no-dowry stance that it has decided to boycott the wedding of anyone who goes against it. "The wedding will not be registered in our books and our *khatib* too will stay away from it", says *Jamaat* secretary S.P. Bashir, regretting that the practice is rampant in the community although it is un-Islamic.

The no-dowry rule will be relaxed only if a girl from the *jamaat* marries a boy from another Muslim sect, where it is still in vogue. The Shekhmale *jamaat* seems to be setting a trend as people of the Bhadriya *Jamaat* too now seem to be keen on banning dowry. "The Shekhamale *jamaat* has taken a very good stand against dowry. We too would like to pass a similar resolution and ban it among our people", says Siddiq of the Bhadriya *jamaat* committee.

Dowry and its Consequences

The effect of dowry is quite far-reaching. Muslim society is still in its slumber. No sincere efforts are made to eradicate this social disease. Muslims know only to suffer. But rarely do they apply their mind to find out a solution. Puttur people have shown the way. This message should spread.

One of the most important consequences is its effect on

girls. If the elder sisters remain unmarried, younger sisters also remain unmarried. Thus it becomes a vicious circle. I met one female lecturer in a private college in Delhi. I had been there for a seminar. I casually asked her about her family background. She gave her name as Anjum Pathak. I was surprised. I asked her why she has kept this name. She informed me that her two elder sisters did not get married because of dowry problem. When a non-Muslim lecturer in the same college expressed his desire to marry, I was surprised.

I informed my eldest sister. She said that if the person is good and reliable, she had no objection. "This is a lesson for our religious and community leaders who talk loudly about Islam, but hardly solve our problems."

Anjum gave her consent. They were married under the Special Marriage Act. She is happy with two children. She has been advocating inter-religious marriages, if inevitable.

V
Fatwas

Fatwa is a religious decree issued by Islamic authorities with the object of preventing or promoting certain actions of Muslims. Darool Uloom Deoband of Uttar Pradesh is the most leading Islamic seminary from where *fatwas* are issued. The way in which *fatwas* are issued, number and frequency of issue of *fatwas* lead to controversies. Even the substance of *fatwas* matters a lot. *Fatwas* are issued on petty issues like insurance policies, using a neck tie, women at work, women's wages and so on. There is also a controversy about fee taken for issue of *fatwas*. Whether *fatwa* is legally binding, whether there is unanimity among Islamic scholars about *fatwas* and the theme of *fatwas*? Can a *fatwa* once issued be withdrawn? What happens if *fatwas* are not respected?

There are various shades of opinion among Islamic scholars and ordinary Muslims on the relevance and themes of *fatwas*. Sometimes, *fatwas* become obstacles to progress and harmony. They also lead to controversies between the people and the Islamic scholars. All these issues are examined in the light of happenings at the grassroot level.

Vande Mataram

The most important *fatwa* is on singing *Vande Mataram*. Though some Muslims do not endorse the views of those who are up against *Vande Mataram*, the minority voice becomes too feeble. Unfortunately a religious colour is given. While Hindus say *Vande Mataram* is not against Islam or Muslims, Muslims, by and large, say it is definitely against Islam which believes in monotheism. There cannot be a second or parallel

God. The argument is based on the reference to 'Durgah' and the very use of the word '*Vande Mataram*'. Muslims do not appreciate the word '*Vande Mataram*' as it amounts to 'mata', Hindu goddess and prostrating before the goddess.

There is also a feeling that it is a song of the RSS and aimed against the Muslims? It exposes the total ignorance of Muslims and Muslim organizations. This song was composed by the Bengali poet, Bankim Chandra Chattopadhyaya when Bengal was partitioned by the Britishers on the basis of population of Hindus and Muslims. It was a patriotic song to inspire Bengali youths. Many Muslims also joined. This was in the nineteenth century. In 1937 the Congress Working Committee adopted this song. This song was almost adopted as National Anthem. But the then Prime Minister chose Tagore's '*Jana gana mana...*". Out of high regards to the great poet who had also achieved Knighthood by this time. The Constituent Assembly adopted this as the National Anthem and *Vande Mataram* as the National song. Both are on par with each other. The Indian National Congress party is now using this song on many occasions.

Those who oppose this will have to be educated properly. They can sing at least the first-two stanzas where there is no reference to 'Durga'. Further, the famous music director, A.R Rahman has composed a new version without altering the original text. He calls *Vande Mataram* '*ma tujhe salam*'.

If Muslims refuse even to sing the first two stanzas where there is no reference to Durga, then there is a need to have a dispassionate discussion among Islamic scholars, religious leaders and enlightened public leaders. There is no meaning in forcing children in schools or elders in public gatherings to sing *Vande Mataram*. The fact that it is a National song almost on par with Gurudev Rabindranath Tagore's *Jana gana mana Adhinayak Jayahe* .... which is the National Anthem. There is constitutional support to it. As said earlier, it is not a BJP or RSS song. In fact, it has more Congress support. The question is why to colour this National song with political parties. *Mullas* and *moulanas* are divided. There are both supporters and opponents. Muslims should tread a safe path and pay more importance to rationality rather than emotionality.

In any case, I am convinced that nothing can be gained out of compulsion in any direction, for or against. Wisdom rather than selfdom should be the guideline. When some hardcore groups try to impose, Muslims should exercise their individual thinking and see if there is any threat or problem to the community on the religious tenets. Let Muslim thinkers ponder over the issue whether *Vande Mataram* is anti-Islam. Are Muslims compelled or influenced to support parallel God? As Muslims firmly believe that Islam believes in monotheism, Hindus also believe in it. Vedas have ample material to support the view that god is only one and has no shape. If *Vande Mataram* is given a religious colour, no Hindu can support it. But *Vande Mataram* has nothing to do with religion. Bengalis never disassociate themselves with *rasgollas*, Ravindranath Tagore and *Durga* in their daily life. Let us not give too much importance to the reference of the word '*Durga*' in the song.

Strictly speaking even the National Anthem, Jana gana mana . . . . is not totally free from reference to Hindu religious thinking. Nature worship is the Hindu way of life. Let us review another issue of similar type. This is the State song of Karnataka, "*Jaya he Karnataka Maate*". This is a song composed by the National poet Dr. K.V. Puttappa, popularly called Kuvempu. We find some words like '*maate*' here also. While *Vande Mataram* has reference to Durga, the deity of Bengalis, this State song has also brought in the reference to Chamundeshwari, or Bhuvaneshwari. Who is this Karnataka *maate*?

It is the responsibility of Islamic scholars and *ulemas* to rise to the occasion and promote a new thinking which fits into the requirement of a pluralist society. India is a land dominated by the Hindus. Our Constitution provides for religious freedom of expression, movement and even conversion. All religious groups are equally treated in all walks of life. There is no discrimination. Hindus and Muslims live happily and sustain brotherhood. This equality is denied in Pakistan to religious minorities.

Since singing of *Vande Mataram* has become a bit controversial, and social harmony between the majority Hindus and minority Muslims is disturbed, it is the responsibility of every Indian, be Hindu or Muslim, to maintain religious harmony and National integration. *Vande Mataram* is Constitutionally a National song and every citizen is bound to accept, respect and sing. Islam also mandates that Muslims should respect the law of the land unless it affects Islamic tenets. There are many Islamic scholars who support *Vande Mataram*. It should be separated from religious consideration. The word 'Durga' does not appear in the first two stanzas and, therefore, these two stanzas can be sung. Let there be open minded discussions among different groups of Muslims. I raise a few topics for a dialogue:

1. Is *Vande Mataram* anti-Islam?
2. If so, where and how?
3. Should Muslims sing or avoid the National song?
4. If not totally anti-Islam, what can be done to enable Muslims to sing this voluntarily?
5. Are all the religious leaders in Muslim society unanimous in opposing *Vande Mataram*?
6. If not, why some oppose and some support?
7. When Muslim religious leaders are divided, is it not natural that individuals are also divided?
8. Is not opposition to *Vande Mataram*, a National song with some changes against the great image of Islam in a pluralist society, particularly in view of the fact that Islam is elastic, not static, it is dynamic, but not dogmatic?

In any case, my view is as long as it is not against religion, particularly with regard to the first-two stanzas, there should be no opposition. If there is unanimity among Islamic scholars and intellectuals that it hurts religious sentiments, there shall not be any force.

***Fatwa*: It's illegal for Women to Work, Earn**

Darul Uloom Deoband, the self-appointed guardian for Indian Muslims, in a Talibaneseque *fatwa* that reeks of tribal patriarchy, has decreed it as *haram* and illegal in *Shariat* for a family to accept a woman's earnings. Clerics at the largest Sunni Muslim seminary after Cairo's al-Azhar said the decree flowed from the fact that the *Shariat* prohibits proximity of men and women in the workplace.

"It is unlawful (under the *Shariat* law) for Muslim women to work in government/private sectors where men and women work together and women have to talk with men frankly and without a veil", said the *fatwa* issued by a bench of three clerics.

The *fatwa*, although unlikely to be heeded, is clearly detrimental. Even the most conservative Islamic countries, which restrict activities of women, including preventing them from driving, do not bar women from working. At the peak of its power, the Taliban only barred women in professions like medicine from treating men and *vice versa*. But there was never a blanket ban on working.

Edict on Women's Wages shocks Lucknow

The Darul Uloom Deoband's *fatwa* that it is *haram* and illegal in *Shariat* for a family to accept a woman's earnings has created a storm. "Men and women in *Shariat* are entitled to equal rights. If men follow the *Shariat*, there is no reason why women can't work with them", says Rasheed, the Naib Imam of Lucknow's main Eidgah Mosque in Aishbagh. Mufti Maulana Khalid Rasheed of Darul Ifta Firangi Meheli, another radical Islamic body which also issues *fatwas*, has criticized the Deoband *fatwa* as a retrograde restriction on Muslim women. The *fatwa* was in response to a question whether Muslim women can go for government/private jobs and whether their salary should be termed as *halal* (permissible under the *Shariat*) or *haram* (forbidden).

Well-known Shia cleric Maulana Kalbe Jawwad, however, justified the *fatwa*. "Women in Islam are not supposed to go out and earn a living. It is the responsibility of the males in the family", he said. "If a woman has to go for a job, she must make sure that the *Shariat* restrictions are not compromised with", he added, citing the example of Iran, where Muslim women work in offices but have separate seating areas, away from their male counterparts. In Lucknow, a city with strong secular and progressive traditions, where Muslim families train their daughters to be doctors, engineers and executives, there is a sense of shocked disbelief even in conservative quarters that such a decree could come from those who consider themselves to be advocates of the community.

Fatwa against Birthday Celebrations

In a fresh *fatwa*, Islamic seminary Darul Uloom Deoband has said that Islam does not permit celebrating birthdays. Responding to a query posed by a woman, the country's biggest Islamic seminary observed that the tradition to celebrate birthdays was started by the Jews and Christians, but Islam does not permit this practice. Jamiat Ulema-e-Hind's maintained *fatwas* should not be generalized.

Housewife seeks Refuge from *Fatwa* in Law

It was a desperate bid to escape torture, but Reshma, 24, now finds her whole community ranged against her. Heads of the community (*Jamaat*) summoned Reshma and her parents to a mosque, where she was beaten in front of nearly 300 onlookers. A *fatwa* was later issued that Reshma should leave the city in three days; her parents were told to leave in three months. If they did not do as they were told, the *Jamaat* threatened that Reshma's father would have to crawl around the locality on his knees; Reshma would be paraded on a donkey, her head shaved. Sounds like a bizarre medieval tale? This is a real-life news, from Vidyaranyapura in North Bangalore.

And what was the young housewife's crime? Nothing, she says. Her husband Dastagir suspects her of infidelity. Married in 2005, the physical abuse had started early. "However, he also said he loves me", Reshma said. Things spun out of control when the couple took in a tenant Nagaraj. Dastagir and Nagaraj grew close, and the tenant often had meals with the family. In time, Dastagir began to suspect that he was being cuckolded by his tenant and kept an obsessive watch over his wife's movements. He would rope in children in the neighbourhood to spy on her. "He beat me often, for no reason. He pretended to leave for work, then got on the neighbour's terrace to watch", says Reshma.

As it grew unbearable, Reshma reached out to her parents. They suggested that she ask the tenant to vacate. Even after Nagaraj moved out, the torture continued without cease. In a bid to commit suicide, Reshma went to the railway tracks near Yelahanka station. Nagaraj found her there, and persuaded her to escape to his aunt's house in Raichur, where she stayed for a fortnight. Dastagir got wind of where she was, and brought her back. He complained to leaders, who refused to hear his wife's side of the story. Reshma has since approached the Vidyaranyapura police, who took up a complaint against the men who issued the *fatwa* only after Deputy Commissioner of Police H.S. Revanna intervened. A petition has also been filed with the State Human Rights Commission.

Fatwa and a Khushboo Judgement

The Darul Uloom Deoband is one of India's well respected Islamic seminaries. Its *fatwa* against suicide attacks and its condemnation of killing of innocent persons were most welcome. Of late it has issued *fatwas* that Muslim women should not work in offices where men too are employed and also that working in banks is un-Islamic. The Deoband has also declared that opting for an insurance policy is against the tenets of Islam because insurance policy is unlawful as it is based on interest and gambling. In the present age of trade and commerce and globalization do these *fatwas* make sense? Realistically, will they be implemented by Muslim business and industrial houses? Are these *fatwas* recommendatory or mandatory? What penalty can be imposed for their breach? What is the response of the Muslim business community and Muslim civil society? An enlightened Muslim, Javed Akhtar, criticized these *fatwas* in moderate times. The result was a huge hate-mail and aspersion that he is an irreligious Muslim. Fortunately there were voices in his support. More such voices are needed. These *fatwas* do no good to the Muslim community. They offer fodder to those who wish to defame Islam. The Deoband which is highly regarded even by non-

Muslims may shed light on the subject in the interest of its own credibility.

SC Judgement in Khushboo: It is unfortunate that the Supreme Court judgement in Khushboo's case has been grossly misunderstood by some well-meaning persons as promoting immorality by encouraging live-in relationship and pre-marital sex. The judgement does nothing of the sort. It recognizes that in India marriage is an important social institution and that the mainstream view in our society is that sexual contact should take place only between marital partners. But as pointed out by Justice Dr. B.S. Chauhan speaking for the Bench, live-in marriages and engaging in sexual relations outside the marital setting, with the exception of adultery, is not an offence. Besides in the societal mainstream, there is a significant number of people who see nothing wrong in engaging in premarital sex. Notions of social morality are subjective. Criminal law cannot be used to interfere with the domain of personal autonomy when the acts complained of are not offences. The thrust of the judgement is that "we must lay stress on the need to tolerate unpopular views in the socio-cultural space. Under our democratic constitutional scheme different views are allowed to be expressed by the proponents and opponents". Expression of opinion which is contrary to conventional notions of decency and morality has to be tolerated and the same cannot be a ground to penalize the author. Viewed in proper perspective the judgement highlights the need for tolerance, deprecates moral policing and attempts by intolerant bigots to penalize people holding contrary views by recourse to criminal law. And therein lies the real merit of the judgement.

Fatwa Effect : College Teacher quits her job for marriage

The controversy over the recent *fatwa* issued by the Darul uloom Deoband against working Muslim women refuses to lie down. Just days after the seminary invited the wrath of liberal Muslims and civil society in general, forcing it to reword the *fatwa*, a case has come to light where a college teacher has quit her job citing the edict. The woman, who taught at the Burhani College, Mazgaon, as an *ad hoc* member, was due for permanent posting this year. "But she is also up for marriage. She said her prospective in-laws consider her earning to be *haram* as per the *fatwa*," said Farrukh Waris, Vice-Principal of the college. "We tried to convince her, but neither she nor her parents relented."

The teacher who quit was entitled to a handsome salary, as per the Sixth Pay Commission, which would have worked out to over Rs. 30,000 per month. Also, two students of the college's arts faculty have quit. "They did not (cite the *fatwa* as the reason), but we put two and two together. We even tried to convince the parents of one, but it was futile", Waris said. "This will have a detrimental effect on women. It is difficult to fight something when religious sanctity is given to it through *fatwas*. Lately, more women are opting for studies . . . . and then we have these cases too!"

"This way, one day there will be no scope for coeducation. Most women in the community are self-employed but a section of (Muslim) men are against it", said Farida Lambay, Vice-President, Nirmala Niketan and member of the Maharashtra Study Group, a body formed by the State government for the implementation of the Sachhar Committee report. "This (Issuing such *fatwas*) is a matter of great concern as it is shaming Islam. The way Islam is practised in India is a blot (on society). Not even in Islamic countries do we have the kind of marriage laws we have here", said Javed Anand, editor, Communalism Combat. Waris, Lambay and Anand were speaking at a press conference at the Press Club. It was organized by the *Aawaz-e-Niswaan* (Voices of Women). Reacting to the press conference, All India Ulema Council General Secretary Mahmood Ahmed Khan Daryabadi said: "Darul Uloom has not even issued a *fatwa* that says women's earnings are *haram*. This is a conspiracy to defame the seminary. One should first check what the (Burhani College) management has done. It could be that they forced her to leave and are now blaming it on a *fatwa* that does not exist".

Fatwa against taking Oath to Vote

Mufti Mohd. Irfan, a Muslim cleric of madrasas, at Fulat has issued a *fatwa* according to which taking oath in the name of Allah to vote for a particular candidate is un-Islamic, reports PTI from Muzaffarnagar. The *fatwa* was issued after some Muslim voters have been affirmed oath in the name of Allah or *Quran* to vote for a particular candidate by their supporters.

Female Foeticide 'un-Islamic', says *Fatwa*

In a *fatwa*, the Lucknow-based "Darul Uloom Firangimahal" has said that it is "un-Islamic to abort the foetus after determining its sex. "Islam does not permit abortion", said Maulana Khalid Rashid Firangimahali, chief of the institution and a senior member of the All India Muslim Personal Law Board, an apex organization of the Muslim community in the country. The *fatwa* was issued in response to a query by one Dr. Huma Khwaja, who wanted to know what the *shariat* (Islamic law) stand is on termination of pregnancy after determining the sex of the foetus.

"Just as a murder is a sin, to cut off a part of the body (foetus) is also a sin in the eyes of Islam", Maulana Firangimahali said in the *fatwa*. He said that it was the duty of the human beings to consider the "girls" (female foetuses) as gifts of the god. "Society will progress only if the girls survive", the well-known Sunni cleric said in his *fatwa*. The Maulana has also called for stern punishment to those indulging in female foeticide. The *fatwa* assumes significance in view of the recent Census report, which pointed out that 63 districts in Uttar Pradesh had disproportionate male-female ratio. The Census also reported that the number of girls in 0-6 age group in the State had dropped by 10 lakh even though the population of the State went up by three crores.

Fatwa against Salman's Family

A Muslim religious outfit Darul-Uloom Hijaziya Chisti of Mumbai has issued a *fatwa* calling for boycott on the family of veteran Bollywood scriptwriter Salim Khan for performing Ganeshotsav at their home. Last week, the television channels showed the Khans, including Salim's actor son Salman Khan, offering *aarti* to Lord Ganesha and even participating in the immersion of the idol.

Violated Islam: The celebration angered Mufti Manjar Hassan Khan Ashrafi Misbahi, chief of the outfit, and he issued the edict for boycotting the family. In a media conversation, the Mufti defended his decision and said all Muslim actors, who had performed idol *pooja* on screen in various roles, have violated Islam. Notwithstanding the edict, Salim Khan hit back at the Mufti and said, "Who are they to question people's religious beliefs? Why don't they issue such a *fatwa* against terrorists and terrorism, which is un-Islamic? The clerics are talking nonsense", he thundered. The Khans celebrate Ganeshotsav every year. Salim Khan said his wife is a Maharashtrian Hindu and to worship Lord Ganesh is their family tradition.

Neck-tie is Un-Islamic says *Fatwa*

Wearing a tie to school or to work is un-Islamic. The Darul Ifta in Deoband has now issued a *fatwa* claiming that wearing a tie is against the tenets of Islam. Replying to a query posed by a student of class eighth, the Darul Ifta has said, "Tie is an emblem of Christians, and adopting the emblem of any religion is not only unlawful but also is against Islamic spirit". "When tie is compulsory in your school, you should get admission in a school where such thing is not in force", the *fatwa* said.

Fatwa against Scholar backing Osama bin Laden

A *fatwa* has been issued against a well known Islamic scholar and owner of Peace TV Channel, Dr. Zakir Naik by the Qazi of Lucknow, Maulana Mufti Abdul Irfan Qadvi for allegedly supporting Osama bin Laden and asking youths to join terrorism. The Qazi demanded an immediate ban on the channel and a thorough probe into the sources from where Naik received funds. The *fatwa* issued here, has branded Naik as Qafir and recommends his excommunication from the Muslim community. Popularly known for his critical analysis of Islam and teachings of *Quran*, Naik is an orator in Peace TV, an Islamic television channel. Earlier, the Deoband had also issued a similar *fatwa* against Naik.

Maulana Qadvi said he had issued the *fatwa* following a demand from several clerics and Muslims, who took strong exception to Naik's support for terrorism and openly asking youths to join it. The *fatwa* however received flak from a section of Sunni clerics. Sunni religious scholar and All India Muslim Personal Law Board member Maulana Khalid Rashid defended Naik, saying that the emerging Islamic orator had been targeted. He also dismissed the allegation against Naik.

Fatwas against Freedom of Women

Fatwas have become daily function of some *maulanas*. These *fatwas* have no place in a modern society. They have lost their meaning and relevance today. My opinion on some *fatwas* is;

1. Modelling and exhibiting bodies is un-Islamic. This is a very serious issue which has a strong bearing on the development of the personality of the youths. This is totally against Islamic culture. This is intolerable.
2. Not to speak so loud that a woman's voice carries to men not related to them. I feel that it is always better than woman's voice is low. A woman has her own cultural behaviour.
3. Not to work in a government or private sector in male company and without a veil: I feel that this condition is impractical in a country like India where Muslims constitute a small percentage of total population. Educated women do work. The question of separate office for women is out of question. Even in Urdu medium schools only for girls, presence of two-three male teachers cannot be ruled out. Veil is definitely impossible in offices. It is also to be noted that even in Islamic countries there is a change. Rigidity is being slowly relaxed.
4. No cycling for adolescent girls or applying of

perfumes: Cycling is unavoidable. Girls go to schools using cycles. Even State Government is providing cycles freely to girl students. However applying of perfumes is not essential. It is better perfume is avoided by girls when they go out of homes.

5. A woman cannot be a judge: This is the view of hard-core *maulvis*. Even in Islamic/Muslim countries quite a few women have become judges of High Court. It is a noble and dignified profession. In India a Muslim woman was a judge of the Supreme Court. Barring a few hardcore *maulanas* no other Muslim would ever support this stand.
6. No talking to one's fiancé before marriage: This view of some *maulanas* goes against the spirit and letter of Islam and the message of the Holy Prophet. Islam permits boys and girls to meet each other and to express their choice of marriage. All this has to be within limits. While meeting face of the girl should be open so that the boy can form his opinion and inform his parents.

Insurance Policy is against Islam, rules Darul Uloom

After its *fatwa* that working in banks is un-Islamic, the Darul Uloom Deoband has now declared that opting for an insurance policy too, goes against the tenets of Islam. The "insurance policy is unlawful as it is based on interest and gambling", claimed the *fatwa* issued by the country's largest Islamic seminary. The edict issued by Darul Ifta department of Darul Uloom seminary was in response to a query whether it is lawful to take an insurance policy in the light of the *Shariat*. Millions of Muslims in India opt for insurance policies which is a contract that pledges payment of an amount of a person assured or his nominee against losses or perils.

"The clerics who issue *fatwas* should explain the context in which it is being issued to avoid confusion". Maulana Afroz Mujtaba, a Delhi-based cleric, said. Leading Islamic body Jamiat Ulema-e-Hind's spokesman Abdul Hameed Nomani said *fatwas* should not be generalized and they should be seen in the context in which they have been issued. Earlier, Darul Uloom had declared the job of writing and calculating interest in bank or insurance company unlawful.

Talaq uttered Thrice on Cellphone valid, says *Fatwa*

Talaq uttered thrice by a Muslim man on a mobile phone will be considered valid even if his wife is unable to hear it all the three times due to network and other problems, a fresh *fatwa* has ruled. The *fatwa* was given by Darul-Ifta, the *fatwa* department of leading Sunni Islamic seminary Dar-ul-Uloom Deoband, in reply to a query by a man. The man in his query had asked if no witness was present when he utters *talaq* thrice to his wife over the phone, whether it would be considered valid or not. "I angrily said *talaq* three times to my wife on cell phone but she claimed that she didn't hear it even once and nobody was around us. Please tell me whether *talaq* has taken place", he asked.

In its reply, Dar-ul-Ifta said, "If you have given three *talaqs* to your wife, all the three took place and she became *haram* (forbidden) for you", the *fatwa* said the woman will be free to marry anywhere she likes after her *iddat* (three months period after divorce) is over. "For *talaq* to take place, it is not necessary that the wife hears it or the witnesses are present", it ruled. In October, the seminary had ruled that saying *talaq* three times even on a humourous note is valid as per the *Shariat* (Islamic law) and the marriage stands nullified. A youth in his query had stated that while chatting with his wife over net, he had jokingly typed *talaq* thrice.

Claiming to have less knowledge about Islam, the youth said he didn't know how *talaq* is executed. The youth had stated that he was happily living with his wife and wanted to live with her in the future as well. Dar-ul-Ifta in its reply had said once *talaq* is put out three times it amounts to divorce and her wife was *haram* for him. The *fatwa* section in its reply stated that in the process it does not matter whether the man had enough knowledge of Islam or not. Under such circumstances the youth was neither allowed to take his wife nor to marry her again. It stated, adding now she would be required to go through *nikah* "*halalah*". As per the ruling, the woman would be required to complete *iddat* period after which she would be required to marry another man. The woman would be then required to divorce her second husband and go through *iddat* period again.

"Then only the woman would be allowed to remarry her former husband", it stated. "When you gave three *talaqs*, all the three took place. No matter whether the woman hears *talaq* or not, your wife became *haram* for you whether you are aware of the commandments of Islam or not", the *fatwa* read. "Neither do you have the right to take her back nor solemnise new *nikah* without a valid *nikah halalah*. After the completion of *iddat* period, the woman can marry where she wishes except you", it said, citing references from the books such as *Bukhari* and *Fatawa al-Hindiyah,* etc. Senior mufti of Darul-ul-Uloom Waqf Arif Kasmi said that under *Shariat talaq* even if made out in a lighter vein amounts to divorce.

Taliban shave Men for listening to Music : Victim

Taliban militants in northwest Buner district shaved the heads and moustaches of four Pakistani men as punishment for listening to music, one of the men said on Sunday. On Saturday, Taliban hardliners shaved the heads and moustaches of four men for listening to music, a young man from Buner said by telephone, requesting not to be identified. "I was with three other friends in my car listening to music when armed Taliban stopped us and, after smashing cassettes and the cassette player; they shaved half our heads and moustaches", he said. "The Taliban also beat us and asked us not to listen to music ever again", said the terrified man. Local police said they had no information about the incident. The victim said neither he nor his friends lodged a complaint with police, as this would have been "useless".

"It might have annoyed the Taliban further and I fear for my life", the man said. Residents in Mingora, the main town in Swat, said Taliban posters had been put up in streets and markets ordering women not to go shopping. The posters had appeared after the Taliban's controversial agreement with the government to enforce Islamic law in the region. "We will take action against women who go out shopping in the markets and any shopkeeper seen dealing with women shoppers will be dealt with severely", read the poster from the Swat branch of Tehreek-e-Taliban. "The peace agreement does not mean that obscenity should be reborn", it added. Hardline Islamists in the extremist Taliban consider it "obscene" for women to leave their homes, and ban females from venturing out in public without an immediate male relative – father, brother, son or husband. For years, Swat was a popular ski resort frequented by Westerners but the government lost control of it.

Fatwa calls for educating Muslim Girls

After a series of *fatwas* against Muslim women, an Islamic seminary has issued a *fatwa* saying that education for Muslim girls was 'mandatory' under *Shariat* (Islamic laws). The *fatwa* has been issued by the prestigious Lucknow-based Darul Uloom, Firangi Mahal in reply to a query with regard to education for Muslim girls. "Educating Muslim girls is mandatory in accordance with the *Shariat*," the *fatwa* said, adding, that the *Quran* laid great emphasis on education. The *fatwa* said that it is the responsibility of every Muslim man to provide education to his daughters and sisters and treat them well. "Such a person gets a place in *jannat* (heaven)". It added that the *Shariat* provides that maid servants should also be given education.

Reactions of *fatwas*

Muslims are generally not in favour of *fatwas*. *Fatwas* on certain types of behavioural culture may be good to the society. Rarely do we come across *fatwas* on gambling, smoking, debauchery, racing, usuary, dowry, violence, negligence of aged parents, desertion of wives, bribe, land grabbing, etc. We do need *fatwas* on these social concerns. Muslim society is at cross-roads today.

Sale of *fatwas* for a small amount has disgraced the Muslim society. *fatwas* are recklessly issued for a song. Some views against *fatwas* are presented here. Even religious leaders are divided over issue of *fatwas*. Some say *fatwa* is only an advice. It may be accepted or rejected. It means there is no rigidity. Some say that when *fatwa* is issued, it cannot be withdrawn. Thus, we find contradictions and conflicts of opinion. Youths are misled. They become emotional. Some of them believe that every *fatwa* has Islamic sanction and therefore, every Muslim should follow. The historical perspective of *fatwa* is not known to the majority of Muslims. Unless they are educated properly, this division and conflict will continue. This is not good to a positive development of thinking among Muslims.

Ulemas divided over *Fatwa*

"We must first properly understand the wordings of the song (*Vande Mataram*) and then decide whether reciting it is un-Islamic or not," Shia cleric Maulana Hamidaul Hasan said after meeting former RSS chief K.P. Sudarshan. He said to recite the song for worshipping someone was wrong, but if it is sung in honour of the country then there was nothing wrong with it. Sudarshan said the controversy over *Vande Mataram* was meaningless. He said Muslims were not a minority in the country and attributed the conflict between the two to the "communication gap".

Another senior Shia cleric Maulana Kalbe also echoed similar sentiments and called for a debate over *Vande Mataram*. It should be clarified by language experts if the word "*Vande*", on which the entire controversy rests, meant worship or just respect, the *maulana* said. "If it is worship, it could be objected, but in case of latter, there is no room for opposition", he added.

Deoband issues *Fatwa* against Birthday Celebrations

After the eviction of reformist rector Ghulam Muhammad Vastanvi over his remarks on Gujarat Chief Minister Narendra Modi, leading Islamic seminary Darul Uloom Deoband seems to have gone back to its ultra-conservative position. The country's biggest Islamic seminary has issued a *fatwa* against celebrating birthdays. Advising Muslims not to celebrate birthdays, the *fatwa* says that Islam does not permit such a practice which is a tradition of the western countries.

Responding to a query of an AMU student, Darul Uloom's *Fatwa* department said, "Islam does not permit such celebrations as they are against the *Shariat* law". The query was made in reference to the birthday celebration of founder of the Aligarh Muslim University Sir Syed Ahmed Khan. Maulana Abul Kasim Noomani who had replaced Vastanvi as the Darul Uloom VC, said that even the Islamic seminary does not celebrate the birth anniversary of founder of the religion Prophet Muhammad.

Former Rector Vastanvi was aware of the harm that the controversial *fatwas* were doing to Islam in the country and had plans for an image makeover for the century-old seminary. He had tried to reform the Darul Ifta (*fatwa* department) by putting some control over issuing *fatwas*, which were not in tune with the current days. "Vastanvi was determined to take the Darul Uloom to a next level by bringing in fresh reforms and modern practices. He wanted the seminary to be much more than a regressive *fatwa* issuing factory. But the conservatives wanted to stop him at any cost and succeeded in it. Now, the institution is back to its backward looking trail", said a Mufti within the seminary.

Fatwas only for Guidance, says Darul Uloom

Known for issuing *fatwas* even on trivial issues concerning Muslims, the prestigious Islamic seminary Darul Uloom in Deoband has clarified that *fatwas* are aimed only at providing guidance to society and no one can be forced to obey them. "It is up to the individual to accept the directions given in *fatwa* or reject them. He cannot be coerced or forced to obey them", said senior cleric Mufti Habibur Rehman who is in charge of the seminary's *Darul Ifta* (department of *fatwa*). The seminary has drawn flak from different quarters for issuing *fatwas* affecting the lives of Muslims.

Rehman said *fatwas* are issued only in response to specific queries and they contain specific instructions pertaining to the issue raised. "*Fatwas* are issued in the light of *shariat* (Islamic edicts) and they specify the position of the religion", he said. Rehman said it was wrong to force the people to obey *fatwas*. The cleric blamed the media for "blowing" *fatwas* out of proportion. Rehman also defended the sacking of former *mohtamin* (Vice-Chancellor) of Darul Uloom Maulana Ghulam Muhammad Vastanvi, Rehman said Vastanvi was sacked only after he refused to resign. The seminary, in the past, has issued, *fatwas* on whether Muslim girls should wear jeans or whether Muslim women should work in offices. It has once said the earnings of Muslim women working in offices was *haram* (illegal in the eyes of Islam) as they (Muslim women) cannot wear veil in the offices. In another *fatwa* the seminary had banned cycling by Muslim girls above the age of 13 saying they cannot remain in veil while cycling and it was un-Islamic.

Islamic Scholars Question Relevance of *Fatwas*

From banning wearing of wig during prayers to prohibiting having test tube babies, Islamic scholars are now raising questions on the relevance of a number of such *fatwas* issued by the country's largest seminary the Darul Uloom Deoband. Islamic scholar Maulana Wahiuddin Khan said it was not proper to issue *fatwas* "on every issue". "It is essential to understand that these *fatwas* are merely a point of view and it depends on an individual whether to follow them or not", he said.

On the seminary's *fatwa* website, the edicts have been divided in 39 categories. In one such query to the clerics, a man asked if it was appropriate for him to wear his wig during the *namaz* to which they replied that it was inappropriate. In another case, a man had asked that if he goes to another planet and finds an alien there should he click its picture, the reply was that Islam forbids clicking pictures of living beings. A man sought the seminary's advice when his six-year old daughter wanted to learn to ride the bicycle. The clerics said that the girl can ride the bicycle till the age of nine, not beyond that.

The Darul Uloom has also issued *fatwas* stating that it is forbidden under religion to donate organs or to have test tube babies. According to a *fatwa*, a condom can be used by a man only if his wife is unwell or too weak to bear a child. Also a person can work in a bank only as a watchman or as a messenger but not at any other post, the seminary said. Ashgar Ali Engineer, an Islamic scholar and social worker, said that these days Muslims do not blindly follow such edicts.

"Such *fatwas* create confusion among people. The Ulemas speak bookish language and don't consider the problem practically", he said. "Our ancestors were living in different conditions and whatever they said is considered holy by our clerics and they feel that these should be followed. But the reality is that society has changed", he said. Engineer said there were several instances from the life of Prophet Muhammad where men and women worked together.

Bangalore gives Deoband Fatwa a Thumbs Down

What *fatwa*: Darul Uloom of Deoband denied asking Muslim women not to work along with men and said it only suggested that working women should dress "properly". "We had only given an opinion based on *Shariat* that women need to be properly covered in government and private offices", said Maulana Adnan Munshi, spokesman for the seminary in Uttar Pradesh. He denied a report that the seminary was opposed to men and women working together. "No new *fatwa* was issued", Munshi said. Even the opinion on dress code was given when one asked if women could go to work without *purdah*, he said.

There are few takers for Darul Uloom of Deoband's latest *fatwa* in the city. The *fatwa* that asks Muslim women to wear veil at office has been castigated by professionals as well as activists. Theatre person and leadership development practitioner Munira Sen says *fatwa* is a regressive step. She says: "At a time when Parliament is poised to see more participation of women, it is unfortunate to have such a Diktat. It is an emotionally unintelligent response when Islam is being equated with fundamentalism and extremism the world over."

Nishi Rahman of Kahawa boutique says Islam is a very practical religion. She says: "It does not say women cannot work. But Islam mentions the practice of *hijab*. In fact, a girl has to wear veil even in the presence of her father. It is a personal choice and can't be forced". Artist Nilofer Suleman calls the new *fatwa* ridiculous. Nilofer feels women should work irrespective of their financial situation, as it is "better for the financial and intellectual growth of not just women but their children too". Calling the *fatwa* an infringement on individual rights, she says: "Gender biases have to be done away with". Madhu Bhushan of Vimochana said it is high time we ignored *fatwas*. "There is a subtle transformation happening among the Indian Muslims. The trick is not to take these *fatwas* at face values since it will only give credence to the men behind them".

Khurshid Downplays *Fatwas*

A majority of Muslims in the country are not much affected by *fatwas* like the one issued by Darul Uloom, Deoband, on the community going for insurance and its women working with men, Minorities Affairs Minister Salman Khursheed said. "Hence, it does not affect me as a Muslim", Khursheed said. And the feedback that he got on the matter showed the community was also not much affected by the edict. Darul Uloom, Deoband, the most influential Sunni seminary in the subcontinent had recently issued a *fatwa* against Muslims opting for an insurance policy, saying it went against Islamic tenets, as "it is based on interest and gambling." Darul Uloom issued the edict in response to a query as to whether it was lawful to take an insurance policy on the light of the *Shariat*.

Deoband's Fatwa Contradicts Islam

Deoband ulema: Is anybody listening? : The collapse of the 1857 mutiny – also considered India's first battle for independence from British rule – left the subcontinent's Muslims, and particularly their elite, in a political vaccum. In 1886, within nine years of the mutiny and the decline of Muslim political pre-eminence in India, a congregation of Islamic scholars led by Maulana Muhammad Qasim Nanautawi established the Darul Uloom at Deoband, UP. Today, Islamic schools are modelled after Deoband – notwithstanding the institution's wrangling with modernity. Deoband Ulema, for instance, had issued a *fatwa* against the founder of AMU, Sir

Syed Ahmed Khan, for promoting western education. Over the decades, there have been numerous instances of Deoband failing to see things in an enlightened manner. There were many within Deoband who rejected petition. But Muslims have never taken its *fatwas* seriously.

Dar-ul-Uloom Deoband's *fatwa* describing the earnings of a working woman as *haram* (forbidden) under the *Shariat* has left many people fuming. Waris Mazhari, Jamia Millia Islamia research scholar and a former Deoband student, says, "The life of the Prophet and his companions provides us a standard that Muslims should follow. In the light of their way of life, the *fatwa* is completely unjustified. Our second Caliph Hazrat Umar Farooq had appointed several women to high posts. One of the, Shifa bin Abdullah, was the supervisor of the markets. It is obvious that as the market supervisor she had to interact and deal with the men. Similarly, during the Prophet's time, women used to worship in mosques and work along with men. No such restrictions were imposed. Men used to even seek guidance from the Prophet's wife, Ayesha, who has also fought in a war Jang-e-Jamal."

Zafar-ul Islam, a reader at the Department of Islamic Studies, Aligarh Muslim University, writes in his book, *Fatwa Literature of the Sultanate Period* about Razia Sultana, the thirteenth century slave dynasty ruler. "From all available material, it can be safely concluded that Razia did not wear a veil. There is not a single known instance in any research work or history book that condemns or talks adversely about her rule. On the contrary, Qazim Vinhajud Siraj, an authority in Islamic scriptures, speaks highly of her administrative instincts and tact in his book *Tabaquat-e-Nasiri*. "One need not go too far back into history", says another scholar Ashfaque Khan.

Deoband says it only advised proper dress code – "No fatwa issued against working women"

Fatwas, or advice, are issued by clerics in response to questions put to them by people seeking solutions to problems they may be facing. While sometimes the replies are politically correct and in keeping with the times, some are not.

A look at some *fatwas* issued by the Darul Uloom of Deoband to specific queries:

Can a woman whose husband was in jail and has no financial support work without a veil?

It is allowable to work with open face in case of emergency if there is no fear of any evil.

Can woman wear burqua that are fit, from which the shape of boys is seen? Can woman wear transparent burqua, from which inside cloths are seen? Can woman wear burqua of different colours, e.g., white, blue, green?

Wearing such a dress which exposes the body structure is prohibited. The cloth of *burqua* should not be so thin which reflects the clothes of body. Yes, she can wear coloured burqua.

Is it permissible for a woman to apply any type of perfume in public?

It is unlawful for women to go out after applying perfume.

Is it allowed for a woman to cut and colour her hair for her husband? Is it allowed for a woman to behave as western woman for her husband?

It is unlawful and *haram* for a woman to cut hair of her head. But she can colour it with colours other than black. Imitating western-styled women and adopting their resemblance in matters against *Shariat* is unlawful. It is not lawful even for husband.

My husband chats with other girls on internet. Is it correct?

A married man should pass his life with chastity. In the presence of a good wife, paying attention towards other girls and chatting with them is against Islamic rules and unlawful. Make your husband understand through any respected person of your family.

Since I work in the Gulf, can I have sex talk with my wife over the phone?

There is no problem if you talk on phone in secrecy.

The Darul Uloom of Deoband, India's foremost Islamic seminary, denied that it has asked Muslim women not to work alongside men, saying it had only suggested that working women should dress properly. "We had only given an opinion based on *Shariat* that women need to be properly covered in government and private offices." Said Maulana Adnan Munshi, spokesman for the seminary in Saharanpur in U.P.

He denied a media report that the seminary was opposed together. "No new *fatwa* was issued", Maulana Munshi said, adding that the opinion was to a query on whether women could go to work without a veil, and issued over a month ago. Earlier, in the day, activists and lawyers criticized the *fatwa* (religious advice) saying Muslim women should not work since in doing so, they would be interacting with men, which was against Islamic tenets.

Former Minister for women and child development Renuka Choudhary ridiculed the Deoband *fatwa*, saying women don't need *fatwas* on how to conduct themselves. "Women are sensible enough and have inherent common sense when it comes to dealing with men or conducting themselves. In fact, it is men who need *fatwas* on how to conduct themselves before women and how to behave with us. Men like these *maulvis* (religious teachers) who issue *fatwas* must respect our independence," she said.

Professor Zoya Hasan of Centre for Political Studies, Jawaharlal Nehru University, pointed out that *fatwas* do not matter since they have no utility. "Nobody quits jobs and sits at home just because a *fatwa* has been issued to stay away from men or women and not talk to each other", she added. Meanwhile, an Allahabad High Court judgment that held a marriage between a Muslim and a non-Muslim was invalid unless the non-Muslim first converted to Islam evoked mixed reactions.

Well known lawyer Yusuf Muchhala pointed out that a *nikaah*, or marriage as per Islamic religious laws, can only be between two Muslims. "That is why we have the Special Marriage Act, so that if a non-Muslim and a Muslim want to marry without converting, they can do so. But for a *nikaah* to be valid, both have to be Muslims", he averred.

Yet, some would say it is time to move and a broader view needed. "There are many instances where people have retained their religion despite marrying a person of another religion", said Urvashi Butalia, a historian and founder of Zubaan, a publishing house. "People operating in the present time have to keep up with modern time".

Incidentally, the court had also quoted the *Hadiths* (traditions), which lists nine conditions for a bride. One of them is marriage to a widow or divorcee, both permitted and practiced in Muslim societies, would also be illegal. Clearly the last on this judgment hasn't been heard.

Fatwa to Cast Vote

Irrespective of their political leanings, Muslims must come out and vote, says a *fatwa* from Darul Uloom of Deoband. "A vote is as important as a testimony or witness is in Islam, hence, it must be utilized and corrected. A vote must not be kept back and wasted", says the *fatwa*. The *fatwa* gains salience considering the receding voter turnout across the country during the first two phases of elections. Although a number of organizations have launched campaigns showcasing filmstars and other celebrities appealing people to vote, the exercise has failed to make an impact in urban regions. Issued by Dr. Darul Ifta, the *fatwa* division of Darul Uloom, the flat came on a question seeking guidance for Muslims on voting in a country which isn't governed by *Shariat*. The question sought details about whether a Muslim could vote for a candidate who is a criminal and if Muslims should make their choice after testing the candidate or the party on the fundamentals of the *Quran*.

The Darul Ifta replied: "India is not an Islamic country but a secular democracy, hence, it would be out of place to look at its politics in Islamic perspective and test the parties and political leaders on the principles of the *Quran* and *Hadith*. This would bring nothing but disturbance and confusion". Restraining from commenting on the political character of the parties and candidates, the *fatwa* says: "One should vote for the party and the leader supported the *fatwa* appealing to Muslims and non-Muslims alike to vote on the polling day in large numbers. "It's our duty to vote. In a democracy, since we choose our own leaders, we can't blame anyone else for the state of affairs", says well-known Sunni cleric Maulana Khalid Rasheed, the Naib Imam of Eidgah Aishbagh and member of the executive committee of All India Muslim Personal Law Board (AIMPLB). Prominent Shia cleric Maulana Kalbe Sadiq, too, emphasized the importance of votes. "We must make the right choice instead of sitting back and lamenting on the state of affairs. Casting a vote doesn't take more than 20 minutes. This is all that tour system wants for us to deliver for the next five years. But we often do not realize the value of votes and let them go waste", Maulana Sadiq said.

Everyone Loves a Bad Fatwa!

"Everyone loves a bad *fatwa*", rues journalist Kashif-ul-Huda. *Fatwa* is arguably one of Islam's most misunderstood words. Say "*fatwa*" and it conjures up an image of hardline, extremist Islamism. In 1989, when Ayatollah Ruhollah Khomeini passed a death sentence on Salman Rushdie, the *fatwa* attracted worldwide negative publicity. In 2007, an India *fatwa* sought to put exiled Bangladeshi author Taslima Nasreen to the death for defaming Islam. Osama bin Laden issued two *fatwas* in 1996 and 1998. Both were targeted at civilians and military personnel from the US and allied countries and were meant to remain current until the West withdrew support for Israel and its army from Muslim countries.

Small wonder the *fatwa* has such a bad press and has promoted "learned ignorance" about Islam. Arshad Alam, Assistant Professor at Jamia Millia Islamia University, believes such depiction of *fatwas* and Muslims in general is a product of Western Orientalism. "They think Muslims can be best understood through the *Quran*." This is why the West has created the homogeneous "Islamic mind", he says. For the West, Islam continues to be the great "Asian Mystery", the variety and difference within are brushed aside and it is given a monolithic character. India has borrowed such typecasting from the West and a senior bureaucrat explains this as "helping certain vested interests here".

So what is a *fatwa* exactly? Maulana Abdul Khalik Madrasi, deputy Vice-Chancellor of Darul Uloom of Deoband, says "a *fatwa* is an advice or an opinion given in response to questions asked by an individual on a personal or religious matter. It is not binding on anyone. Whether the person who sought the advice follows it or not is his or her wish." *Fatwas* are based on Islamic law. Faizan Mustafa, Vice-Chancellor of the National Law University in Orissa, points out, "*Fiqh* (Islamic jurisprudence) is not sacred, *Shariat* is. *Fiqh* developed around 200 years after the death of the Prophet. Various schools of thought within Islam have differing views on it. Nobody can say authoritatively that this view is wrong and that is right".

It is all about interpretation. Arshad Alam says, "In India, the *Quran* is interpreted in a way that makes family planning un-Islamic. But, Indonesia draws upon the *Quran* to justify family planning". Differences are the hallmark of democratic debate. "The Prophet had said, "I am happy there is disagreement among my people," says Faizan Mustafa. A *fatwa* from a mufti of one sect is not considered binding in any way by other sects. Abdur Rauf, columnist and social activist in Kolkata, says, "Bengali Muslims in West Bengal, for instance, largely follow the *peer gharana* or Sufi Islam. A *fatwa* issued by, say a Deoband mufti, has no impact on most. The *fatwa* culture is rare in Bengal". Bangladesh banned *fatwas* by a High Court judgment. "Anyone who violates the ban and issues a *fatwa* is immediately arrested", says Tahmina Khatun, senior lawyer associated with Bangladesh National Women's Lawyers Association. Theologians believe that *fatwas* are not really meant for public consumption. Maulana Mubarak Hossain Misbahi of the Barelvi sect Tanzeem Abnae Ashrafia at Mubarakpur in Uttar Pradesh says, "The frequent publicity in the media makes a mockery of *fatwas*. *Imams* and *muftis* should act responsibly and refrain from pronouncing *fatwas*, say, during elections asking Muslims to vote for a particular candidate".

Many Muslims lament that news reports about *fatwas* affect non-Muslims more. "It is human psychology. People like to hear ill of others. In reality, *fatwas* have no effect on Muslims, especially those who are educated", says Shai religious scholar Kalbe Sadiq. His views are echoed by Ayaz Muhammad, a Chennai-based HR consultant. "*Fatwa* is a suggestion. I will mull over it. Ultimately the decision is mine whether I accept or reject it. *Fatwas* are not a restrictive or punitive device as is often made out to be. The hype created by the media irks Ayaz. Many Muslims share his angst. "The essence of *fatwa* is being distorted by the media", says Salman Sultan, Associate Professor of Chemistry at Azamgarh's Shibley National College. Kalbe Sadiq feels the media is playing a negative role. A senior IAS officer agrees that "when a *fatwa* is issued about making education mandatory for women, newspapers bury it on the inside pages. But, the *fatwa* forbidding women to work with men is splashed on the front page of all newspapers".

Such reports reinforce carefully crafted stereotypes about Muslims, adds Arshad Alam. It's a misconception that Muslims follow every diktat from every *maulvi*, says Abdul Wahid, associate professor of sociology at Aligarh Muslim University. "There is a gap between precepts and practices of Muslims. What Muslims practise in their daily lives is often contrary to Islam. For instance, dowry is anti-Islam. But, in many Muslim marriages, especially in north India, dowry is prevalent", he says. Generalizations about Muslims stem from the assumption they are a homogeneous group. To a great extent, the media has helped cement such views. After 9/11, the veil of propriety came off and the stereotyping became more blatant. Experts say India too is following in the footsteps of the West. "That is absolutely wrong. If you look around, you will see that behaviour of a rich Muslim is very similar to a rich Hindu's. It is imperative to consider a host of factors – socio-economic, spatial, political while analyzing a community", says Abdul Wahid.

The media is also blamed for according undue importance to the ulema and theologians. "Nobody asks the opinion of a Muslim intellectual. Theologians of any religion will propagate conservative views", says Faizan Mustaza. He says the conservative nature of Indian Islam is undoubtedly part of the problem. "In India, the Muslim personal law is stuck in the eleventh century. It is not even *Shariat* complaint. It was given by British judges". Indian Muslims missed an opportunity post-independence when Jawaharlal Nehru reformed Hindu marriage laws. Mustafa says Muslims could not muster the courage to reform Muslim laws. "Nehru understood secularism as an assurance of protection to minorities, their customs and laws. In the West, secularism entails a wall of separation between religion and State. Mustafa believes Islamic jurisprudence needs to be looked at again. "*Fiqh* was developed considering Islam as a State religion where Muslims are rulers. It has become redundant today when 80 per cent of Muslims live as minorities in a world that talks gender justice, equality and secularism.

Deoband Fatwa is Unconstitutional

The year 2010 marks the 60th anniversary of our Constitution, given wider meaning and content to the freedoms enshrined in it and tried to inject fresh life into core constitutional values like equity and equality. Despite these achievements, there are forces within this country which tend to pull us back. Every time we take a step forward, these forces push us two steps backward. Among those who fail to see value in our Constitution and tend to take us back to medieval ages are some Muslim clerics who view everything through the prism of religion. These clerics often issue ridiculous *fatwas* that are not only regressive but also against the letter and spirit of the Constitution. The latest example of this unfortunate trend is a *fatwa* issued by Darul Uloom of Deoband which said that "under the shariat it is unlawful for Muslim women to work in the government or private sector where men and women work together and women have to talk with men frankly and without a veil". This *fatwa*, which is a chilling reminder of the continued incompatibility of Muslim clerics with the core values in our Constitution, created such revulsion across the land that the seminary has been forced to offer explanations and downplay its implications.

A spokesperson of Darul Uloom later claimed that the

seminary did not intend to bar women from working alongside men in offices and factories. It only wanted them to be "*properly covered*". Further, although the seminary did not withdraw the *fatwa* or re-word it, it sought to soften the blow by claiming that this was not a *fatwa* but only an 'opinion'. Whether this is a '*fatwa*' or an 'opinion', we need to tell clerics in Deoband that their explanations are unconvincing and that we just cannot allow the tenets of any religion to override constitutional principles. For example, Article 14 guarantees equality before law and says the state shall not deny this to any citizen and Article 15 prohibits the state from discriminating against any citizen on grounds of religion, race, caste, sex, etc. Article 16 declares that there shall be equality of opportunity for all citizens in matters relating to employment and says no citizen shall be discriminated against on grounds of religion, race, caste, sex, etc., in regard to employment under the state. Thereafter, we have a clutch of rights Article 19 including the right to practice any profession or to carry on any occupation trade or business.

All these provisions underline the principle of equality, which is at the foundation of a democratic society. Another significant provision in regard to employment is Article 19(1)(g) which gives every citizen the right to practice any profession or to carry on any occupation, trade or business. The Deoband *fatwa* violates all these provisions which deal with Fundamental Rights in Chapter III of our Constitution and guarantee gender equality. Those who defend the issuance of such *fatwas* argue that the Constitution gives every religion the right to manage its affairs. This is only partly correct. While Article 25 gives every citizen the right to freely profess and practice his religion and Article 26 gives every religious denomination the right "to manage its own affairs", these are not unbridled rights. As Article 25 states, it is subject to public order, morality and health "and to other provisions of this Part", which means that these rights cannot override Fundamental Rights under Part III.

This principle was first enunciated with a great deal of firmness in 1952 by two of India's great jurists. In the State of Bombay *vs* Narasu Appa Mali, Chief Justice Chagla and

Justice Gajendragadkar of the Bombay High Court declared that the right conferred under Article 25(1) "was not an absolute or unlimited right". It is subject to public order, morality and health and other provisions of Part III of the Constitution (that contains Fundamental Rights). This principle — that the Constitution is above everything else – has been most forcefully asserted by the Supreme Court of the United States in 1879. It said that if the professed doctrines of religious belief were deemed to be superior to the law of the land, it would amount to permitting "every citizen to become a law unto himself".

The court said that while the laws cannot interfere with religious beliefs, they may interfere with religious practices, ". . . . if a wife religiously believed that it was her duty to burn herself upon the funeral pyre of her dead husband, would it be beyond the power of the civil government to prevent her carrying her belief into practice"? These principles constitute the bedrock of our Constitution too and if we allow religious leaders to tinker with it, we expose our Constitution and our secular way of life to the gravest danger. Seen in this light, the *fatwa* issued by the clerics of Deoband is grossly unconstitutional, because it hits at a basic premise — gender equality — and the right of every citizen to work and practice his or her profession or trade. Finally, we need to remind Muslim clerics again and again that India is not an Islamic state. In democracies like India, terms like *ahl-e-kitab* (People of the Book) acquire a different meaning. The *kitab* in our context is our Constitution and only those who respect it in letter and spirit are worthy of the bountiful rights that it confers on citizens. Will Muslim clerics ever understand this? In the larger interest of our democracy, it may be a good idea for the Ministry of Law to institute a basic course in Constitution law for religious leaders of all hues.

What Fatwa? I wasn't there, says Chidambaram

Home Minister P. Chidambaram probably visited Deoband and addressed a Jamiat Ulema-e-Hind (JUH) rally in the hope of mustering Muslim support for the government's battle against terrorism. What he did not bargain for, however, was the controversy generated by a JUH resolution asking Muslims not to sing national song *Vande Mataram.*

The BJP was quick to attack the Home Minister, with party Vice-President Mukhtar Abbas Naqvi accusing Chidambaram of providing legitimacy to the *fatwa*. The Minister, however, claimed innocence. A statement issued by his office said he was not present at Deoband when the resolution was adopted. "The Minister was at the JUH conference at Deoband on November 3 between 10 am and noon. No resolution was adopted in that period. When he spoke, he was not aware of any resolution relating to *Vande Mataram* or women's reservation and television."

In response to Naqvi's allegations, Chidambaram's aides also pointed out that he was reading from a prepared text. The Congress too rushed to the aid of the Minister, with party spokesman Shakeel Ahmad asserting, "He was not present when the resolution was adopted". The Congress said the BJP was unnecessarily raking up a two-year old resolution to spoil its chances of reconciling with Muslims. Even the Samajwadi Party, normally critical of the government, came to the Minister's rescue. It urged the BJP not to politicize the issue.

Bone of Contention: JUD reiterated a resolution it had passed in 2006, urging Muslims not to recite *Vande Mataram* as "parts of the song are against the tenets of Islam", at its 30th Conference at the Deoband seminary in Uttar Pradesh's Saharanpur. The Jamiat, however, made it clear that the opposition to *Vande Mataram* did not in any way reflect on the loyalty and love of Muslims for the country.

VI
Violence in Muslim Society : A General Perspective

Islam means peace, tolerance, submission, patience and so on. Violence in any form is quite alien to Islamic culture. But today we see violence and intolerance throughout the world. There is no sight of any improvement. Burning mosques by Muslims, terrorism, infighting among members of the *jamaat* in the mosques and other areas are all common. Even some *maulanas* provoke youngsters to spread violence. A few *maulanas* behave like pseudo politicians and this leads to a disturbed Muslim society. In other words violence is patronized and Islamic mandate is sidetracked. Perhaps barring a few exceptions, all Muslim countries are involved in violence, mostly against Muslims only. It is just a question of Muslims *Vs* Muslims and ultimately Islam *Vs* Muslims.

A few instances are presented here by way of illustration.

"Pro-Pak" Graffiti creates Tension

Alleged pro-Pakistan writings by miscreants on walls of some old temples at Murugamala, near Chintamani in Chickballapur district triggered tension. The slogan "Pakistan Zindabad" on the walls of three shrines near the famous Murugamal Dargah, came to light in the morning. Written in Kannada script, the slogan created discomfiture among people leading to an instant protest. An irate mob allegedly damaged a vehicle and tyres were burnt in protest against the incident. Some pro-Hindu activists led by Bharatiya Janata Party Chickballapur district unit president Satyanarayana Mahesh staged a protest at Chelur Circle demanding that the authorities nab the miscreants.

The sources ruled out any hand of local people in the incident since Hindus and Muslims are living in amity for long time. Vehicular movement came to a grinding halt in the area following the protests. Superintendent of Police and Deputy Superintendent of Police rushed to the spot. Security has been tightened in the village. "A peace committee meeting has been held. The situation is under control." Mr. Ravindraprasad, SP said. The peace committee appealed to the people to maintain communal harmony and peace.

Radical Muslims warn of another September 11

Muslim extremists have held a meeting at the heart of the area where the liquid bombers lived in which they warned of a September 11. One speaker at the meeting, held on the anniversary of the attacks in America, told the assembled crowd that the West should "listen to the warnings." The meeting, in front of a 100-strong crowd at a community centre on the Lea Bridge Road in Walthamstow, east London, was also addressed by the exiled preacher Omar Bakri Muhammad *via* video link from the Lebanon.

His appearance was greeted by cheers of "faith" and "god is great" as he claimed to have foiled a bomb plot against him by agents of the British Government, although much of his Speech was inaudible due to technical difficulties. Walthamstow was home to two of the three members of a gang found guilty of conspiracy to murder. They face a retrial over allegations they were targeting trans-Atlantic flights. Among the speakers were a number of former members of the banned group Al-Muhajiroun, once led by Bakri from his council home in Edmonton, North London.

The most incendiary speech was delivered by Saiful Islam, from Luton, Bedfordshire, who praised Osama bin Laden and Al-Qaeda for their "courage" in retaliating against the "dictatorship and oppression" of the West. He said: "The blame of 9/11 belongs to no one but the American government. They are the terrorists. Sheikh Osama warned America numerous times, it was because of their own arrogance, because they thought they are a superpower and nobody could match them, that Sheikh Osama taught them a lesson — a lesson they still have not learned." Saiful Islam warned that unless British and American troops were withdrawn from "Muslim lands" they would be blamed for the consequences, saying the West would "never achieve security until our own lands achieve security".

Clashes at Goripalya, Bangalore

Three people were injured in group clashes that erupted in Goripalya, Bangalore. According to the locals, the fight was sparked off after heated exchanges between former corporator Aarif's men and some members of a group that was going door-to-door to collect money for charity after the afternoon *namaz*. The injured were admitted to Victoria and NIMHANS hospitals. Nazni Begum, Councillor of Padarayanapura, told *Indian Express* that people with ex-corporator thrashed the group that was collecting money.

The clashes intensified as the evening progressed, and the attackers also ransacked 10 shops in the area. One government-run pharmacy also attracted the mob's ire. There are unconfirmed reports of some women being beaten up. Some people in the area, who spoke to *Indian Express*, said that when the people went to complain to Jagjivanramanagar police, they were turned away. The police dismissed the complaint saying that it was a "minor incident". The police, however, were forced to register a complaint after a large crowd gathered in the police station and refused to budge till a case was filed.

Gaza in Shock as Islamists Kill Kidnapped Italian Activist

Gaza was in shock and mourning after a radical Islamist group killed an Italian activist just hours after kidnapping him in an act deplored by Rome as "barbaric." The victim, 36-year old Vittorio Arrigoni who was working with the pro-Palestinian International Solidarity Movement (ISM), was found dead by the security forces in a house in northern Gaza. He had been hanged, Hamas security officials said.

Arrigoni had been kidnapped a day earlier by a Salafist group which had demanded that Hamas release Salafist prisoners within a 30-hour deadline that was to be expired on Friday afternoon. It was not clear why they killed him. The murder drew widespread condemnation from Gaza City to Rome. Hamas called the murder a "heinous crime" and vowed to hunt down the perpetrators, while Italy decried what it said was an "act of vile and senseless violence". Arrigoni's friends and family were devastated, and spoke of their shock that the killers had targeted a man described as "a real activist for Palestinian human rights".

In a video posted on YouTube, the kidnappers said Arrigoni had been taken hostage in order to secure the release of an unspecified number of Salafists detained by Hamas security forces, including Hisham al-Saedini, a leader of the radical group Tawhid wal Jihad. The kidnappers, who said they belonged to the Brigade of the Gallant Companion said they would execute Arrigoni if their demands were not met by 5.00 pm on Friday.

Tawhid wal Jihad denied it had anything to do with the kidnapping, while acknowledging that the murder was the result of Hamas's "repression" of Salafists. "What happened is the natural result of the repressive policy of Hamas and its government against the Salafists", it said. "We and others have for a long time warned the Hamas government against the risks of acting.... against the Salafist trend". In Gaza City, Hamas officials said two people had been arrested on suspicion of involvement in the kidnapping and said they were hunting further accomplices to what spokesman Ihabal-Ghussein called a "heinous crime which has nothing to do with our values, our religion, our customs and traditions.

Pak Taliban Kill Couple in Public for 'Adultery'

A man and a woman accused of committing adultery have been gunned down by the Taliban in restive North West Pakistan, showed a chilling footage of the public execution that surfaced just two weeks after a video of a teenage girl being flogged by the militants sent shockwaves across the country. The new video, sent to the *Dawn* newspaper by unidentified persons, shows a Taliban firing squad killing the man and woman, both apparently in their forties, after accusing them of having committed adultery.

The two persons were gunned down in the presence of their relatives. The newspaper quoted its sources as saying that the incident took place in Hangu district of North West Province a few days ago. In the video, the woman is heard appealing to the Taliban for mercy. "Have mercy on me, please have mercy. The charges against me are false and no man has ever touched me", she is heard saying. The Taliban militants first pumped several bullets into the woman's chest and then fired a burst from assault rifles at her and the man. As the woman was apparently still alive after being shot, some Taliban are heard shouting: "She is alive, kill her".

Pakistani political leaders and rights activists had condemned the public flogging of teenager Chand Bibi in the restive Swat valley after the emergence of the earlier two-minute mobile phone video. That video showed the *burqua*-clad 17-year old girl being held face down on the ground by three men while a fourth whipped her repeatedly. A large crowd of men watched the flogging, which reportedly occurred in the Matta area of Swat some weeks ago. Prime Minister Yousuf Raza Gilani ordered an inquiry into the matter and the Chief Justice of Supreme Court Iftikhar Chaudhry took *suo moto* notice of the issue and sought fortnightly reports from the government on its inquiry.

However, federal interior secretary told a news conference at Saidu Sharief in Swat that an investigating team had concluded the earlier video was fake. The team, headed by a senior police official, had submitted a report on its probe that will be handed over to the apex court, he said. The team had also concluded that no incident of flogging had occurred, Shah said. The team and the judge of an Islamic court had recorded the statements of Chand Bibi and her husband, and they had both denied the incident. Shah said he had visited the area in compliance with the directives of the apex court, which had asked him to go to Swat to inquire about the incident.

Lahore Blasts Toll Rises to 43

Pakistan's second city Lahore was on high alert after two suicide bombers blew themselves up in an Islamic shrine packed with worshippers, killing 42 people and wounding scores more. Pakistan's Taliban, which has been instrumental in deadly attacks over the past three years, denied it was involved in Thursday's bombing. Footage from the scene of the carnage at the shrine dedicated to a Sufi saint showed crowds of panicked worshippers fleeing in all directions as a huge blast sent clouds of smoke into the air.

Television pictures showed bloodstained clothes strewn on the ground outside the heavily damaged shrine and people crying and beating their chests in despair. A spokesman for Tehreek-e-Taliban Pakistan denied involvement in the attack. "We condemn this brutal act. Our target is very clear and we only attack police, army and other security personnel", Azam Tariq told AFP by telephone from an undisclosed location.

Thousands of people were at the shrine in the crowded centre of Lahore dedicated to Sufi saint Hazrat Syed Ali bin Usman Hajweri, popularly known as Data Ganj Bakhsh, at the time of the blasts. "A total of 42 people have been martyred", senior rescue official Mazhar Ahmad said. Authorities had found the heads of two suicide bombers, and were investigating how they had entered the area despite strict security measures. "We were searching everyone walking through the gate. One bomber crossed the gate and ran to catch him but in the meantime he blew himself up", Rao Fazul-ur-Rahman, an administrator at the shrine, told AFP. Hours after the blasts, two firecrackers exploded near the American consulate and Lahore Press Club, adding to jitters in the city, but none was hurt.

Classical Example of Violence : Killing Imams

Killing has been well accepted by the society as the desperate act of the frustrated individual or group. But killing should also be sensible. Can an Imam behind whom we offer *namaaz* be mercilessly killed? If Imam is killed, who else cannot be? Here is a classical example of not one Imam, but two

Imam being killed on the same day and under similar circumstances.

Uttar Pradesh is the well recognized Islamic cultural State. It has its own history of Muslim rule. Here we have two globally known Islamic study centres. One is the Deoband centre and the other is Bareilly centre. While one is known for its liberal nature, the other is known for its conservative nature. Both are bitterly pitched against each other. The whole atmosphere is surcharged with diacritically opposite views.

The Imam of Deoband offered Fajar *namaaz* in the mosque and was returning home. Some vandals for Bareilly attacked and killed him on the spot and fled away. Blood of the supporters of Deoband Imam was boiling. They were waiting for time. The same evening, the Imam of Bareilly mosque offered Maghrib *namaaz* and was returning home. He was attacked and killed by the Deoband supporters.

Two killings of Imams in one day is something very innovative, strange and perhaps must have created a world record. If this is the way in which vengeance and vendetta play havoc, how can we raise our head and say, "we are the followers of Prophet Muhammad who taught us the meaning and principles of Islam? Not only two human beings were butchered, the essence of Islam was battered. We are just bogus followers of Great Islam. We are discreditors of Islam. We have lost our moral rights to be called Muslims. Where is Islam and where are we?

Infighting

The Holy Prophet has said, "All Muslims are brothers. They constitute one brotherhood . . . . You will observe that the believers are like the parts of the body in relation to each other in matters of kindness, love and affection. When one part of the body is afflicted, the entire body feels it; there is loss of sleep and a fever develops". He has further said, "It is not proper for a man to keep away from his brother for more than three days, and then when they meet they turn their faces away from each other".

This message can also be called a mandate. But it is a pity

that this is ignored, disrespected, violated at all levels of human social interaction. An observance of this message is very rare. Straight from family to the international level we find Muslims are miserably divided. Hatred has no bounds. Killing one another is common. At the international level, Iran *Vs* Iraq, Kuwait *Vs* Iran, Pakistan *Vs* Bangladesh are displaying their enmity openly. Conflicts between Sunnis and Shias are common. Sunnis and Tableeq-e-*Jamaat* show dreaded poisonous attitudes. At the family level in-laws play havoc. In the mosques we find groups fighting for their control over mosque management. Anjumans are in conflict and often approach the government or court for settlement of their dispute. There are instances of a *mutawalli* of a mosque being beaten up in the mosque itself.

There was another conflicting situation in western part of Karnataka. Two groups of *mutavallis* had acute differences over the management of the mosque. I tried my best to bring about reconciliation. My efforts failed. I appointed a government officer as the Administrator. One day both the groups resorted to infighting. One group wanted me to close the door of the mosque on a Friday so that no group can enter the mosque and offer Friday prayer. I was annoyed. I felt disgusted. I asked the leader why the group takes such painful and un-Islamic decision. I refused to oblige. I told the leaders I do not want to become a sinner. I allowed the door open. Friday prayer was offered. No untoward event took place, perhaps because of heavy police force with police vans.

Sunni-Tableeq-e-*Jamaat* Conflicts

Sunnis are not allowed to offer prayers in a mosque managed by Tableeq-e-*Jamaat*. In many places conflicts have taken place. Two years ago it happened in Chitradurga. Some Sunnis wanted to offer prayers in the mosque under the management of Tableeq. Some Tableeq youths opposed. Differences were expressed and the atmosphere became too hot in the very premises of the mosque.

There was a theatre nearby. Both the groups faced each other and bitterly fought. Properties were damaged. The whole area was disturbed. There was tension. Some thought it was a communal clash. But was a clash between two groups of Muslims over the issue relating to offering *namaaz*.

Such clashes between Sunnis and Tableeq are not uncommon. In Bangalore a couple of years ago such a clash took place during the holy month of Ramzan. Police services were summoned. How can such mad and poisonous action could take place. Where is the fear of God and Rasool? The words of the Prophet are totally neglected.

Clash over Issue of *Janaza* (Coffin)

In a village in Arasikere taluk of Hassan district, Karnataka, another most painful event happened. In the village Mohammadpur sizeable Muslims live. But the Hindus are in majority. They have good relationship. But Muslims are divided into two groups. One group had less number than the other group. Former was headed by one Rahman and the latter was headed by Kareem. Some members of Rahman group had not paid the annual chanda (contribution). Therefore, they were not allowed to offer prayers. This went on for some time.

One day an elderly man from Rahman group died in the morning. *Janaza* was required. Rehman group requested several times. But Kareem group refused to give until the arrears amount was paid. Dispute went on till 2 pm. Funeral had to be completed by 5.30 pm. Both the groups remained very adamant. There were shouting and counter shouting. This scenario disturbed peace in the village.

Finally the chairman of the Gram Panchayat was briefed about the matter. He felt bad. He summoned the leaders of both the groups and heard them. He requested the leaders to resolve the matter later and hand over the *janaza* immediately. But Kareem group did not agree. Time was running out. Therefore, the Chairman, a Hindu asked Kareem group leader as to how much the amount due. The amount of just Rs. 1500. The Chairman gave this amount to Kareem group leader and strictly directed the leader to hand over the *janaza* immediately. This was done. The funeral was over. But bitter relationship continued.

This small case exposes the narrow mentality of some

Muslims. I do agree both the groups were at fault. But the tragic situation on hand required a different solution. It is a great sin if some one obstructs funeral ritual. It is unfortunate that no action was taken up by Muslim leaders to patch up the differences. Obstructers should have been punished by the religious leaders. It is also a shame that a Hindu leader came to the rescue of Muslims.

Two held for Chopping Off Ernakulam Professor's Palm

Two activists of the Popular Front of India (PFI) were arrested on Monday in connection with the attack on a professor at Muvattupuzha in Ernakulam district. Sources said 12 others, most of them with extremist links, were also taken into custody for interrogation. Ashraf, 37, of Mundeth, Mekalady, and Jaffar, 28 of Eramaloor, Kothamangalam, were remanded to judicial custody by the Judicial First Class Magistrate Court, Muvattupuzha.

The right palm of T.J. Joseph, 53, professor of Malayalam in the Newman College, Thodupuzha, was chopped of by the assailants. He, along with his mother and sister, was returning home from church when a gang of six waylaid his car and attacked him with an axe. Professor Joseph underwent two lengthy micro-vascular surgeries at the Specialists Hospital, Kochi, and the severed palm was "reconstructed and re-grafted". Hospital sources said he was conscious and that his condition was stable. He is recovering in the intensive care unit. Professor Joseph has been under suspension following a controversy over disparaging remarks about religious beliefs in an examination question paper he prepared for undergraduate students in the college.

A team led by Muvattupuzha Deputy Superintendent of Police Sabu Mathew is probing the attack. T. Vikram, Superintendent of Police, Ernakulam Rural, who was camping in the area, said: "We have talked to church leaders to convince them an all-out effort is being made to nab the culprits". Meanwhile, the Muslim Aikya Vedi took out a march to the Muvattupuzha police station claiming that its activists did not have any role in the attack. Police presence was intensified at Muvattupuzha and Thodupuzha. The attack has caused widespread shock and outrage across Kerala. Several organizations, cutting across political and religious divides, have condemned it and called for stern steps to prevent recurrence of such incidents. Many Muslim organizations, including the Indian Union Muslim League, condemned the attack and urged the government to take action against the culprits.

After the controversy over the question paper arose, Prof. Joseph was arrested for allegedly fomenting communal disturbances. In the question paper, he had used a passage about an imaginary dialogue between God and Muhammad, and the students were asked to comment. Certain Muslim organizations, assuming that 'Muhammad' in the passage was Prophet Muhammad, took offence and staged protest rallies and clamoured for action against the professor. Stones were thrown at the college run by the Christian church. The college management apologized and, on the government's instruction, Prof. Joseph was placed under suspension for a year. The police registered a case against him. He went into hiding, but after a couple of weeks he was arrested under Section 295 of the Indian Penal Code (for causing communal hatred). He was later released on bail.

Attack against Islamic Tenets : Muslim Leaders

Several Muslim organizations have condemned the violent attack on and chopping off of the hand of T.J. Joseph, a professor in Kerala's Ernakulam district by some miscreants on the pretext of avenging blasphemy. In a joint statement, they said: "We feel that law was taking its due course against the professor for his misdeed and he was already suspended from his college for a year due to his insult to the Prophet of Islam". The signatories are Manzoor Alam, Secretary-General, All India Milli Council, Muhammad Jafar, Naib Ameer, *Jamaat*-e-Islami Hind and acting President, All India Muslim Majilis-e-Mushawarat; Zafarul-Islam Khan, former President, All India Muslim Majlis-e-Mushawarat and Editor of The *Milli Gazetteer*; Niaz Farouqui, Secretary, Jamiat Ulama-e-Hind; Navaid Hamid, General Secretary, Movement for Empowerment of Muslim Indians and member of the National Integration Council.

The statement said: "Those who attacked Mr. Joseph forgot that the Prophet of Islam, upon whom be peace, in his own life had pardoned a Jewess who used to throw garbage on him and when she did not do so one day, the Prophet enquired about her and upon being told that she was ill, went to wish her early recovery and good health. The Prophet forgave the people of Mecca after its conquest although they had pained him, expelled him from his hometown and had waged war against him for years". The attack on the professor was against the basic tenets of Islam and the Sunnah of the Prophet which laid emphasis on forgiveness. Islam explicitly forbade one from taking the law into one's own hands when there were competent authorities to deal with an issue.

"We hope that the law will take its due course to punish the criminals who attacked Mr. Joseph. They have clearly sinned and defamed Islam by committing this crime which we condemn without reservations. We also appreciate the youth wing of the Jamat-e-Islami Hind and workers of Solidarity for donating blood for Mr. Joseph in hospital", the statement said. Condemning that attack, Citizens for Justice and Peace Secretary Teesta Setalvad said: "Though the identity of the assailants is still under investigation, media reports suggest that the professor was attacked by three persons armed with swords — who police reports say, belonged to the Popular Front of India".

If his remarks in the question paper were either inflammatory or defamatory, there were saner and democratic means to deal with them. "Are we so fickly in our convictions and in our faith that we cannot tolerate discussion and debate? If the words or thoughts or sentiments of anyone hurt us, do we have the right to resort to barbaric and unlawful means of redressal", she asked in a statement. "Outfits like the PDP and NDF in Kerala have been allowed to carry out a brand of intolerant acts unchecked. This is dangerous to syncretic traditions of Kerala and the secular traditions of the country as a whole."

Eid Day Protests in Kashmir Turn Violent, Two Injured

Violence marred Bakr Eid celebrations in Kashmir. Police said miscreants assembled outside a mosque at Janglat Mandi in Anantnag after Eid prayers and began torching police vehicles passing by and pelting stones at security forces. Two people, including a police man, were injured in the violence. "We exercised maximum restraint and brought the situation under control. Constable Ghulam Muhammad suffered a head injury in the stone-pelting", a police spokesman said.

Protestors clashed with police in Srinagar's old city area as well. The clash took place when police tried to prevent an anti-India march on Nalamar road. Protestors pelted stones and tried to cross barricades, but security forces dispersed the mob by lobbing smoke shells and using cane charge. As news of the police action spread to neighbouring areas, more people took to the streets and pelted stones. "Some miscreants tried to disrupt pace at Nawa Kadal and Sekidafar in old Srinagar by pelting stones. They were chased away and situation brought to normal." The police spokesman said.

Demonstrations were also held in other parts of the Valley. Some protestors raised pro-freedom slogans after prayers at the revered Hazratbal shrine. The violence erupted despite police putting chairmen of the two Hurriyat factions, Syed Ali Shah Geelani and Mirwaiz Umar Farooq, under house arrest. Last Eid, Mirwaiz had taken police by surprise when he marched to Lal Chowk, sparking violence in which a power department building and a crime branch office were set ablaze.

Terrorists targeting Mosques in Pakistan

Jihadi groups have attacked or destroyed at least 40 mosques in Pakistan in recent years, killing hundreds of worshippers, a move that is being dubbed by a former Indian envoy as random terrorism. "This is random terrorism. Taliban wants to spread their extremists Deoband brand of Islam which is different from what people in India follow. They have aligned with a number of Sunni extremist groups like SS, LeJ and JeM", former Indian High Commissioner to Pakistan G. Parthasarthy said.

The strategy of targeting mosques at prayer time is now increasingly being used by the terrorist groups across Pakistan, as this has become a lethal way to create terror. According to the available data, about 40 mosques have been targeted either by Taliban or other terror groups like Sipah-e-Sahaba (SS), Lashkar-e-Jhangvi (LeJ) and Jaish-e-Muhammad (JeM), since 2002 across Pakistan with four being attacked this year so far. Former diplomat Satish Chandra says, "There is lot of sectarian violence in Pakistan mainly fomented by the Taliban".

The recent in the series was the April 5 attack on a mosque in Punjab's Chakwal town which claimed 30 lives. On March 27, a suicide bomber blew himself up in a mosque packed with worshippers in Jamrud in the North-West Frontier Province (NWFP) killing 76 people and reducing the roadside mosque to rubble. On February 5, over 32 people were killed when a suicide bomber blew himself up amidst a crowd of worshippers outside the Al Hussainia mosque in Dera Ghazi Khan in Punjab. So far over 200 people have been killed in the attacks on mosques in 2009.

"Taliban has killed thousands of Shias in Afghanistan and these groups in Pakistan are doing similar things against Shias and Sunni Barelvi Muslims to create terror", Parthasarthy said. Pakistan's Interior Ministry chief Rehman Malik has said in the past that Al-Qaeda has been using the LeJ and SS to execute terrorist attacks in Pakistan. Islamic scholar and Jamiat-Ulema-e-Hind spokesman Maulana Abdul Hameed Nomani said, "A true Muslim can never target a religious shrine. This kind of acts are inhumane and the culprits must be punished. This is un-Islamic act". All India Muslim Personal Law Board Vice President and Islamic scholar Maulana Kalbe Sadiq said, "Those who carry out such attacks do not deserve to be called Muslims. Such acts are against the basic Islamic principles".

"When Babri mosque was demolished, there was hue and cry everywhere but why the same people are now silent when mosques are being destroyed and innocents are being killed", Sadiq asked. In 2008, the mosques were targeted on 12 occasions, with major being in Tull Tehsil of NWFP in Badan village of Bajaur agency and in the Maskanai area of lower Dir in the NWFP. Over 80 people were killed in these attacks. In 2007, over half a dozen mosques were targeted in which more than 100 people were killed. The major attack was near Qasim Ali Khan mosque in the Dilgaran area of Qissa Khawani bazaar in Peshawar which claimed 15 lives in January. In December, over 50 people were killed when a suicide bomber blew himself up in the midst of worshippers offering Id-ul-Adha prayers in Charsadda in the NWFP. In 2005, the major terror attack took place in May in which 25 people including the suicide bomber were killed at the Bari Imam shrine located in the vicinity of the diplomatic enclave in Islamabad.

Angry over Question, Imam assaults Journalist

A sufi activist and editor of a weekly Wahid Chishti was assaulted by the *Imam* of Delhi's Jama Masjid Syed Ahmed Shah Bukhari and his supporters at a press conference after the scribe asked Bukhari, a seemingly "uncomfortable" question. A furious Bukhari allegedly slapped Chishti and grabbed him by collar as the battery of mediamen tried to intervene and rescue the sufi activist. Bukhari's supporters also manhandled the journalist who was somehow whisked away from the scene by his fraternity members.

Bukhari who was addressing a press conference, lost his cool when Chishti asked him about the name of one Dasarath in the record of the disputed land before 1528. He also asked the *Imam* why the land in Ayodhya could not be given to the Hindus for constructing a temple. Terming Chishti as an agent of the Congress Party, Bukhari used abusing language against him and also asked his supporters to thrash him. Earlier addressing the media, the *Imam* of Jama masjid said trifurcation of the disputed land was not acceptable to the Muslims and that the High Court verdict must be challenged in the Supreme Court.

Muslim kids Exposed to Extremism

Muslim children are being taught how to chop off thieves'

hands and that Jews are plotting to take over the world at a network of Islamic schools, it has been disclosed. Up to 5,000 pupils attending weekend schools across Britain are being exposed to textbooks claiming that some Jews were transformed into pigs and apes, and that some offences could be punished with stoning. One book for six year-old warns that those who do not believe in Islam will be condemned to "hellfire" in death.

Another text for 15-year old teaches that thieves who break *Shariat* law should have their hands cut off for a first offence and their feet amputated for a subsequent crime. Teenagers are presented with diagrams showing where the cuts should be made. Panorama on BBC One will claim that the books were discovered at a network of 40 private schools teaching the Saudi Arabian national curriculum. The programme claims to have upcovered evidence apparently linking the schools to the Saudi embassy. Officials at the embassy deny any link.

Panorama also found examples of private Muslim schools using extremist sentiments of their websites. Researchers claimed in a separate report that the education system was "not equipped" to deal with the threats posed by extremist organizations. The Policy Exchange think-tank said the Coalition's new free schools, run by parents, teachers and charities, could be exploited by organizations seeking to indoctrinate young people. It also claimed that checks on groups running private schools were "piecemeal, partial and lack depth".

Taliban in *Burquas* Blast Government Offices

Taliban attackers, some in *burquas*, stormed government offices in Afghanistan in a spurt of suicide blasts and gunfire that killed at least six people, officials said. At least 13 Afghans were wounded in the attacks in Khost, as was a US soldier and several police personnel who tried to stop the militants, officials said. The Taliban said it was responsible for the attack, claiming to have dispatched 30 militants into the small town about 20 km from the border with Pakistan.

At 10 am, five "terrorists wearing burquas" pulled up at

the gates of the provincial governor's compound in a four-wheeled-drive vehicle, Khost provincial police Chief Abdul Qayoum Baqizoi said. Some exchanged fire with police. The car, rigged with explosives, blew up, added interior ministry spokesman Zemarai Bashary. "Two police and two security guards were martyred on the spot," Bashary said. Three of the attackers then tried to enter the nearby municipality but were killed by security forces.

There were, however, reports that two had been able to get inside the building. Provincial public health director Amir Padshah Rahmatzal Mangal said that six bodies of Afghan security forces and civilians were brought to the main hospital as well as 13 wounded people. The US military said one US soldier was wounded. In Washington, US President Barack Obama authorized the firing of General David McKiernan, NATO Commander in Afghanistan, after his Pentagon Chief concluded that the US forces "Can and must do better" in the war. US Defence Secretary Robert Gates said "nothing went wrong and there was nothing specific". General Stanley McChrystal will take over command of the 45,000 US troops and 32,000 others from other nations in Afghanistan.

Violence against Women

Though Islam has amply made it clear through the message revealed in the Holy *Quran* and the words of the Holy Prophet, women today find it difficult to survive at the brutal behaviour of man. They have become animals for hunters. Their life depends upon the mercy of the man. They are killed like rats raped like dogs, molested like beasts. They are treated as bitches. For no fault of her, she suffers at the hands of man. The way in which the Prophet treated women with all dignity and honour, mercy and kindness, today Muslim men behave like wild animals and beasts. A few instances of harassment of Muslim women by the so-called followers of Islam are quoted. Let me clear it that what I have just said is not a general statement covering all Muslims. Some Muslim males are involved. It is not a question of number. The apathy of Muslim community leaders to rescue women and ensure punishment to the accused is questioned.

Rape

Raping a girl or a woman by force is the worst form of crime against woman, often helpless. This action violates all principles of humanism. Neither religion nor law would ever tolerate this barbarian action.

But what is disturbing more is the attempt by the father to rape his own daughter, sometimes producing children from her. In this case, the daughter becomes the wife and father becomes the husband. There are instances of father-in-law raping the daughter-in-law. In this case the father-in-law becomes the husband and the daughter-in-law becomes the wife. Husband has to just leave the relationship and go away.

This is not ruled out in Muslim society too in villages. The community panchayat hears the parties and often announces the judgement in favour of the accused who becomes the husband of either daughter or daughter-in-law. We just cannot think of such happenings. This violates all principles and sanctity attached to husband-wife relationship and also father-daughter relationship. What is worse is that the administration does not take any action against the accused. Muslim religious institutions remain silent. Great Islamic centres like Deoband are mute spectators. There could be many cases of this type not reported. Poor women are the worst sufferers, mentally and physically. In what way we civilized people are better than the dogs?

A few such cases are mentioned her by way of illustrations:

Father rapes Daughter and Daughter-in-law

There are quite a few sensational cases where unnatural sexual behaviour is noticed. In a district headquarters of Karnataka State a drunken father raped his daughter aged 18. The wife was not at home. Daughter was in the bathroom. Unfortunately she had not bolted the door from inside. The drunken father just opened the door. He saw his grown up daughter in her total nudity. He dragged the daughter to the bedroom. She started shouting. He switched on the TV and raised the voice so that her voice is not heard by outsiders. He put cloth in the mouth of the daughter and raped her. After another half an hour he raped her again.

Meanwhile his wife entered the house as the main door had not been bolted from inside. She tried to enter the bedroom. Husband was not allowing the door to be opened. Finally she pushed the door with force. The door opened. She was shocked to see her daughter and husband without clothes. Daughter started crying. She allowed the daughter to wear clothes. She took some wooden rod and started hitting the husband. She allowed him to dress up. Then he ran away.

Mother started counselling the daughter. Both agreed to collect their belongings and settle down in Bangalore. They did not want to lodge police complaint as this would affect the future of the girl Then they came to Bangalore. They were in search of a job for the girl, who had completed matriculation. I got her a job. I also helped the mother. My wife is from their place. The case is known to me and my wife. We have fully guarded the incident.

Hasina's Case

This is a famous case where father-in-law raped the daughter-in-law a number of times for quite some time. This affair went on for some time unnoticed, unheard. She bore two children from him. But one day the issue became public. Matter was taken to community panchayat. Since it was a Muslim case, only Muslim members were on the committee. Members made a thorough enquiry and were convinced. They took a decision that Hasina should be with the father-in-law and treat him as husband and the real husband should be treated as a son. This decision was a shock for the community. Nobody had courage to interfere and challenge.

This un-Islamic episode was tolerated even by the religious leaders. If punishment is not inflicted, this becomes a licence and the entire significance of marriage as understood in Islam becomes a laughing stock.

Gang Raping

It has become a common practice in some parts of India as well as Pakistan to punish girls who have affairs with men outside the marriage. Even if brothers have affair with some girls, the sisters are subjected to rape in public view by a few men. This looks very heinous crime, barbarous and unbelievable. But this is real.

The community panchayat members take this collective decision after making a thorough enquiry. This committee is least bothered about Islamic principles. They are generally tribal people who have retained their own traditions even in modern days. The village people do not have courage to challenge. They are all Muslims by birth, not by practice. The Panchayat members feel the girl deserves this punishment for her fault or for the fault of her brother.

Man arrested for raping Daughter-in-law

A middle-aged person was arrested for allegedly raping his daughter-in-law in Nagrota area in Jammu. Noor Hussain has been accused of sexually abusing his maternal daughter-in-law during a marriage party.

Caste Panchayat and Harassment

There are several instances of caste panchayats at village level harassing poor Muslims for different reasons. Caste panchayat is not an official organization. It has no legal sanctity. It is a customary body to resolve disputes arising in the village. It may have only Muslim members or only Hindu members or a mixed group of Hindus and Muslims. It derives power not out of Law books, but out of traditional sentiments and customs. They do render some service to the people. But the problem arises only when a set of hardcore, unreasonable and tough persons are members. Their decisions are binding on all concerned. There is no excapism. Rarely concerned people challenge the verdict in courts of law. A few instances of their most inhuman decisions are presented here purely from Muslim perspective.

Faizabad is a village in Uttar Pradesh. It so happened that a youth had eloped with a girl of the same village. The local elders were enraged. They summoned the father of the boy and showered their tempers on him. They finally decided to impose a hefty penalty on him. But poor man had no means to pay this, unthinkable for him. He pleaded with local elderly persons. But the appeals did not fall on the deaf ears of the members. This mercy was more heinous than cash penalty.

They ordered him to pledge their minor daughter instead as a guarantee. Father obliged. The girl was repeatedly abused. One day she escaped from captivity.

In another case in Mohamedpur village a minor girl had an affair with a boy of a different village. He eloped with her. She was traced and brought back. A fine of Rs. 55,000 was imposed. Father repeatedly pleaded to waive off the fine. But the caste panchayat did not agree. Panchayat wanted the girl to be pledged. Father refused. He picked up courage and went to court. Police arrested the caste panchayat members.

Remarried Woman asked to return to First Husband

In a throwback to the Gudiya case, a community panchayat has asked a Muslim woman who had remarried 'to go back to her first husband" who returned after remaining missing for five years. Roshan got married with Irshad eleven years ago and had two children. Irshad then went missing for five years. Meanwhile, Roshan got married to another man Gaffar. However, the community panchayat of Miranpur town pronounced her second marriage as "illegal" and directed Roshan to return to her first husband.

The case is similar to that of Gudiya of a Meerut village, who had remarried after her husband Arif went missing in Kargil war. On returning to his village, Arif and Gudia were reunited following a decision by the village council.

Pak's Mai married for Women's Rights

Ensconced in a bungalow with air conditioning, sofas and a computer, the woman who can read only some of Pakistan's national language Urdu admits that the English alphabet is beyond her knowlodge. Seven years after her ordeal, she may still be a pariah among illiterate and older women but her transformation from victim to queen of her own destiny is complete since becoming the second wife of Nasir Abbas Gabol. "Marriage gives you a sense of responsibility. It is a sacred relationship. You also get a sense of security and protection and a woman gets the status of mother", the 39-year old said. "He says he fell head over heels for me", she gushed of her new husband.

Mai runs three schools — two for girls and one for boys —

where around 1,000 children from poor families get an education. She heads a staff of 38, half of them teachers, the rest working in her office and welfare centres. They shelter female victims of violence who trek far and wide to seek refuge with Mai, organize seminars to boost awareness of rights, dispense legal aid and operate a mobile unit that reaches out to women in their communities.

Mai was gang-raped in June 2002 on the orders of a village council as a punishment when her younger brother, who was 12 or 13 years old at the time, was wrongly accused of having illicit relationship with a woman from a rival clan. In conservative and patriarchal Pakistan, rape victims frequently kill themselves. Those who don't live as social outcasts abandoned by their families, there is no prospect of marriage. But Mai has defied the norm.

Husband's Harassment

Nasreen's Case

Nasreen was residing in Rahmatnagar, Bangalore. She had completed X standard. She was interested in going to college. She was just 16 years. Her parents forced her to get married to one auto-rickshaw driver who had not even passed VI standard. After marriage she was staying with her husband in a different locality. Her mother-in-law and sister-in-law (husband's sister) were also staying in that house. She was always harassed and forced to bring dowry in cash. She could not oblige for long. She had two children. Her life became miserable.

She used to tell me all her problems as I was a social worker. I used to help her financially whenever she was in trouble. Her husband and mother used to beat her too much. They threatened that they would kill her. I told her to go back to her mother's place for some time. She stayed with her mother. After two months her husband pleaded for her return to his house. He made all promises. She went with her husband.

This time husband, mother-in-law and sister-in-law tried to finish her off. They beat her severely. They took a towel and tried to block her throat. Somehow she managed to escape and got into an auto-rickshaw and rushed to her mother's house. News reached me. I went to her house immediately, consoled her and warned her not to go back to her husband's house at any cost.

One day her husband came home. He was not allowed to get in. He sat outside for half a day. He appealed to the neighbours. Some of them intervened and advised the mother to reconcile and give him a last chance. On my advise, mother refused. Finally, he said he would stay here only and maintain the wife. Mother agreed. He used to earn and bring money to be given to his wife. But harassment became part of life. He was a drunkard. He used to drink day and night. A large portion of his earning was spent on drinks.

One day he asked his wife to prepare breakfast early. She had no money to purchase wheat, egg, etc. She went to a nearby shop and purchased whatever needed on loan basis. She was preparing the breakfast. He came home. Breakfast was not ready. He took his wife to task. She said, "you have not given money for three days. I had to borrow and prepare. Please wait". He lost his temper. He scolded his wife and threatened to kill her. He was fully drunk. Then suddenly she observed some liquid falling on her. She could not realize what it was. In just two minutes he threw a burning beedi on her. Immediately there was flame. She was being burnt. She shouted at the top of her voice. Neighbours entered the house and tried to save with a woollen blanket. Flame was put off. But her body was burnt to the extent of 75 per cent.

Immediately she was taken to the hospital in the auto-rickshaw by the husband. On the way he threatened her that he would kill her if she opened her mouth before the doctor. She was admitted. He ran away. After a few days Nasreen died. The husband was arrested, tried in a court and was sentenced to 10 years jail.

Thus ended the life of young Nasreen. Society did nothing to protect and protest.

Mother-in-law elopes with son-in-law

Gulnaz was a middle aged widow. She had one daughter and two sons. Daughter Razia was married to Ibrahim. She had two children. Razia was working as an attender in a private school. Her husband was a cleaner in a bus. They were all staying in the same house. While having food they used to sit together. Gulnaaz, the mother-in-law, used to sit with Ibrahim, the son-in-law and eat together. She used to give special attention to Ibrahim. Sometimes she used to feed him with her hands. No one ever suspected her. They thought mother-in-law is actually a mother.

But it was not so. Gulnaaz had developed love for the son-in-law. She tempted him a number of times. He did try to avoid. But one day when they were at home and all had gone out, Gulnaaz took Ibrahim inside the bedroom and started love affair. Ibrahim just yielded. They had sex. That day onwards they used to have sex whenever the occasions permitted. Thus it became a regular affair. Nobody suspected about their affair. In a short time the mother-in-law consumed. After one month it was confirmed that she was pregnant.

Now they decided to quit the house. Ibrahim purchased an old auto-rickshaw. He was running it for some time. Mother-in-law told daughter that she was in her sister's house in a neighbouring town for 8-10 days and would come back. She agreed. Son-in-law told his wife that he would take her to her sister's house and return the next day. Everything was planned. The exact time was not disclosed. The daughter had a duplicate key. On that day, by 1 pm, both left the house by auto. They collected their belongings.

In the evening the daughter and her children returned home. Children were asking for the grand-mother and their father. Mother told the children they would return the next day. The daughter noticed that belongings of the husband were missing. But she stopped thinking about all that. Next day arrived and husband did not arrive. Eight days were over, no trace. She was worried and restless. She was under the impression that some accident must have taken place. Anyway, she lodged a complaint in the area police station.

On the 10th day a call came from the husband. He plainly told her that her mother and himself would not return as they got married and he was becoming a father soon. She almost fainted. She did not tell anyone. She came to me for advice. I was also surprised. I asked her a few question.

Self: Razia how it could be that your mother fell in love with your husband. What is the age of your mother? Is she so attractive?

Razia: My mother 35 years, but looks 30 years. Her looks are pretty and attractive. My husband is 30 years old.

Self: How did this happen? Was there any suspicion about them at home?

Razia: No. They were very close. They used to sit together sometimes even on the bed. If my husband was tired, she used to ask him to lay on the bed and she would massage him with her hands. She used to keep his head on her lap and apply some ointment. She used to give him bath and wipe his body with a towel. One day he was almost naked. She gave him a towel to cover up his body in the bathroom. Though her actions were surprising, I never mistook all this.

Self: Now what do you want to do?

Razia: Sir, you advise me. The matter is very-serious.

Self: Please forget your husband and mother. Leave them to their fate. It is very harmful to raise the issue and make it public. You will be the loser and sufferer. If the police asks you, simply say that they are in their relatives house and ask them to close the matter.

Razia agreed and gradually forgot both and also informed the police accordingly.

Time passed on. Razia's two brothers grew up and they were able to understand the whole affair of their mother. They decided to trace their mother. Finally they got some clues and traced the house. The house was located in an isolated place. They saw their mother alone in the house. They knocked at the door. It was opened. Mother took a few minutes to recognize the sons as they had grown up after a distance of 8 years. She became nervous. She pretended to be innocent. She said that she had come out of the house to recoup her health. Sons knew the whole story. They just pulled out one knife and stabbed her in the stomach and chest. She collapsed instantly. They stayed for five minutes, removed blood stains in the room and pulled the body into the bathroom and dumped there. They washed their hands.

Then they went out of the house after closing the door and were hiding. They were waiting for the arrival of their brother-in-law. It was dark. He entered the house. Their brother-in-law wanted to know their identity. Dagger was pulled out from the bag and immediately pierced into the abdomen and chest as done in the case of their mother. Blood stains were removed. The body was dumped in the bathroom. Bucket full of water was poured. Then they left the scene. As it was dark, nobody could see them.

They reached Bangalore. They informed their sister all that they did. They decided to behave as usual. Total normalcy prevailed.

Women who rally against "rape" law termed bawds

The young women stepped off the bus and moved toward the protest march just beginning on the other side of the street when they were spotted by a mob of men. "Get out of here, you whores!" the men shouted. "Get out". The women scattered as the men moved in. "We want our rights!" one of the women shouted, turning to face them. "We want equality."

The women ran to the bus and dived inside as it rumbled away, with the men smashing the tail lights and banging on the sides. "Whores!" But the march continued anyway. About 300 Afghan women, facing an angry throng three times larger than their own, walked the streets of the capital to demand that Parliament repeal a new law that introduces a range of Taliban-like restrictions on women, and permits, among other things, marital rape.

It was an extraordinary scene. Women are mostly illiterate in this impoverished country, and they do not, generally speaking, enjoy anything near the freedom accorded to men. But there they were, most of them young, many in jeans, defying a threatening crowd and calling out slogans heavy with meaning. With the Afghan police keeping the mob at bay, the women walked two miles to Parliament, where they delivered a petition calling for the law's repeal.

"Whenever a man wants sex, we cannot refuse", said Fatima Husseini, 26, one of the marchers. "It means a woman is a kind of property, to be used by the man in any way that he wants." The law, approved by both houses of Parliament and signed by President Hamid Karzai, applies to the Shiite minority only. Women here and governments and rights groups abroad have protested three parts of the law especially. One provision makes it illegal for a woman to resist her husband's sexual advances. A second provision requires a husband's permission for a woman to work outside the home or go to school. And a third makes it illegal for a woman to refuse to "make herself up" or "dress up" if that is what her husband wants.

Killing of Married Women

Marriage today has become a highly risky affair. It is accepted that husbands and wives do quarrel. This is part of married life. But there is a limit to this strained relationship. It is also true that marriage is a blissful act. Prophet has said that every youth should get married and lead a blissful life. Lust for sex among the youths should not be misdirected. Marriage provides sexual pleasure, comforts and also enables procreation of children for sustenance of the society.

It is desirable to ensure peace at home. Differences have to be resolved. Both husband and wife should sacrifice a little. If differences become acute and can no longer be tolerated, the best course of action is to resort to divorce. But neither the husband nor the wife has any right, moral or legal to kill the spouse directly or through outside agencies. This is now called "*supari* killing". Either spouse can find out this agency and agree for certain amount to be paid when the work is done faithfully. The trend is increasing and now Muslim society is also covered.

This trend is generally confined to the upper-middle and the higher class. Since the amount is heavy, it is outside the purse of ordinary Muslims. But the question is; where is the fear of Islam? Where is the fear of the society? What is the benefit derived? What are our leaders of all kind doing?

Honour Killings

Honour killing is also a new sociological concept. It was not heard so far. If a person commits a crime and gets punished, not only the concerned person, but the whole family would suffer from the family prestige point of view. "Honour" is the most guarded wealth of the family. But what we now learn about "Honour killing" is entirely different. It is ridiculous and irrational if the girl of the house is eloped or otherwise married by a boy of either different religion or caste without the permission of the parents, the parents feel disgraced. It amounts to killing the honour of the family. It becomes intolerable. Therefore, they take hard decisions to kill the couple or at least their daughter. I know one typical case that happened in Bangalore. A Muslim girl married a Christian boy very secretly. When parents came to know they became furious. Father and brother went in search of them. Finally they traced the house. As they were approaching the house, the couple ran away from the house. They used to keep limited luggage which can be carried by any of them. They would change the house once in two months because of the fear. One day the husband had gone out. Father-brother traced the house. They had come fully prepared to kill the girl. They managed to enter the house, caught hold of the girl and within a few minutes cut her into pieces. They put the cut pieces in a gunny bag and dropped outside as it was dark. They cleaned the premises to remove blood stain and washed their hands and ran away.

The husband returned home and did not find his wife. He was afraid. He thought the father of his wife might have come and taken her away. He lodged police complaint. He could not sleep. Next morning a large number of people had assembled near his house. He went out and was surprised to see the crowd. He saw his wife's father too. His so-called father-in-law advanced towards him, all the way shouting at him. He told the police that his daughter was killed by him. John, the Christian husband was shocked. Police asked him whether he killed his wife. He pleaded his total ignorance and innocence. But police took him to the station for further interrogation. But fortunately for him there was another constable with whom he had gone for a function. Police let him off, after recording all details. Now the police suspected the father. After one hour's grilling the father admitted to the crime. He said, "I have done no wrong. I wanted to save the honour of our family. This is a lesson for all girls who go away from the house like this. I don't mind facing the consequences". He surrendered himself to the police.

There are many such cases of harassment to women as reported in various newspapers. I have organized a few important cases which are presented here. Merciless killings of various kinds and for various reasons are reported. All these cases finally throw light on the unassailable conclusion that Islamic spirit of harmony, adjustment and tolerance is hardly respected and practised. The community leaders including religious leaders have remained mute spectators. They have almost failed to protect the image of Islam. What impression it creates on the mind of non-Muslims?

Brutal Justice : Pak Woman loses Nose, Hair to Extramarital Affair

A Pakistani woman's nose and hair were chopped off by her brother-in-law and his family after they accused her of having an extramarital affair with a neighbour in Gujranwala city. Police officials have registered separate cases against the accused and have taken them into custody, the *Express Tribune* said. According to police, Awalkah Bhaike resident Aasiya Bibi was locked up for three days in a room after her brother-in-law Anwar, his wife Kalsoom and sons Waqas and Awais teamed up and chopped off her nose and shaved off her head in Noshehra Virkan area in Punjab province.

She was in a terrible condition when the police, with the help of another neighbour, discovered and rushed her to the district hospital where her facial wounds were stitched up. According to the doctors, Aasiya narrowly managed to avoid an infection. "We were surprised that her open wounds have not gotten infected even though they were not treated for three days", medical superintendent Azam Sheikh said, adding, "She is currently receiving treatment and we expect her to make a full recovery".

An unrepentant Anwar said, "she was having illicit relations with a neighbour. We caught her and this was her punishment. She deserved it. I should have killed her on the spot". According to Aasiya's neighbour; there were frequent fights and Anwar's family was "cruel" to her. "Aasiya has been living with her in-laws for over seven years and her husband works in Multan, so he rarely manages to visit", her neighbour Nida said.

Businessman slits Wife's Throat

A 40-year old man allegedly killed his wife after a heated argument over various issues including her extra-marital affair. Accused Muhammad Rafiq, a resident of J.J. Nagar, slit his wife' throat resulting in her death. Rafiq, a cloth merchant, was married to Parvin Taj for the last 15 years and they had two children Sheeyab Pasha (14) and Arvin Taju (12). While the son stayed with his grandparents, the daughter stayed with Parvin.

The couple had an argument after Rafiq returned home. A heated argument ensued and within some time neighbours heard Parvin screaming for help. By the time, the neighbours managed to break open the doors, Rafiq had fled after slitting his wife's throat. A neighbour informed the police and took her to Victoria hospital, where she was declared brought dead. The police nabbed Rafiq within an hour. On interrogation, he said his wife was having an affair with some other man for quite some time now.

"I used to work in Dubai as a clerk in a private hotel. It was only because of my wife that I left my job and came here. Initially, for about six years, I was really happy with her, but soon things stated becoming bad", said Rafiq. He went on to add, "We were living in the apartment that was given by her father but she wanted an independent house. I asked her to wait till I earn enough money. I started working as a real estate broker and also started a textile business. But she started pressurizing me for more money. She used to humiliate me even before my children. Sometime back, I found out that there was another person who used to come home regularly in my absence". But Parvin's brother, Shabeer Pasha, said Rafiq used to harass his sister and not the other way round. Parvin's was the 66th killing in the city in 2009.

Denied Sex, Gay Teen Stones Cousin to Death

An 18-year old gay allegedly stoned his 11-year old cousin to death when the latter refused to yield to his sexual advances. Zaffar Ali, a class X student in Sidhra, Jammu was arrested for murdering Asif Iqbal, a class IV student. A case under

Sections 302 and 377 Ranbir Panel Code (RPC) was registered against him.

DSP (headquarters) Mohan Lal Kaiph said Asif's family lodged a missing report at the local police station after their son did not return home. "During investigation we rounded up some boys for questioning. One of the boys said he had seen Asif with his cousin on the evening he went missing. We immediately brought Zaffar to the police station. Under sustained questioning, he broke down and confessed to the crime", Kaiph said.

Zaffar's confession sent shivers down the interrogators. Kaiph said Zaffar had developed sexual relation with Asif for some days. "On the fateful day, he took Asif to a dingy underground hall housing bathrooms. Zaffar was in an inebriated state and tried to make advances. But Asif resisted and threatened to disclose the matter to the family.

An infuriated Zaffar hit him with a stone, killing him instantly. "He later dumped Asif's body in the hall and left for home without anyone suspecting", said Kaiph. After confessing to the crime, Zaffar took the police to the spot where he had dumped the body. "We have conducted the *post mortem* and the report is awaited. We have formally arrested Zaffar under section 302 and 377 RPC" he said.

The families of both boys have gone into a shell. "Zaffar's father is a lineman in the State government. We are also questioning him. Asif's father, too, is a government employee and both are brothers. The families are in a state of shock", said the DSP. "We need to revive the old system of Samaj Sudhar Committees in *mohallas*. The youth should come forward to head these committees", said Zareef Ahmad Zareef, chairman of the Valley Citizen Council. Zareef called on local *imams* to focus on social reforms in their sermons in mosques.

Opposed to Love Affair, Man Kills Daughter

In yet another case of honour killing in western Uttar Pradesh, an 18-year old girl died of burns after her father allegedly threw acid on her when she refused to leave her lover. The girl's father, Asgar, was arrested on the basis of her initial statement. But in her dying statement given before a magistrate she said she poured acid on her body to commit suicide as she was fed up with her life. Gulistan, a resident of Chaurara village in Bulandshahr district, was in love with a boy living nearby. The police, however, could not identify the boy. Fifty-year old Asgar and his son were opposed to her relationship.

Officiating Bulandshahr SSP J.K. Shahi said: "The girl was found lying on the side of a nearby canal with burns on her body". She was rushed to hospital, where she succumbed to her burns. Bulandshahr Chief Medical Superintendent Dr. S.P. Ahuja said the victim was brought to the hospital with 55 per cent burns. Meanwhile, the alleged murder of an 18-year old girl in Baghpat district on April 3 turned out to be a case of honour killing after a letter purportedly written by her to the police was recovered. Police said the girl was allegedly strangulated to death by her father and brother.

Woman hanged for killing Husband with Lover's Help

A woman and three men have been hanged in the southern Iranian city of Shiraz, a newspaper reported. The woman, identified only by her fist name Afsaneh, was executed for killing her husband with the help of her lover, the Etemad newspaper said. The other convicts hanged were an Afghan man found guilty of raping a 50-year old woman, an Iranian drug trafficker and a murderer, the report said.

Women's Forum decries HC Order on Runaway Girl

In the backdrop of a recent school of thought that propagates fears of Hindu women being lured by Muslim men into love and conversion to Islam, the Karnataka High Court recently directed a 23-year old woman to stay with her Hindu parents after she eloped with a Muslim man. Siljaraj said that she converted to Islam on her own will. However, certain groups have called her a victim of "Love Jihad" — an alleged Islamic conspiracy to "brainwash" Hindu women to be instruments of anti-social and anti-national activities. The All India

Progressive Women's Association (AIPWA) opposed the High Court order. In a release, AIPWA state president E Rati Rao said: "The Karnataka High Court has chosen to suspect the veracity of Siljarajs statement by aksing the girl to stay with her parents, and ordering a probe into the incident".

She said the Court has no right to order an adult woman to stay with her parents. "The Court has been highly irresponsible to take such statements on the basis for sweeping orders that perpetuate communal myths without a shred of evidence. Any enquiry into a marriage between a Muslim and a Hindu woman violate the Constitutional right to privacy and choice in matters of marriage", said Rao.

Rati Rao also said that the "Love Jihad" theory propagated by the Sangh Parivar and other Hindu right-wing organizations have been disproved in the missing cases of women who were allegedly poisoned by accuse serial killer Mohan Kumar. "The High Court's observations provide a shot in the arm for Sri Ram Sena, Bajrang Dal and the Sangh Parivar Pramod Muthalik", she said. Terming "Love Jihad" a communal fantasy, Rati Rao said: "The AIPWA will launch a nation-wide campaign against every attempt, be it by Court or any government to police women's freedom."

"Love Jihad" Couple gets Court's Nod

It was a moment of great joy for Neethu, aka Sarah Khan. The Karnataka High Court let her go with her husband, Sameer Khan. Sarah, a 20-year old student was said to have been a victim of love-jihad. Sarah, originally a Hindu, was in love with Sameer since high school days and had married him against her family's wishes. She had later converted to Islam to be with her husband. A division bench, headed by Justice K.L. Manjunath, said that since Neethu was a major, she could take her own decision and had all the rights to live with her husband.

On May 24, the bench had sent her to a remand home after she failed to explain the meanings of a few Urdu words. Neethu's father Ram Lal had filed a *habeas corpus* petition in the High Court alleging that Sameer Khan had kidnapped his daughter. On May 17, he had filed a complaint with the

K.G. Halli police station saying his daughter was missing from May 3. He alleged that Neethu was kidnapped and converted to Islam by force. But, Neethu, *alias* Sarah Khan, was produced in the court. She submitted to the court the certificate showing her conversion to Islam, her marriage certificate and also her SSLC marks sheet.

She told the court that she and her husband were High School mates. She was in the first year of her degree course, she said. She also told the court that had married him of her own will and that she was not forcibly converted. The division bench then asked her the meanings of a few words written in Urdu in her conversion certificate, after Ram Lal alleged that Neethu was made to learn the Urdu language using force. She could not give the meanings of all the words.

Neethu grew emotional outside the court hall when the media surrounded her after the court gave its verdict. She said she wanted her family members to pardon her since she could not inform them about her marriage. She apologized to her mother. As she became emotional, her father-in-law consoled her. Sameer said he was happy that his wife was back with him from the remand home.

Iran Court allows Woman to Blind Spurned Lover

An Iranian court has given out "an eye for an eye" judgment, allowing a 32-year old woman to inject acid to blind the person who had done almost the same act after she turned down his marriage proposal in 2004. The woman, Ameneh Bahrani, was left blind and disfigured after Majid Movahedi threw sulphuric acid in her eyes at a bus stand after he•had begged her in vain to marry him. She later underwent 19 operations following the attack, and the court awarded her $ 19,000 as compensation besides sending Majid to jail, but Ameneh turned down the compensation offer saying she wanted revenge.

She wanted her attacker to suffer the same anguish that she had undergone for over six years. "His mother phoned my parents. She asked for mercy. She said that Majid would always work for me if he could keep his eyes. But now it's too late," the *Daily Mail* quoted her. Ameneh said she also received death threats because of her determination to exact revenge, adding: "The police have told me not to go out on the street alone. My parents are scared. They think the judges are wrong".

Mothers Kill Daughters, All for Honour

In yet another case of "honour" killing, two Muslim girls were allegedly killed by their mothers for eloping with Hindu youths in Uttar Pradesh's Baghpat district. Zahida (19) and Husna (26) both residents of Mughalpura, were allegedly tied to the cots and strangulated, the police said. The girls recently eloped with two Bihari youths and got married, the police said. They came back to their locality and approached the police for security. However, their mothers gave some undertakings in this regard and the two girls were sent back to their homes by administration officials.

Married Man throws Acid on a Widow

A widowed woman was reportedly attacked with acid by a married man after she refused to marry him. A relative of the victim and a four-year old, accompanying the woman, also sustained burns in the incident that occurred at Urdigere village near Tumkur. The accused, Sadiq Pasha came on a two-wheeler and allegedly threw acid on Sultana and managed to escape. Sultana, who received 20 per cent burns, was admitted at the district hospital here and is reportedly out of danger. Her elder sister Parveen and Juha (4) are being treated for injuries.

The incident occurred while they were on their way to their uncle's house. According to sources, Sultana of Islampura area in Madhugir town got married three years ago. The untimely death of her husband made her return to her parents house in Madhugiri town. Sadiq Pasha from Bangalore wished to marry her, but Sultana's marriage was fixed somewhere else. Following this, Sadiq had frequent altercations with her family and allegedly hatched a plot to kill them. There were several cases registered against him.

Man "harasses" wife for share in property

A woman in the city has approached Police Commissioner Shankar Bidari seeking protection against her husband and relatives citing threat to life. She has accused her husband and relatives of hiring goons, including rowdy-sheeter Tanwir, to kill her. Nargis Ahmed, a resident of Yelahanka New Town who has five daughters, said she was being harassed and threatened by goons who were hired by her husband and son-in-law for share in property.

In a petition to the city Police Commissioner, she said she lived in a house that was gifted by her father. The property was jointly registered in the name of husband and wife. She has stated in her letter that her husband was an alcoholic and gambler. She said she had managed to arrange the weddings of three daughters and lived with two daughters.

Her husband, Rafiq, allegedly was harassing her for seven years to sell the house. When Nargis did not agree to it, he engaged goons to threaten her, she said in the complaint. One day some goons reportedly barged into her house and beat her up when she did not agree to give her share of property. They slapped her so hard that she feel unconscious and took away gold worth Rs. 3 lakh, she has alleged.

The complaint says she managed to call an acquaintance for help who informed the New Yelahanka town police about the incident. Police reportedly came and returned saying they did not see anything uncommon. She said when she went to the police station the next day, police turned her away stating that they could not file a complaint as they did not find any evidence of assault or robbery. The complaint says the goons also threatened to kill her if she did not vacate the house. "Since then, I am living in a relative's house", she said in the complaint.

Suspecting Fidelity, Man chops off Wife's Hand

A doubting husband chopped off the left hand of his wife after tying her to a tree in front of his house. He then threw the severed limb on his neighbour's terrace. The incident happened at Idaman in Kollam district of Kerala. Accused Hashim (35), a fish seller, is on the run. His wife Nasiya is recuperating at Government Medical College Hospital, Thiruvananthapuram.

Hashim, told the police that he suspected his wife of having a physical relationship with the neighbour. He had apparently warned both of them of dire consequences if he saw them in suspicious circumstances. On the fateful night, Hashim returned home to see them both in the backyard. Furious, he beat up Nasiya and tied her to a tree before chopping off the left hand with a sharp-edged weapon. He then threw the severed limb on the terrace of the neighbour.

Other neighbours rushed to the spot upon hearing the cries, only to find her profusely bleeding. They rushed her to the nearby taluk hospital from where she was sent to the Government Medical College Hospital. The severed limb was recovered after hours of search. They put it in a polythene bag and gave it to the hospital. The couple have two children, a seven-year old girl and a five-year old boy.

This is the fourth such incident in Kerala. Anti-socials had chopped off the hand of a bank employee after an altercation, in Pathanamthitta district. In August, goons chopped off the hand of a youth following an "alleged" dispute over eve-teasing in Alappuzha district. In July, Muslim radicals chopped off the hand of a college lecturer accusing him of blasphemy.

99 lashes for Iran Woman Facing Death by Stoning

Sakineh Muhammadi-Ashtiani, an Iranian woman sentenced to death by stoning for adultery, has also been sentenced to 99 lashes for a photo published of her without a headscarf, according to her son. In an interview published on the website of the French magazine *La Regle Du Jeu and the blog Dentelles et Tchador*, Muhammadi-Ashtiani's son Sajjad said they learned of the new punishment from released inmates.

He said that a prison judge confirmed that she was to be lashed for spreading "corruption and indecency" by the publication of a photograph of her without a headscarf that appeared in a British newspaper. *The Times* of London published a photo of a woman without a headscarf that it said was Muhammadi-Ashtiani. However, it said the attribution of the photo which it received from one of her lawyers that has fled Iran, was incorrect. The photo "is certainly not that of my mother", said Sajjad.

What gave her Husband "Passport" for Acid Attack

The victim wanted to stay with her brother, Dr. Syed Siddique, an eye specialist in Riyadh, as she was "too scared" to live in Bangalore and feared a backlash from her husband, Abdul Wakeel. Not surprisingly, Rahatunnisa's worst fear came true as Wakeel, in a sudden act of vengeance, threw acid on her when she was about to take bath at her home in Bhuvaneshwari Nagar.

The victim's elder sister Syeda Ishrat wishes mournfully that if only Rahatunnisa's passport was in order, she would not have to go through the horrendous time she is having at the moment. But the attack was destined. "I wish she had got her passport and flown to Saudi Arabia. Alas, that didn't happen", Ishrat told Deccan Herald. Throwing light on the couple's courtship which led them to tie the knot, Ishrat said that her family got to know about the marriage only a month after it was solemnized in September 1998.

Wakeel's grand-father used to teach *Quran* to Rahatunnisa's family members at their house in Tiptur. Thus both families came closer. So did Rahatunnisa and Wakeel. When the victim was pursuing BE (Architecture) in Tumkur, her relationship with Wakeel blossomed and she had discontinued studies to enter into wedlock.

Even as her father, Syed Siraj-ul-Hasan, suffered a stroke, Rahatunnissa eloped with Wakeel and got married in a low profile ceremony in Bangalore. Her family, however, continued to oppose the marriage and stayed away from the couple initially. It was only after Sufia, the first child of Rahatunnissa and Wakeel, was born in 2000 that the victim's family decided to reconcile with their son-in-law, Ishrat recalled. But the marriage hardly worked. Wakeel used to frequently quarrel with his wife. His unsteady earnings only worsened the matter. Things were so bad that Rahatunnisa applied for *khula* (the right of a woman to separate from her husband) at the Darul-ul-Uloom Sabeelur Rashad, an Arabic College in Govindpur.

Wakeel, however, apologized for his behaviour and promised to reform, Ishrat said. The victim's sister says Wakeel hardly kept the promise and continued to torture

Rahatunnisa. In May 2011, Rahtunnisa approached a local mosque in Minhaj Nagar, Kadirenhalli, and applied again for *khula* which was upheld. The couple was to separate, a day after the acid attack. Rahatunnisa is still in the ICU of DG Hospital. Dr. Deepak Shetty, who is treating her, said that she will be in the ICU for two to three weeks for observation. "But she is out of danger", he said. The doctors are still unable to confirm the type of acid used in the attack. She is presently on a diet of gruel. Ishrat says her sister will undergo plastic surgery. Meanwhile, Wakeel is still at large. Ishrat suspects that he might be hiding in Bangalore or Tumkur.

Outrage as Iran executes Celebrity Jail Artist

Execution of an Iranian artist, who had allegedly committed a murder when she was a juvenile, has sparked an outcry. Delara Darabi, 23, knew the end was close when she made a panic filled call to her mother from prison to say that she could see the hangman's noose from her window. She was executed for a murder allegedly committed when she was 17 and for which she retracted her brief confession, claiming she was covering up for her boyfriend.

The prison authorities hanged Darabi even though the head of Iran's judiciary granted her a two-month stay of execution amid international outrage over her case, *The Daily Telegraph* reported. They also did not give her lawyer the required 48 hours' notice. Horrific new details have merged of her last desperate plea for help from Rasht prison as jail guards came to lead her away. Darabi made a tearful call to her parents to say she could see the gallows and noose, according to media reports from Tehran.

"Mother, they are going to execute me, please save me", she pleaded. But a prison official then grabbed the phone and told her distraught mother: "We are going to execute your daughter and there's nothing you can do about it". The execution of a young woman whose case has become an international cause célèbre is a further damaging blow to President Barack Obama's attempts to thaw US relations with the Islamic regime. Roxana Sabri, an American-Iranian journalist, is on hunger strike in a Tehran prison after being convicted of espionage in a show trial last month.

Darabi's case gained widespread attention after moving paintings and drawings that she made in her prison cell were shown around the world. She developed her talent as a painter behind bars. Iran, Saudi Arabia and Yemen are the only countries to execute people for crimes committed when they are under 18.

Women harassing Men

Though commonly men are held responsible for harassing women, it cannot be held that women are totally free from harassing men. There are several examples of women beating and harassing men too. Anti-Dowry Act is said to be in favour of women. But let us not ignore the fact that in some cases even women harass the husbands and mothers-in-law by lodging false complaints relating to forced dowry. This Act is a very easily available weapon to beat husbands and mothers-in-law. Law is not blind. If complaints are lodged by women with sufficient evidence, police will certainly go ahead against the husbands and in-laws.

Similarly, women can also play a foul game. One day I was having a morning walk in a park. I came across a woman wearing *burqua*. She was also walking fast. I just said, "*salam-o-alaikum*, you are walking very fast". The lady remained unconcerned. The next day when I was walking two men known to me came close to me. One of them said, "why did you say salam to the lady". I said I thought it was my duty. The gentleman said, "no, you are a stranger to her. You are not supposed to wish her".

The lady in question did not stop. She told quite a few people about this. I felt very bad. When I said *salam* with good intention she should have ignored. But she carried a malicious propaganda against me. Since that day I stopped saying *salam* to women unless they first greet me.

I present a few cases of Muslim women's misbehaviour with men. There are; a Saudi woman hitting a cop. In Saudi Arabia, a woman beating up *maulvis* over *talaq*, Bangalore city police arresting an Iranain woman for assault in

Bangalore. In Lucknow divorced women jolt *maulvis* because of too much of interference in women's minimum freedom. A woman with ten husbands hired goons to get her way.

Saudi Woman hits Cop

A Saudi religious policeman who stopped a young woman for walking with a man in an amusement park received a rude shock — the woman lost her cool and repeatedly punched him. The policeman was from the Commission for the Promotion of Virtue and Prevention of Vice. He asked the man and woman, who was in mid-twenties, to confirm their identities and relationship to one another. The man collapsed on being questioned. Even before the policeman could react, the woman began hitting him. She punched him repeatedly on the head and upper torso.

City Police Arrest Iranian Woman for Assault

An Iranian woman, studying in a local college, was arrested by the D.J. Halli police for allegedly assaulting a Bangalore Metropolitan Transport Corporation (BMTC) bus conductor. According to a complaint filed by Muhammad (35), a bus conductor attached to the BMTC 14th Depot, he was assigned to duty on bus route number 176 (KA 01 F1352) on March 3, when the incident occurred.

The woman student, identified as Kamali Azadeh, got into the Hennur-Nagarbhavi bus. But when the conductor asked her to buy a ticket, she refused on the ground that she was holding a pass. The conductor checked the pass only to find that the pass was not meant for buses plying through the particular route. An argument ensued between the two, and the bus was taken to a police station, where she was let off with a warning. But if the conductor thought that the story would end there, he was sadly mistaken. Because Azadeh certainly didn't seem to want to give up without a fight.

Around 8.30 pm, when the bus reached Kaval Byrasandra, Muhammad looked out only to see Azadeh waiting for him with a couple of her friends. As soon as he had alighted from the bus, she caught hold of the conductor and assaulted him. The intimidated government servant decided to take the matter up with the appropriate authorities.

Following this, he filed a complaint against her with the Devarajeevanahalli police station for criminal intimidation and preventing a government servant from performing his duties. The police traced the Iranian national in the Padmashree nursing college in Nagarabhavi and nabbed her. Soon after her arrest, Azadeh filed a counter-complaint against the conductor. According to her, the conductor had misbehaved with her in the bus. The medical student was released on bail later in the day, police said, adding that they have intimated the immigration department about the incident. The Iranian embassy will be informed through the Ministry of Home Affairs at New Delhi to take appropriate steps against the woman student.

Divorced Women jolt Maulvis

Muslim women are beginning to demur with patriarchal notions of bias and control. At least this much was evident when 100-odd angry women marched down the congested alleys of Old City here, waving placards and shouting slogans. It was a sight none must have ever seen before. The 1.5 km walk in this uber-conservative neighbourhood ended at the residence of Abdees and marital home of Hina and Arshi, the two among three women who had roughed up some *maulvis* of the *Shariat* court in June for issuing *ex parte talaqnama*. Amid tight security and after much drama, the two muscled their way in, leaving their morose-looking in-laws with no option but to watch them in silence. The fierce army of chaperones then left, promising to keep in touch.

"The incident proves that Muslim women have had enough of *mullah* interference", declared State convener of Bharatiya Muslim Mahila Andolan, Naaz Raza, who led the march. This could just be the beginning, warned her colleague Naish Hasan. The feisty woman spells big trouble for the *maulvis* with her outspokenness. This year has seen at least a dozen anti-women *fatwas* from Dar-ul-Uloom of Deoband. Women are forbidden to ride bicycles, join public office without *hijab*, talk loudly, join judiciary or even talk to their fiancé before marriage. Now they have one question, said Naish, "Just why not"?

"When a woman puts a "daliya" (wicker basket) on her head and carries bricks, no *mullah* advises her not to work beside men. But the moment she dons a stethoscope or a black coat, there are restrictions galore", Shahnaz Begum said. The semi-literate *chikan* worker from Bansmandi says, "Maulvis are scared they may lose their importance once women begin to exercise their brains. And each issue, from condoning triple *talaq* to pronouncing anti-woman *fatwa*, only shows their insecurity". "My daughter is studying to be a graduate. She cycles down to her college and observes no *purdah*, said Shama Azhar, a school teacher. "I did the same in a place like Azamgarh. Why such restrictions in this time and age", she asked.

The rise in *fatwas* could be linked with the Imrana case, feels convener of Bazme Khawateen, Begum Shahnaz Sidrat. Imrana was raped by her father-in-law and the clergy had declared her husband as her son. Imrana stood up to the edict and fought for justice. With each passing day, this insecurity of clergy, according to some people, is increasing.

Woman with Ten Husbands hired Goons to get her way

Kausar Begum "allegedly" demanded a flat worth Rs. one crore and Rs. 50 lakh in cash as the price to let her ninth husband, Sayyed Ahmed, go. Begum and her parents made these demands only three days after she got married to Ahmed in June 2006. Matters apparently worsened when Ahmed didn't respond to their demands. "It crossed limits when hired goons sent by Begum attacked me with sharp weapons at Santa Cruz on December 5, 2006. The goons claimed I spoiled Begum's life and demanded that I settle the matter soon. I lost the little finger of the left hand in the incident", Ahmed told TOI.

Ahmed said he initially agreed to meet their demands. "I visited Bangalore in July 2007 to settle the matter. She signed the divorce form and assured me that she would not harass me and my family. But I was shocked when I landed in

Mumbai. Cops were at my Powai home to arrest me after Begum and her parents lodged a dowry complaint against me and my family," Ahmed recounted. Sion cops arrested Begum after a magistrate's order and claimed to have found that Begum married 10 businessmen in Mumbai and Bangalore and harassed them. Cops also arrested Begum's parents from Bangalore for allegedly duping Ahmed.

"Ahmed received threatening phone calls for three months in 2006. We lodged a complaint with the court in April 2007 when cops in Mumbai failed to lodge an FIR against them", Ahmed's lawyer, Ganesh Iyer, said. Iyer said a complaint was lodged against Rahmatullah and Babubhai, goons who threatened Ahmed. "A person called Tanveer, who married Begum before I married her, is in severe financial crisis. He has sold his entire Bangalore property to divorce Begum. He now sells DVD and VCD players in Bangalore. Begum has trapped Tanveer and 16 members of his family by lodging a false dowry complaint against them", Ahmed claimed.

He also said that another victim, Abdul Rafeeq alias Kutty, was forced to sell his property in Bangalore to get Begum divorced. He, too, is on the streets after losing all the money he earned in Saudi Arabia. Deputy commissioner of police (zone IV) said: "We are interrogating the accused and her family to get details about the number of crimes they have committed."

Imams and Political Affiliation

Mosque is a sacred place meant for a particular function. That is a place for offering daily prayers. The *imam* is the person who conducts prayers and offers sermons. The subject matter for the sermon (*Khutba*) may be from the *Quran* and *Hadiths* generally related to social concern, life here and hereafter. The sermon has profound influence in shaping the personality of children and youths in particular and old people to correct themselves to stand trial in the court of the Lord.

But the *imam* has absolutely no role to play in politics. He is not supposed to take sides between two political parties as an *imam*. In his personal capacity as a citizen he has a right.

But he shall not bring it to the mosque. I have seen and I have heard from others that some *imams* support Congress party and oppose BJP. They openly appeal to the gathering to exercise their votes in favour of one party of their liking. He behaves like paid agent of a political party. Then he has to be pulled up and be given marching orders. Among those who come to the mosque, there are people having their own political affiliation. They may protest and create conflicts. Then the peaceful and sacred atmosphere gets spoiled.

Some *imams* also allow political parties to canvas for their parties. This is un-Islamic. Both the candidates and the voters should not use the mosque atmosphere to be polluted. One day I was present in a mosque to offer Jumma *namaaz*. There is a custom in many mosques to invite leading *imams* to conduct Friday congregational prayers. Mosque will be full. *Imam* is expected to offer special *khutba*. But this *imam* not only did not deliver useful and educative sermon, but also behaved like a committed supporter of a leading political party. I was shocked when he condemned one party and appreciated another party and appealed to the people to vote for that party. I was very unhappy. I wanted to stand and ask him to behave like an *imam*. But I controlled myself to avoid any possible commotion and disturbance in the mosque.

I met the chairman of the mosque committee and reminded him about the way in which the *imam* conducted himself. He also agreed with me. Among those who offer prayers, there will be Muslims belonging to various political parties. There could be tension and conflict. Moreover, it is not the business of the *imam* to act as a political party's agent. Sanctity of the mosque has to be maintained.

Sufi Maha Panchayat denounces Wahabi Extremism

The All India Ulama and Mashaikh Board (ALUMB) gave a call to Sunni Muslims across India to reject and rebuff hardline Wahabism so that Islam could reform to its tolerant, Sufi roots: "When an extremist turns up at your door seeking your support, when anyone tries to recruit you into terrorism, hand him over to the nearest police station", said Board General Secretary Maulana Syed Mohd. Ashraf Kachochavi, addressing a large-sized Maha Panchayat of Sunni Muslims here.

The Maulana also asked the government to immediately pass legislation to set up a Central Madarsa Board so that fundings to madarsas could be audited and a watch kept on the flow of Saudi petro-dollars into madarsa education. The Maha Panchayat was a sort of "coming out" event for the AIUMB, which claims to represent 80 per cent of Sunni Muslims (themselves accounting for the largest share of Indian Muslims) and yet has been barely visible on the Indian Muslim political and cultural scene. The AIUMB's case is that despite their huge numbers, they have not been able to assert themselves because the Deobandis and the Wahabis have captured key Muslim institutions such as the Wakf Board and the madarsas, and also wield political influence far beyond their size: "The government listens only to the hardliners. It has handed over Wakf properties and Masjids which belong to us, to them".

Board members stressed the threat from Wahabi extremism over and over in their speeches to the Maha Panchayat, arguing that a small group of people had succeeded in giving a bad name to Islam and Muslims, most of whom were Sunni Sufis and, therefore, peace-loving, tolerant and intensely patriotic. Speakers also emphasized the essentially inclusive nature of Sufism which did not differentiate between Muslims and non-Muslims and allowed all communities to pray in their shrines. The Deobandis, on the other hand, did not allow their followers to go to Sufi *dargahs*.

"The time has come for us to come out and claim our rights. Let us take a pledge that we will never support Wahabi extremism — not today, not tomorrow. Let us take a pledge that we will work for the unity and integrity of our motherland", Maulana Kachochavi told the gathering. Later talking to the press, the Maulana made a strong pitch for a Madarsa Board saying: "Right now the madarsas are under the control of Wahabi-inspired organizations which run on Saudi money. The ideology they teach and spread is hardline Wahabism. These organizations have put pressure on the government not to enact the Act. We want the funds to go to the really needy and poor".

Remarkably, the Maha Panchayat appeared to have been boycotted by the influential Urdu press. Last week, when the Board held a Press Conference in Delhi, Urdu journalists were openly hostile to the organizers, arguing that the AIUMB was trying to divide Muslims, and was no different from the Sangh Parivar, which saw all Muslims as terrorists.

Opposed to Congress

When journalists brought up the issue of the AIUMB's political learnings, AIUMB members insisted that they were apolitical. However, Maulana Kachochavi made it clear that the AIUMB was opposed to the Congress, "which propped up hard-line organisation like the Jamiat Ulama-e-Hindi." Asked if the AIUMB would put up its own candidates in the Uttar Pradesh Assembly elections, he admitted that it was an idea they were considering, as "that seems to be the only way to make people and the government hear us". But for now, "we will vote whoever supports all our demands".

VII
Summary and Conclusions

Sociologists are concerned with many current social problems. They are duty bound to make a systematic analysis of these problems. The reasons and consequent solutions form a part of their social responsibilities. Economists who are also social scientists do present a scientific analysis of the economy of the country. Poverty and unemployment may form a significant part of their research studies. But they do not generally come under a public scrutiny resulting in lots of criticisms. Whereas, sociologists have to face such criticisms. Vested interest groups who are bent upon traditional values, mores, *status quo*, narrow minded thinking and totally opposed to social change create havoc. They attack anyone who ventures to speak or write in support of new values, broad interpretation and who stands for objectivity. He has to either give up his role as a reformer or supporter of a reformer or be prepared to accept the change and go ahead.

This is particularly so in Muslim society. Generally there are differences between the religious leaders and rationalists. Many religious leaders are conservatives. They firmly argue for *status quo*. They think their interpretation of the Holy *Quran* and *Hadith* is final and should not be questioned. They hardly realize that when once an attempt is made to interpret Quranic verses or the *Hadith*, there can be scope for others to offer their own interpretation. As a result of this, many schools of thought have surfaced. Consequently many groups have emerged. Each group feels that its interpretation is the best. Thus arise group clashes. The society gets terrifically divided so much so that there will be severe social restrictions. The problem of inclusiveness and exclusiveness kills the basic mandates of Islam.

The present study is based mostly on secondary source of information and partly on primary source. Care is taken to avoid subjective analysis. The subject matter is very sensitive because of the general tendency in Muslim society to misunderstand anything that one says on Islam. Every reference to the word 'Islam' or 'the Prophet' is taken as an attempt to attack Islam and the Prophet. Many people lack the capacity to read and understand. Some people read with a mischievous mind and create stories about the authors. Islam stands for patience, whereas in general Muslims are known for impatience. They are more emotional than rational. Therefore, the author appeals to the readers not to misread and offer wrong interpretation and mislead the public.

The subject matter of the study centres round certain basic tenets of Islam as enshrined in the Holy *Quran* and *Hadith*. Since *Quran* is a revealed sacred book and *Hadith* contains the utterances and actions of the holiest among the holy Prophets, every message is for the happiness, safety and progress of mankind. *Quran* and *Hadith* are not exclusively meant for Muslims. They are for the entire mankind. The subject matter includes the 'words of the Prophet'. This is not exhaustive, but is selective. But this is like a mirror that reflects all that stands for a peaceful, just, moral bound life of people. In theory, Muslims seem to be bent upon respecting every word of the Prophet. Every word is a gospel truth. They do not give room for violation of whatever the Prophet has said. Any word or sign that insults the Prophet cannot be tolerated. Whenever any negative reference is made to humiliate or violate what the Prophet has said will lead to clashes throughout the world. Any sketch of the Prophet is prohibited in Muslim society. Some mischievous elements draw his picture. Lakhs of Muslims come to the street, attempt to commit suicide and resort to violence. Any slightest remark against the Holy Prophet is intolerable. But when Prophet's words are violated by Muslims themselves, why does this spirit be dispirited?

As pointed above, the primary source of data is obtained through individual contacts and group discussions. A list of individuals who are knowledgeable was prepared. This included both known to be liberals and conservatives. From each category one-third was picked at random. The total came to 998. This group had some female respondents too. They were personally contacted and information was obtained by administrating prepared questionnaire. A list of illiterates and semi-literates was also prepared and selected few were contacted to see whether they could furnish information. It was found that they were absolutely ignorant of the basics of *Quran* and Prophet, accounting for nearly 5 per cent. Individual respondents list contained religious leaders, political leaders and the elite.

Group discussions were held in several places and with representative groups. Men and women were included. Non-participant observation technique was also used. Group discussions were found very useful.

Secondary sources included published books on Islam. Besides this, public views expressed by educated Muslims in leading newspapers for the last twenty years were liberally made use of. Infact, this source formed the major source of information. Based on the need for personal verification and cross-checking, I went to a few places and found the information obtained through newspapers was correct and reliable. Moreover as the Minister in-charge of Ḥaj, Wakf and Minority welfare, I had ample opportunities to meet cross-sections of Muslims who used to contact me in my chamber and my visits to their places. It took nearly one year to collect the data.

Collection of data, verification, classification, editing and analysis took six months. To repeat, care was taken at every step to contain the emotions of the youths and hardcore elements in the Muslim society. I had one advantage in containing misunderstanding. I had done my best to serve the religious and secular needs of the Muslim community most honestly and sincerely. People, by and large, reposed confidence in me and respected me. I had proved to be their trusted friend. Of late, researchers find it difficult to get the wholehearted support from respondents. "Why should we waste our time and furnish information? What do we get? Sometimes, researchers have to offer some financial assistance to the respondents or their leaders to solicit data from them. But I had the advantage being a committed minister.

The data were edited and classified under seven chapters as follows:

Chapter I	–	Introduction and research methodology;
Chapter II	–	Words of the Holy Prophet Muhammad;
Chapter III	–	Burqua system;
Chapter IV	–	Status of women;
Chapter V	–	Fatwas;
Chapter VI	–	Violence in Muslim society: A general perspective; and
Chapter VII	–	Brief summary and conclusions

About the Title

Some people say that the title of the book is a bit disturbing factor. It is quite strong and it offends Muslims. Some are happy and say it is the most appropriate title keeping in mind the anti-Islam behaviour of a large number of Muslims. Those who deviate from the basic values of Islam have to face to anything. They lack moral strength. I have already clarified that my intention is to uphold the glorious principles and values of Islam. Many non-Muslim scholars have appreciated Islam and the action and sayings of the Holy Prophet. Islam is the fastest growing religion in Europe. But if the majority of Muslims behave contrary to what the Holy Prophet has said, can we remain mute and pocket all wrong images about *Quran* and the Holy Prophet. We have to correct the situation and tell those who have got wrong perception of Islam that the deviants' are wrong. Many have not even seen the Holy *Quran* in any language or their understanding of *Quran* and the Prophet is very poor. Therefore, some strong words are needed. In good faith I have given the title "Tall Islam and Short Muslims".

There are quite a few books authored by well read people. They have given some titles to their books which also uphold the fact that Islam and Muslims are different today. Suzanne Haneef's book, *Islam and Muslims*, Maryam Jameela's book,

Islam and the Modern Man, Dr. K.K. Usman's edited book, *This is Islam*, Mahmoud M. Ayub's book, *Faith and Practice* throw light on deviation of Muslims from the faith.

All these books lend valuable support to my selection of the title. Therefore, neither me nor any other Muslims should feel bad. No one in the world, whether a Muslim or a non-Muslim can say one word against the Holy *Quran* and the Holy Prophet. The fault lies with the followers of Islam.

I have drawn inspiration and some substance from many authors. Moulana Wahiduddin Khan's books on many issues have helped me a lot. Similarly, there are many books on status of woman. Of these, I was impressed with Jamal A. Badwani, Dr's book, *The status of woman in Islam* and Mazheruddin Siddique's book, *Women in Islam. Rights of Women in Islam* authored by Mutude Mutabbari is also a very useful book. The famous Dr. Zakir Naik's book and speeches should awaken Muslims. He gives the answer to the question: Are Muslims and Islam poles apart today?

As pointed out, this topic is very sensitive. There are many who have no knowledge of *Quran* and *Hadith*, but mistake secular views as anti-Islam. They have utterly failed to understand what Islam really stands for. It is very difficult to make them understand the real message of the Holy Prophet. Here comes the question of real Islam and misunderstood Islam. Glorious Islam and short sighted Muslims create a world of difference. This is what I call, "Tall Islam and Short Muslims."

I would like to present a small case-study to illustrate my problem with some people who cannot understand the real Islam. They rarely follow Islamic tenets. But they are extremely sensitive to the very utterance of the word, "Islam". Once Mr. C.K. Jaffar Sharrief sahib former Union Minister for Railways had arranged a meeting with intellectuals in a hotel in Bangalore. I was one of the invitees. I was sitting in the auditorium far away from the stage where Jaffar Sheriff sahib and a few senior politicians of the Congress party. I was not a member of any political party.

Jaffar Shariff sahib noted me. He immediately asked someone on the dais to invite me to the dais. I was invited. I went to the dais. A chair next to Shariff sahib was offered to me. I sat in the chair. After some time, Shariff sahib asked me to speak on the outcome of a recent study on "Muslim children in Bangalore city." I referred to drop-outs, child-labour, early marriages, loss of values, etc. I concluded that all these social concerns have emerged and spoiled the image of Muslim society because of deviation from the basic values and teachings of Islam. The moment I said "Islam", a group of elderly people. looking not educated, stood up and shouted at me, "What, are you blaming Islam? Who are you to speak against Islam?" They started threatening me. Sheriff sahib felt bad and asked me to stop speaking. Then someone explained to these people about the gist of my talk which was in favour of Islam. Another group of 15 persons shouted at the first group which misbehaved with me. There was a possibility of group clash. But nothing untoward happened.

The reason for misunderstanding and tension was communication problem. I spoke in English as it was supposed to be an intellectuals gathering. But illiterates had also come. They mistook my reference to Islam. I decided not to speak in a gathering which has ignorant and illiterate people while addressing the educated people.

Syed Abul A'la Maududi, internationally well-known Islamic scholar for his depth of knowledge, penetrative attitude, fearlessness have earned a great name for him. He is totally opposed to borrowing alien values and culture and dump them upon Muslims. Muslims are slowly getting away from the basic values of Islam. Some question whether Islam is a practicable creed in the present day world is clearly absurd. Islam has always been a practicable religion. It remains so in future also.

Maududi is very skeptical about the survival as well as expanding boundaries of Islam at this rate. He questions whether we have any unquestionable leader whose commands are respected from all and all listen to him. Similarly, if any community of men today adopts Islam in its entirety, organizes its life and conduct fully in accordance with Islamic principles, and dedicates itself totally to the cause, there is no reason why the rest of mankind should not be persuaded to embrace and adopt Islam today. He rightly says that, merely through discourses, discussions and pugilistic writings this is not possible. Sincere in efforts, practice are needed. Every individual should have the proud privilege of leading an Islamic revolution in the present age.

In other words, the constant internal squabbles, committed and faithful leaders are conspicuous by their absence. In a clash of interest between the self and the community, it is the latter that is totally sidelined. My stand that Muslim society has today bogus leaders who are committed to corruption, not to the community. Political leaders are self-centered are plunged into the ocean of corruption. There are some who do not hesitate to capture even the Wakf land dedicated to Allah. There are officers who receive bribe from the beneficiaries before giving cheques from the government to enable them to carry on some business for survival. Mosques are used for political campaign in some places. Some Imams openly ask those who come for prayers to vote in favour of a particular candidate or party. Do many of our *imams* preach in favour of youths following Islamic ways of life by adjusting to modern society? Is it not possible to reconcile between Islamic basic tenets and needs of modern society. Is Islam dynamic or dogmatic? If the religious leaders are outdated in their knowledge of twenty-first century, can they be fit for the younger generation?

There was an *imam* who used to deliver special Jumma message in the mosque. He chose the topic of Yousuff-Zuleikha. Instead of telling the significance and morality in the story, he romanticised the story. Every Friday people had to listen to the love story — rather he converted the entire story into a love story provoking the youngsters. The mosque management received many complaints and finally the *moulana* was shown the door. He had plenty of material at his disposal. Dowry, lack of punctuality, corruption, ill-treatment of wives, discouragement of girls education and so on. But the *moulana* was interested only in love stories. What can we expect from such religious leaders?

A few instances of the gap between what Islam says what Muslims do are quoted here to convince the readers that the situation calls for immediate attention to remove the wrong image of Islam. All those who are committed to the Glorious

Quran and the Holy Prophet can never be in rest if they do not purify themselves and fall in line to save Islam.

Bribe

One of the major prohibitions in Islam is that prevalence of the culture of giving and receiving bribe. Islam has mandated that man has to earn his bread only by means of legal and moral methods of acquiring wealth. He cannot sit in arm chair and make money. He has to put in hard efforts and sweat. A man may become quite rich by adopting the dubious method of taking bribe. But this is not permitted. Politicians mint money. Officers and also judges do get involved in this trade. This crime prevails despite of possession of knowledge that this is *haram*. Many of those who love and respect the Holy Prophet are no exception.

Bribe is not something that has crept into the present times whose greed for money is on increase. It was prevalent during the Prophet's time. In the fifteenth century, Ameer Khusro, an eminent scholar in Urdu, philosopher, social worker and a trusted disciple of Hazarat Nizamuddin Owlia in Delhi was a witness to prevalence of bribe even in the judiciary. A poor man complained to Ameer Khusro. He took the complainant within to the court hall. The judge was known for his greed. Behind his chair in the hall he had got a small opening done. The person who wanted to pay bribe would keep the bribe amount in a small bag and push it through the window. The judge would stretch his hand from behind and collect it. The judge thought it was a bag containing bribe amount. But Amir Khusro stretched his hand and caught the hand of the judge. He came into the hall and took the judge to task.

Today Muslim society is an active partner with the Hindu society. There is no difference between the two. While in Islam there is direct anti-bribe mandate, whereas in the Hindu society it is indirectly mentioned. The net result is the same. There are dozens and hundreds of Muslim politicians involved in corruption. Muslim officers are not forgotten. They are also equally corrupt. Some officers have swimming pools in their houses. Though they feel that they are living in glorified bungalows, in reality they are in hell. God will never forgive them for looting the poor and enjoying heavenly comforts.

Do they remember the message of the Holy Prophet that ill begotten wealth will kill them? They will never be peaceful and healthy. The curses of the victims of these wealthy officers and politicians will destroy them. Dignity is lost. Respect is lost. Character is lost. What else is left over? Dreaded and most poisonous snakes will create fear in their houses. When they die they carry nothing. What more description is required? This is the reward in store for these corrupt politicians and officers.

Muslim society is equally guilty. It tolerates, encourages and promotes corruption. I have not come across a single case of inflicting minimum punishment for those who indulge in corruption. They do not bother to know the background of the rich people. Many people escape scott-free. There was a case of a wealthy Muslim politician who performed *yagna* under the direction of a *purohit*. Electronic media covered this. It was a shock of life for lakhs of people who witnessed this. This Hindu culture is totally against the basic faith of Islam. But no Urdu newspaper published this incident. I learn that this rich Muslim politician bribed the press reporters and shut their eyes. This is very unfortunate. Anti-Islamic activity was tolerated and the sinner was spared.

Can we believe that a Muslim who wanted to become the chairman of Haj Committee could bribe the members and solicit their help to get elected as the chairman? How many Hajis are honest? I have seen quite a few Hajis receiving bribe after performing Haj. What is the use of Haj if we cannot wash our sins and crimes?

Divisions in Muslim Society

The Holy Prophet advocated that all Muslims are one. They are totally integrated. One has to share the pain of another. He should never wish another Muslim what he does not want for himself. No Muslim should keep away from another Muslim for more than three days. Allah is one, *Quran* is one, Prophet is one. How can the Muslims be divided?

The principles of equality, egalitarianism and secularism are ingrained in Islam. But are we in our daily life? Prof. Imtiaz Ahmed, a well-known sociologist has produced interesting material in his book, *Caste and Social Stratification among the Muslim.* We all know that caste system is confined to the Hindu society. This is one of the worst features of the Hindu society. It speaks of the high and low caste. It speaks of the touchables and untouchables. There is a great social distance between the two. Practised for hundreds of years, there is no sign of annihilation of the social stigma. Human Rights are totally violated.

But the situation in Muslim society should be different if Muslims adhere to all the dos and don'ts. Muslims have brought shame to themselves by creating and sustaining divisions and sub-divisions. Broadly speaking, Muslims have the Sunnis and the Shias. Then among Sunnis, a number of sub-divisions have surfaced. Nadaf, Ahle Hadis, Pinjares, Quraishs, Mehdis, Cuchi Memons, Saits, and so on. These are not castes, but have caste like features. Intergroup marriages are exceptionally permitted. Shias culture and customs are quite different. These differing features do not bring credit to Muslim society. No efforts are made to put an end to this type of diving culture in total violation of Islam.

There are two diatrically opposed schools of Islamic thought. These are the Darul-uloom Deoband and Bareilvi. While the former is conservative, the latter is liberal. One is dogmatic and the other is pragmatic. Their inter-group infighting and significant differences confuse the Muslims. This is an insult and humiliation to Muslim society. More than this, Islam and the Prophet are totally sidelined. The worst happening that happened a few years ago in their inter-personal relationship is worth mentioning.

The Imam of Deoband's Darul-uloom offered morning prayer and was returning to his house. Suddenly a few vandals of Bareilvi were waiting for the Imam. As soon as he was seen these people pounced upon him and killed him. The situation became tense. In the evening there was retaliation. The Bareilvi mosque Imam offered evening prayer and then he was on his way to his house. Darul-uloom vandals killed the Imam of Bareilvi. How can these ghastly killings be explained and tolerated? Have these vandals learnt the basics of the words of the Prophet? What else insult and humiliation can be done to the Holy Prophet? What image we are sending to non-Muslims? Was there any serious attempt in the country to condemn these two groups of vandals?

Liquor and Smoking

Liquor meaning '*sharab*' is totally prohibited. The Holy Book and the Holy Prophet have warned the people that liquor is the dead enemy of man. Liquor consumers face multiple problems. Health is ruined. Wealth is wrecked. Many deadly diseases attack the health. Cancer, TB, lungs, heart problems will not allow men to be in peace. Similarly, smoking is also equally deadly. Person who smokes will face all health problems faced by liquor consumers. Some people argue that they only produce tobacco leaves. They do not smoke. Some people advance their argument that they only sell, but do not drink or smoke. But they are also equally criminals and sinners. People exhibit their ignorance when they say so. Cultivation of tobacco and preparation of liquor are the root cause for man's ill-health and premature death.

But who cares for the warning in Islam? Where is the respect for the words of the Holy Prophet? Young boys, sometimes at tender age, get involved in both activities. Fathers smoke and drink, children learn. Both liquor and beedi/cigarette have become fashion for the younger generation. Even teenage girls are also victims of these two killers.

Another feature of Muslim society is that some Muslims are involved in illicit liquor. Some kings and queens of this type of liquor are Muslims who violate the total prohibition of liquor and smoke. No serious attempts are made by our elders to correct them.

I had a neighbour years ago. He was a very rich Muslim. He had two daughters. Younger daughter, aged 17 years was seen smoking in the garden. I happened to see this. I advised her. Her answer was quite striking. She said, "when boys smoke, nobody questions. Why this discrimination? What happens to girls happens to boys and *vice versa*". She neither bended nor mended her ways of life.

Mirza Ghalib was a great poet and philosopher. Once an Englishman on duty to spy on the behaviour of Muslims came across Ghalib. He asked him, "are you a Muslim"? Ghalib replied, "yes, but I am a half Muslim". The Englishman was surprised and puzzled. He said, "how can this be"? Ghalib gave a clarification, "Sir, Islam has prohibited two things for a Muslim. These are consumption of liquor and pork. I consume liquor but avoid pork. Thus out of two prohibitions, I avoid pork and consume liquor. Thus, I am half Muslim". The English security man enjoyed the joke of Mirza Ghalib and freed him.

I have highlighted some words of the Prophet and got feedback from the behaviour of Muslims. These words include interest, bribe, violence, repentance, forgiveness, loan and its recovery, anger, trust, education, cruelty, significance of tongue, wealth, *zakat* and charity, gratitude and service to parents. He also refers to the value of our teachers, honesty, treatment to servants, equality, liberty, simplicity, luxury, fear of God, fear of hell, dreaded punishment to sinners. The details are presented in Chapter II.

One of the most controversial social concerns is the *burqua* system. This is presented in Chapter III. There are different and conflicting views on the *burqua* system. Not wearing *burqua* is neither a sin nor a crime. Prophet was in favour of *burqua*. His views on *burqua* are slightly different from what many Muslims of present generation feel. Prophet wants every woman to wear *burqua* from head to feet. But he says face and hands may be kept open. But today we find that face and hands are also covered. Covering face with only two eyes twinkling is not mentioned in Islamic literature. How to reconcile with this conflicting situation? If job seekers cover full face, called *naqab*, employers will refuse to provide jobs. School authorities may refuse to admit girls. There are instances of parents moving the courts.

Burqua is a traditional culture. There is no rule as such even in many Islamic countries. In countries like Turkey, Kuwait, *burqua* is out of question and out of sight. In Saudi Arabia even non-Muslim women have to wear in public. The Prime Minister of Pakistan and Bangladesh did not/do not wear *burqua*. The External Minister of Pakistan, Hina

Rabbani Khar is not only without *burqua*, but also she is quite modern.

In some of the European countries, *burqua* has become a hurdle between the government and Muslim women. The social atmosphere is vitiated. France has taken the lead in prohibiting *burqua*, particularly in schools. The conflict is between the individual liberty and state policy. Some teachers who wear *burqua* in classroom had to leave the job, some students with *burqua* had to leave the school. Some knocked at the doors of courts. Nothing could help the *burquawalis*. Islam allows Muslims to follow the laws of the land, unless the law of the land is anti-Islam. By not wearing *burqua* no sin is committed. *Burqua* is only to safeguard the modesty of the women. Recently I went for Umra. I saw a Hindu couple behind us in Saudi Airlines. I talked to them since they happened to be from Bangalore. My wife and myself were surprised when the Hindu woman started wearing *burqua* as the flight was landing at Jidda airport. I asked why she wears *burqua*. She said this is the law of the land and every woman irrespective of religion has to wear. I was happy. Our Muslim sisters should learn a lesson from this example.

There is nothing mentioned about *naqab* in the Islamic literature. Covering the whole face with two openings through which the eyes are seen twinkling is in a sense against what the Holy Prophet has said, 'Keep your face and hands open', is the message of the Prophet.

There is no uniformity in Muslim society about the *pardha* system. Various Muslim countries or Muslim societies behave differently. They wear *burqua*, headscarf, a fully guarded overcoat. Some women do not wear at all. The woman Prime Minister of Pakistan and Bangladesh do not wear. Hina Rabbani Khar, External Affairs Minister of Pakistan is a young, charming woman who perhaps does not know what *burqua* is.

Marriage and Divorce

Marriage and divorce are two major social institutions which play a sterling role in man's as well as woman's life. The Prophet said that marriage is a must as that is the only opening for a lustful youth to escape from unlawful and unethical temptations. Islam provides for certain procedures and conditions. All this is only to protect the interest of the men and women. Marriage is a civil contract and as such it is not a religious sacrament. But fear of Almighty Allah, and the Holy Prophet and the society should always be observed.

Nikah has to be solemnized by the *Kazi*, a professional. But it is also possible that a non-professional could solemnize. Father, uncle and others could perform the *Nikah*. There should be two witnesses. The boy and the girl should agree and sign in the marriage register called *Nikahnama*. The public present will have to give their consent when the *kazi* asks for their consent. *Dower* amount should be announced by the groom and signed in the register.

But today we find modern mechanisms which are virtually in conflict with the provisions in Islam. Many of these procedures and conditions are given a go-by. Marriages over mobile phone, marriages without the physical presence of the groom and the bride cannot be reconciled. How then our religious leaders have closed their eyes and remained mute needs an explanation.

The spread of poisonous dowry system of the Hindu society is blindly followed by the Muslims. Many girls are ruined. They commit suicide or are burnt to ashes by the husbands and in-laws. Today many young girls are scared of marriage. Some educated girls challenge the Muslim society including the inactive religious leaders and have married non-Muslims. Quite often it is a challenge to our leaders.

Divorce is allowed in Islam. But as the Prophet has said, "God will not be happy to permit, but as a last resort and if inevitable, then it is allowed. God's displeasure is made known to the world".

Islam has prescribed certain procedures for divorce. *Talak* should be pronounced by the husband three times with a break of one month in between. When the third pronouncement is over, divorce becomes irrevocable. The gap of one month in between the first two pronouncements is to enable reconciliation, if possible, with the intervention of relatives, well-wishers and so on.

But if divorce is made known through letters, SMS and

telephone, this is against Islam as these channels defeat the very mandate of Islam. Similarly, divorce obtained at the meeting of the *jamaat* is also not in tune with Islamic prescriptions. If the wife gets divorce and if she gets married again, there is a great risk. If the husband challenges the verdict of *jamaat* and her subsequent marriage, the court is sure to set aside the verdict of the *jamaat*. Then, the wife will be in a precarious condition. Her second marriage will be set aside. If she delivers a baby, what will be the legal status of the child?

Therefore, it should be made clear that the *jamaat* should not take law into its hands. There is no point in challenging the court *vis-à-vis* the *jamaat*. Intervention of *jamaat* is possible only in such countries where *shariat* court and *shariat* laws prevail.

Islam provides opportunity to the wife also to divorce her husband by pronouncing *khula*. It looks as if *talaq* and *khula* have equal force. But this is not correct. Islam ensures equal rights to husband and wife to seek separation from each other. But in practice this does not prevail. Husband has an upper hand and wife suffers. Her *khula* should be agreed to by the husband. But very rarely this is done. Wife suffers from mental torture. Husband and his parents do come in the way. Where is protection to the wife? She has to move the court. If this is so, there is a clear setback to Islamic law or for that matter even for Muhammaden law as it prevails in India. Muslim society represented by the religious leaders and other categories of Muslim leaders have miserably failed to protect the interest of wives and thereby *Quran* and *Hadith*. It means Islam and Muslims are poles apart. Can we accept this conclusion? No, but this is the reality.

Meelad and Violence

It is learnt that one day some youths went to the great film artist Dilip Kumar (Yousuf Khan) and requested him to be the chief guest at a Meelad-un-Nabi function. He asked about the schedule of the function. As usual, they said *Quirath* and then *Naath*. He remarked "*Quirath* is alright. You can say anything about Allah, real or false. But you do not deserve to recite

Naath because your intentions may not be pious. Some of you invite me because you know that I take Saira Banu, my wife, with me wherever I go. Your intention is to see Saira Banu, not to listen to me. You insult the Holy Prophet."

Whenever *Meelad* procession is taken out, atmost decent behaviour is expected. But we observe misbehaviour of the youths. Shouting, dancing and sometimes creating public nuisance and giving room for clashes are some of the ugly features of the processionists. If this is not an insult to the Holy Prophet, what else is this? Prophet is the apostle of peace and non-violence. But some people in the procession create unrest and violence. How can this be justified? For this reason, some sane people say that *Meelad* procession is not necessary. In many Muslim countries this is not observed.

Wealth

Islam is not against wealth. Any person can acquire unlimited wealth. But two conditions are essential and mandatory. The means adopted to acquire wealth and the purpose for which wealth is spent. Means should be legal and ethical. How many Muslims have adopted these means? Lust for wealth is not allowed. Wealth acquired through smuggling, black-marketing, bribe, looting, fooling the poor and so on are totally prohibited. But many Muslims graciously and liberally adopt these means. What is worse is that Muslim society welcomes such wealthy people and spreads red royal carpet to them. Mosques are constructed out of donation offered by these people. There are very rare people who extend financial help out of their legally and ethically coated wealth. There was an interesting case reported. A mosque had to be built in a city. Mosque committee approached a former Minister for help as he was a rich person. He gave in thousands. People expected in lakhs. They told him, "Hazarat Prof. Mumtaz Ali Khan is not a rich person, but he gave two lakhs out of the income he got from his mango trees. But you have given just fifty thousand". He replied, "I have two sources of income. One source is permissible in Islam and the other source is not. What is not permissible is used for election and party expenses. What is permissible is used for charitable purposes.

I have more money from the first category and less from the second category. I do not want to give more donation from the first category for a religious cause. Please accept whatever I have given from the second category". The committee appreciated his logic and accepted his donation.

Fatwas

Issue of *Fatwas* has become a most controversial one. Many Muslims are confused over the nature, purpose and relevance of *fatwas*. Some say it is quite ridiculous. *Fatwa* is a sort of guideline to be followed in day to day life. If it is for guidance and useful, there should be no problem. But often it is negative. *Fatwa* should fit into the modern society. It does not mean ultramodern. It should not mean western culture. *Fatwa* against use of necktie, *fatwa* against women's employment, *fatwa* against insurance, *fatwa* against wearing wigs are some of the examples of *fatwas* which are also rejected by a large number of Muslims. These are all negative *fatwas*.

Sometimes conflicting *fatwas* are issued by different schools of Islamic thought. Sometimes *fatwas* are issued in the morning and withdrawn in the evening. Sometimes *fatwas* are sold. Non-Muslims receive a wrong message. This affects Islamic image.

Restrictions on Women

Women had been subjugated, sidelined for many centuries in all religions. They did not have even minimum human rights. Before the advent of *Quran*, this was their status. After the revelation of the Holy *Quran* and the Prophet's intervention their status began to change. Right to education, public participation, employment, offering prayers in the mosques was granted. Women had the right to choose their partners and also to divorce. They could possess, own property and dispose of. They were the masters of their income and property. In other words they had equality. This is the Islamic image.

But today, in spite of modern thoughts of liberty, equality

and fraternity, women have lost every right which *Quran* and the Prophet had granted. A slavish like situation prevails. This is the fallen image of Islam from woman's point of view.

Blasting Culture

Islam means peace and tranquillity. It promotes non-violence. But this culture has almost vanished. A few Muslims have become experts in bomb culture. Highly educated software engineers have adopted violent methods to spread fear in the society. Bomb culture is deeply rooted among the elders. Bombing in mosques, in public gathering, government offices, trains, airports are widely spread. This has become a world phenomenon. Though all Muslims are not responsible, the fact remains that the majority are Muslims. Mosques are destroyed. In many other Muslim countries like Indonesia, Iraq, Iran bombs and killings are common. Muslims killing Muslims, Muslims destroying the properties of Muslims do not allow us to raise our heads.

Does this scenario lead to the conclusion that Muslim society is decaying and Islam is losing its meaning, significance and relevance? Should there not be self introspection? The situation is going out of control. "*Islam zinda hota hai har karbalake baad*". Shall we allow this prophecy to come true? Why should we? Great thinkers in Muslim society have been alerting Muslims that they have to readjust themselves to fall in line with the message of *Quran* and the Prophet and save themselves. Lakhs of Muslims perform *Haj* and *Umra* every year. But do these people retain the sanctity of these holy performances? We cannot raise our heads before the non-Muslims? Therefore, something should be done immediately to reform ourselves.

Disintegrated Muslim World

Muslims account for 1.67 billion population in the world. Muslims are spread throughout the world. Some Muslim countries are very rich. Allah has been kind enough to provide oil and gold to many Muslim countries. But they are controlled by Western and European countries. One small country which has illegally established a separate state for the Jews by occupying Palestine. Mighty Arabian countries have surrendered to Israel. Control over oil management is in the hands of America.

Muslim world is disintegrated. They are miserably disintegrated. Hatred prevails among them. Pakistan and Bangladesh are not on terms. Iraq and Iran are enemies. Syria and Turkey are not on terms. The result is that Islamic countries are likely to disintegrate. Islam prevailed in almost all countries in Europe and Muslim rule prevailed. But these Muslim states lost their hold.

Are not these symptoms of decay due to falling away from the basic values of Islam? When spiritual wealth is lost, can material wealth sustain Islam? Tears roll down if we say that the days of Islam's survival are numbered? Is it not possible even now to promote unity and strength among all Islamic countries with mutual co-operation and help and thereby ensure survival of Islamic spirit and image? George Bernard Shaw's view that "Islam is good, but Muslims are bad", should be erased. Muslims should save Islam. Otherwise, the doors of Hell are wide open to them.

Bibliography

Ali, Maulana Muhammad, *The Prophet of Islam.*

Ahınadiya, Anjuman, *Isha'at Islam*, Lahore.

Ahmed, Hazaret Mirza Ghulam, *The Philosophy of the Teachings of Islam*, Nazarat Nashro-Ishaat Sadas, Anjuman Ahmadiya, Qadian, 1989.

Ahmad, Hazarat Mirza Ghulam, *Message of Peace,* Pub: Nazarat Dawat-o-Tabliqh Qadian, 1993.

Ahmad, Hazarat Mirza Ghulam, *Testimony of the Holy Quran*, Pub: Ahmadiya Anjuman Isha'at Islam, Lahore, 1989.

Ayoub, Mahmond, M., *Islam: Faith and Practice.*

Badawi Jamal A. Dr., *Polygamy in Islamic Law*, Markazi Maktaba Islami, Delhi, 1986.

Badawi, Jamal A. Dr., *The Status of Women in Islam*, Department of Education and Training MSA of US.

Busool, Assad Nimer, *Forty Hadith*, Goodword Books, Chicago, 2002.

Bakh'sh, Mian Rahim, *The Debt Forgotten,* Ahmadiya Anjuman Ishaat Islam, Lahore, USA, 1993.

Chittick, William C. (ed.), *A Shiite Anthology*, Muhammadi Trust of Great Britain, London, 1980.

Engineer, Ashgar Ali, Dr., *Islam and its Relevance to our Age*, Institute of Islamic Studies, Bombay, 1984.

Engineer, Ashgar Ali, Dr., *The Islamic State*, Vikas Publishing House, New Delhi, 1980.

Elmasry, Muhammad Ibrahim Dr., *1000 Questions on Islam*, Canada, 1995.

Elst, Koenraad, *Negation in India* (concealing the record of Islam), Voice of India, New Delhi, 1992.

Haddad, Yvonne Yazbeck (ed.), *Islam, Gender and Social Change,* Oxford University Press, Oxford 1998.

Haneef, Suzanne, *Islam and Muslims*, Islamic Book Service, New Delhi, 2002.

Haq, Mushir, U., *Islam in Secular India*, Indian Institute of Advanced Study, Simla, 1972.

Hamidulla, M. Dr., *Islam and Communism*, Habib-co, Hyderabad, 1981.

Ghazali, Imam Abu Hamid, *Glory and Grandeur of Man*, Al-Ghazali Institute, Bangalore, 2005.

Iqbal Safia, *What Really is Islam*, International Seerah Academy, Bangalore, 2009.

Jameela, Maryam, *Islam versus the West*, Markaji Maktaba Islami, Delhi, 1973.

Jamil, Javed, Dr., *Islam Means Peace, Mission*, Saharanpur, 2006.

Jameela, Maryam, *Islam and Modern Man*, Crescent Publishing Company, Delhi.

Jackson, Paul, S.J. (ed.), *Muslims of India: Beliefs and Practices*, Islamic Studies Association, Delhi, 1988.

Khader, Syed Abdul, *Gist of Islam*, Alhaj Syed Abdul Khader, Ganganagar, Bangalore.

Khan, Ataulla, Dr., *Extract of Holy Quran*, SAM Fragance, Bangalore, 2005.

Khan, Maulana Wahiduddin, *Islam Stands the Test of History*, Goodword Books, New Delhi, 2001.

Khan, Maulana Wahiduddin, *Conversion: An Intellectual Transformation*, Goodword Books, New Delhi, 2001.

Khan, Maulana Wahiduddin, *Uniform Civil Code: A Critical Study*, The Islamic Centre, New Delhi, 1996.

Khan, Maulana Wahiduddin, *Words of the Prophet Muhammad*, Compiled by Maulana Wahiduddin Khan, New Delhi.

Khan, Maulana Wahiduddin, *Islam and the Modern Man*.

Khan, Maulana Wahiduddin, *Muhammad, The Ideal Character*, Goodword Books, New Delhi, 2005.

Khan, Ibrahim, *Anecdotes from Islam*, Islamic Foundation Bangladesh, Dhaka, 1947.

Kamal, Yusuf, *The Principles of the Islamic Economic System*, Islamic INC, Egypt.

Khan, Mumtaz Ali, Dr., *Modernization among the Muslims*, ISPCK, Delhi, 1988.

Maududi, Syed Abul A'la, *Islam Today*, Crescent Publishing Co., Delhi.

Marcus, Julie, *A World of Difference: Islam, Gender, Hierarchy in Turkey*, ZED Books Ltd., USA, 1992.

Maududi, Abul A'la, *Human Rights in Islam*, Markazi Maktaba Islami, Delhi, 1982.

Maududi, Abul A'la, *The Rights and Duties of Spouses,* Markazi Maktaba Islami, Delhi, 1989.

Maududi, Abul A'la, *Fundamentals of Islam*, Markazi Maktaba Islami, Delhi, 1978.

Maududi, Abul A'la, *Our Message,* Markazi Maktaba Islami, Delhi, 1981.

Maududi, Abul A'la, The Laws of Marriage, Markazi Maktaba Islami, Delhi, 1989.

Maududi, Abul A'la, *Purdah and Status of Women in Islam,* Markazi Maktaba Islami, Delhi, 1974.

Mutabbari, Murtaba, *The Rights of Women in Islam,* World Organization for Islamic Services, Iran, 1981.

Mujahid, Abdul Malik, *Conversion to Islam*, Anima Books, USA, 1989.

Naik, Zakir, Dr., *Answers to Non-Muslims' Common Questions about Islam*, Millat Book Corporation, New Delhi.

Nizami, Khaliq Ahmed, *Secular Traditions*, Aligarh Muslim University, Aligarh, 1991.

Nadvi, Muhammad Shihabuddin, *Quran, Science and Muslims,* Furqania Academy Trust Publisher, Bangalore, 2001.

Omni, Syed Jalaluddin, *Women and Islam*, Idare-e-Tahareeq, Aligarh, 1990.

Quaradawi, Yusuf Ali Dr., *Legislation and Law in Islam,* Islamic INC, Cairo.

Quaradawi, Yusuf Ali Dr., *Wealth and Economy in Islam*, Islamic INC, Cairo.

Rahman, Atiqur, *Islamic Dress: The Protector of Women's Modesty,* Adam Publishers, New Delhi, 2003.

Raza, Muhammad S., *Islam in Britain, Past, Present and Future,* Valcano Press, UK, 1991.

Safi, Omid (ed.), *On Justice, Gender and Pluralism,* One World Publishers, Oxford, 2006.

Shariati, Ali, *On the Sociology of Islam.* Iran Culture House, New Delhi, 1978.

Stobart, J.W.H., *Islam and Its Founder*, Uppal Publishing House, New Delhi, 1989.

Shafeeq, *Faizal Ibn Muhammad (Translator) Don't be Sad*, International Islamic Publishing House, Saudi Arabia, 2002.

Saaleh, Saaleh As, Dr., (Translator) *The Foundations of Faith,* Centre for Islamic Studies, Bangalore, 2006.

Siddiqui, Naeem, *Muhammed: The Benefactor of Humanity*, Markazi Maktaba Islami, Delhi, 1983.

Shourie, Arun, *The World of Fatwas*, ASA Publications, New Delhi, 1995.

Shaik, Anwar, *Islam: The Principality*, Publishers, UK, 1994.

Samad, Ulfat Aziz, *A Comparative Study of Christianity and Islam*, Noor Publishing House, Delhi, 1986.

Siddiqui, Mazheruddin, *Women in Islam*, Adam Publishers and Distributors, Delhi, 1982.

Usmani, Maulana, Imran Ashraf, *What does Jihad mean*, Bilal Books, Mumbai, 1999.

Usman, K.K., Dr. (ed.), *This is Islam*, Forum for Faith and Fraternity, India, 1998.

Ulama of South Africa, Mujlisul, Young Men's Muslim Association Benoni, South Africa, 1995.

Zakaria, Rafiq, Dr., *Sir Syed Ahmed Khan Memorial Lecture*, 2003.

Index